Bread from Stones

The publisher gratefully acknowledges the generous support of the Ahmanson Foundation Humanities Endowment Fund of the University of California Press Foundation.

Bread from Stones

*The Middle East and the Making of
Modern Humanitarianism*

Keith David Watenpaugh

UNIVERSITY OF CALIFORNIA PRESS

University of California Press, one of the most
distinguished university presses in the United States,
enriches lives around the world by advancing scholarship
in the humanities, social sciences, and natural sciences. Its
activities are supported by the UC Press Foundation and
by philanthropic contributions from individuals and
institutions. For more information, visit www.ucpress.edu.

University of California Press
Oakland, California

Library of Congress Cataloging-in-Publication Data

Watenpaugh, Keith David, 1966– author.
    Bread from stones : the Middle East and the making of
modern humanitarianism / Keith David Watenpaugh.
        pages   cm
    Includes bibliographical references and index.
    ISBN 978-0-520-27930-8 (cloth) —
    ISBN 978-0-520-27932-2 (pbk. : alk. paper) —
    ISBN 978-0-520-96080-0 (ebook)
    1. Humanitarianism—Middle East.
2. Humanitarianism—History—20th century.   I. Title.
    BJ1475.3.W38   2015
    361.2'609560904—dc23

                                        2014040823

Manufactured in the United States of America

24   23   22   21   20   19   18   17   16   15
10   9   8   7   6   5   4   3   2   1

In keeping with a commitment to support
environmentally responsible and sustainable printing
practices, UC Press has printed this book on Natures
Natural, a fiber that contains 30% post-consumer waste
and meets the minimum requirements of ANSI/NISO
Z39.48–1992 (R 1997) (Permanence of Paper).

For Aram David and Arda Zabel—my Sun and my Earth

" . . . back there in the good old days when I was nine and the world was full of every imaginable kind of magnificence, and life was still a delightful and mysterious dream . . ."
—William Saroyan, *My Name Is Aram* (1937)

The Tempter came to him and said, "If you are the Son of God, tell these stones to become bread." Jesus answered, "It is written: 'Man shall not live by bread alone . . .'"

—Matthew 4:3–4

Քարէս հաց հանել
To force bread from stone

—Armenian expression

Ekmeğini taştan çıkar
To take bread out from stone

—Turkish expression

Create bread from stones . . .

—Report by Karen Jeppe, Danish administrator of the League of Nations Rescue Home in Aleppo (1922)

. . . اسلّ لهم رغيف الخبز والأثواب والدفتر
من الصخر . . .
— محمود درويش

. . . I secure a loaf of bread, clothes and school notebooks From stone . . .

—Mahmoud Darwish, "Identity Card" (1973)

Contents

Illustrations

TABLE

Preface and Acknowledgments

Bread. Stones. This book has many beginnings.

One was an overcast April day in Syria. My wife, the noted Islamic art historian Heghnar Zeitlian Watenpaugh, and I—both University of California, Los Angeles, graduate students at the time—were visiting Aleppo's Armenian cemetery. Wandering beneath a canopy of *Pinus halepensis* and across the hard-beaten red earth, we found the gravestone of Karen Jeppe and read the Armenian and Danish inscriptions beneath her name, which translate as "Mother of Armenians." I learned that Jeppe, the administrator of the interwar-era League of Nations Rescue Home in the city, was a beloved figure among older Armenians, who had named a high school after her, the Karen Jeppe Jemaran. Yet she had been forgotten in broader Middle East history. This despite the fact that she had played a decisive role in helping recover and rehabilitate a generation of young people, who, having survived genocide, were then subjected to trafficking, rape, slavery, and bearing children against their will.

The history of children, sexual violence, genocide survivors, and humanitarian relief was not among the questions and concepts that drove the historical study of the Eastern Mediterranean at the turn of the twenty-first century. Rather, it was the nationalisms of the dominant ethnicities, the politics of the elite social classes, and French and British colonialism that were the foci of our historiography. And thus my first book focused on early twentieth-century class, colonialism, and urban politics, *Being Modern in the Middle East*. But even so, Jeppe appears briefly in that book. I knew there were many more questions to be asked about people like her who had sought to confront the inhumanity of the wartime and interwar periods, and also about those whom she had helped.

Over the next decade, I started to follow the trail of Jeppe's work. It brought me to the archives of the League of Nations in the Geneva headquarters of the United Nations. There I found the Rescue Home's intake surveys, which included individual photographs of the thousands of young people whose lives Jeppe had touched. I still recall what it felt like sitting in the reading room for two hot summer days, poring over the accounts of loss and survival and looking at the faces of the young people who had told those stories. The stories tore at me.

Perhaps it was because I knew people who could have been their descendants; their names, their places of origin were all familiar. I knew, as a historian of the period, that these were the few who by force of will or circumstance (or both) had escaped. Hundreds of thousands of children were killed during the genocide, and, at the time of the Rescue Home's operation, tens of thousands of Armenian young people were still living in slavery. What I experienced in the archives stayed in my mind even as I left and walked to my apartment, passing under the canopy of the most magnificent cedar of Lebanon I had ever seen. That night I awoke screaming from a dream the details of which I am glad I cannot recall.

Those stories and photographs imposed a burden on me to write a history that neither ennobles the tellers as righteous victims, nor elevates those who helped them as altruistic saviors, but rather looks hard at the causes of suffering and embraces the complex, complicated, and sometimes-failed *humanity* of the efforts to address it.

The title for this work originates in a humanitarian report Jeppe wrote from Baalbeck, Lebanon, in 1922. She had battled depression, what today would be called posttraumatic stress, and the effects of recurring malaria since before World War I, and she often had to convalesce away from the heat and dust of Aleppo. "The Armenian is possessed of a wonderful gift 'to create bread from stones,'" she explained, suggesting that in spite of tough or even impossible circumstances, she was determined to persevere in her work. That year had marked the collapse of efforts to repatriate the vast population of Armenian refugees to their homelands in Anatolia, and the full measure of the cost of permanent displacement was just beginning to dawn on relief workers like Jeppe. The Armenian phrase *karen hats hanel* also occurs in most of the languages of the Eastern Mediterranean; it is best translated as "forcing bread out of a stone" and has very old origins. It certainly predates its occurrence in the Christian Gospel of Matthew, in which we are told that the Tempter asked Jesus to prove that he was the Son of God by turning desert stones into bread, which he refused, saying in a koan-like response that resonates still with the underlying ethos of modern humanitarianism: "Man does not live by bread alone."

In the final years of her life, Jeppe would work with displaced communities to develop agricultural colonies in the stone-covered high steppe of the countryside of northern Syria. And while many of those colonies failed, for a brief period, they did produce harvests of wheat and barley.

Another beginning of this book was a friendship between Ann Z. Kerr and my family. I met Mrs. Kerr first almost thirty years ago, when I was a junior-year-abroad student at the American University in Cairo. She had stepped in to be the academic advisor to a dozen or so University of California students. It had only been a couple of years since the murder of her husband, the political scientist and president of the American University in Beirut, Malcolm Kerr. At the time I had been moved by the fact that, despite what had happened, she had stayed in the region and was still involved in teaching and mentoring young Arab women and men; this was something that, even as an undergraduate, I recognized as special and important.

A few years later, at UCLA, Mrs. Kerr befriended our cadre of Middle East studies graduate students, and it was in that context that she introduced me to the Near East Relief work of her father-in-law, Stanley E. Kerr, and his memoir, *The Lions of Marash*. She also shared with me her daughter Susan Van de Ven's Oberlin College history honor's thesis, based on his letters home in the early 1920s. The impact of those letters, photographs, and memoir are demonstrated throughout this book. I thank the Kerr family for sharing them with me.

More important, for many of us at UCLA, Ann Kerr became our link with a *different path* of American engagement with the Middle East—one built around education, respect, and friendship. This was the 1990s, a historical moment in which it was becoming clear to many of us that the American presence in the Middle East, its demonstrably positive role, and the prestige that two generations of Kerrs had had such an important role in creating was in real decline and would soon collapse altogether in the face of America's war in Iraq.

The final beginning of this work happened on a September 1962 flight from Beirut to Rome, when my father, then a recent university graduate, was returning home to the United States after spending the summer with his parents, my grandparents, in Pakistan. My grandfather, a soil scientist, was in South Asia serving as a consulting technical advisor on various agricultural and water infrastructure development projects on behalf of the United States Agency for International Development (USAID)—which had been established only the year before by President John F. Kennedy. My grandfather had done similar work in the 1950s as part of USAID's predecessor, the Point Four Program's Technical Cooperation Administration, in the lands watered by the streams and rivers that flow from Kurdistan to the Tigris.

On that flight, my father sat next to a newly retired Lebanese-Armenian nurse administrator, Asdghig Avakian, who was traveling to America for the first time. She told my father of her memoir, *A Stranger among Friends* (1960), which chronicles her own history as a genocide orphan, her encounters with Near East Relief education and rehabilitation projects, and her eventual professional career in nursing. Upon her return to Beirut, she forwarded a copy of the book to my father, which he kept and then shared with me. Her memoir is one of the very few first-person recollections of a young person who had survived the 1915 Armenian Genocide and then built a career with the help of American international humanitarianism; her memoir figures prominently in this book.

That trip home was a product of a legacy of my own family's involvement in the Middle East and South Asia in the work of technical assistance, a branch of humanitarianism, which I have come to view with ambivalence. I now see a problem in the way technical assistance can often be a substitute for efforts to extend human rights, empower women and minorities, and achieve justice in unjust societies; in its worst forms it merely helps expand the power and authority of dictators, kings, and military juntas. It has been difficult to reconcile that fact with what I know of my grandfather's sense of social justice and humanity, which was formed in the crucible of the agricultural and social challenges of the American Dust Bowl and the vast reclamation projects made possible by the dams on the rivers of the western United States. I am certain that, in his own mind, my grandfather, like the generations of relief and development workers before and since, were not at all interested in supporting human rights–abusing régimes, but rather were committed to the simple task of *helping* people in need with the most modern techniques and the best science available regardless of the form of government oppressing them. Trying to reconcile the humane intentions of humanitarians with the way that work had possible inhumane outcomes, and what in retrospect seems a painfully naïve belief in "politics-free" technical assistance, is a personal and professional tension that colors this book.

The illusion of "politics-free" humanitarianism is at the heart of another book called *Bread from Stones* (1966), subtitled *Fifty Years of Technical Assistance*. A thin volume on the work of the Near East Foundation, the successor of Near East Relief, it discusses various projects and programs particularly in Iran, but also elsewhere, including Afghanistan and Greece. It is an unambiguous celebration of the heroic American technical assistant, who is at once beyond the political and a physical embodiment of the most modern of modern humanitarianism's impulses. Reading that book backward through the lens of the 1979 Iranian Revolution and its inherent anti-Americanism, one cannot help but imagine how a more reflective and self-conscious vision of that kind of assistance and its relationship to power in its multiple forms could have led to a different outcome. Though published in my lifetime, that *Bread from Stones* is written about a "Middle East" I can no longer recognize.

This *Bread from Stones* was written as the contemporary "Middle East" descended into a humanitarian disaster that, in its degree of suffering and international indifference, resembles the one that occurred during and following World War I. Historians must not draw too many parallels between the past and the present, but as I have looked out across the region over the last few years, I see in the immense refugee flows, human trafficking, sexual violence, and genocide of the current wars in Syria and Iraq echoes of a hundred years ago. Those echoes resound across the same territories of inhumanity and humanitarian response, especially now in the city of Aleppo, which has been subjected to the kinds of unceasing urban violence reminiscent of Madrid in the 1930s or Sarajevo in the 1990s; at the time of this writing the city seems poised to fall into the hands of the most violent of Islamist extremists, whose pitiless and cruel modern ideology has already led to the destruction through genocide of ancient non-Muslim communities in northern Iraq and caused utter misery for countless Muslims throughout the region.

As I finished writing this book, I also led a multifaceted humanitarian project supported by the University of California Davis Human Rights Initiative, the Carnegie Corporation of New York, and the Institute of International Education to try to understand the needs of and ways to help Syrian university students displaced and made refugees by the war in their homeland. It was work that took me to refugee camps, "second-shift" elementary schools, college classrooms, and border cities in Lebanon, Jordan, and Turkey to collect data and write reports, but also, above all, *to listen* to young women and men who told their stories and confided in me their suffering and disappointments, as well as goals and ambitions. They were traumatized but resilient, and despite the depth of their despair, they retained their warmth and even sense of humor. The stories of displaced Syrian students reminded me of those told to Karen Jeppe about extirpation, murder, loss, rape, and torture. Practicing modern humanitarianism in this limited way helped me to reflect on the meaning of suffering, the modes of caring, the production of humanitarian knowledge, and the way that the fears and hopes of refugees can lead to their wanton exploitation by the unscrupulous; it also made me understand the heavy emotional, intellectual, and physical toll the constant exposure to the suffering of others, compounded by a sense of near hopelessness in the face of the enormity of their suffering, can have on even the most consummate professionals, like my close colleagues in that work, Adrienne L. Fricke and James R. King. The experience has made me a better historian and what follows a better book, but it has also left me with a much clearer vision of the vastness of *inhumanity*.

This book would not have been possible without the support of many colleagues, friends, and institutions. There are several in particular I now have the opportunity to thank. The research and writing of this book was supported by two major fellowships. The first was the United States Institute of Peace's Senior Fellowship in International Peace, which, beyond providing support to conduct research and interact with humanitarian and human rights professionals, came with an extraordinary research assistant, Matthew Chandler. I also thank the institute's Steven Heydemann and Lili Cole. Second, the writing of this book was accomplished with the help of the American Council of Learned Societies' International and Area Studies Fellowship, which is underwritten in part by the National Endowment for the Humanities and the Social Science Research Council. I thank Molly McCarthy, Beth Baron, Elizabeth Thompson, Phillip Khoury, and Peter Sluglett for their help in securing that grant. Research was also supported by a stipend from The American Academic Research Institute in Iraq (TAARI). Still other scholars who helped shape this work include Davide Rodogno, Samuel Moyn, Michelle Tusan, Nancy Gallagher, Gerard Daniel Cohen, Dirk Moses, Melanie Schulze Tanielian, Tara Zahra, Francesca Piana, Chris Gratien, Tylor Brand, Amila Becirbegovic, Melissa Bilal, Fatma Müge Göçek, Raymond Kévorkian, Vahé Tachjian, Orit Bashkin, and Bedross Der Matossian. Productive conversations with my colleagues and the graduate students of the University of California Human Rights Collaboration, including Michael Lazzara, Diane Wolf, Alison Brysk, Gershon Shafir, Ev Meade, Bronwyn Leebaw, Andrea Dooley, Nigel Hatton, Nadege Clitandre, and Nancy Postero, played a tremendous role in refining the ideas and content of this work.

My greatest thanks, however, must go to three people. The first is Heghnar Z. Watenpaugh, whose own experiences as a refugee, as a descendant of those who resisted and survived genocide, and as an academic of the highest caliber have left their mark on this work and me. It is no exaggeration to say that without her, this book would not exist. The other two are our children, the hero twins Arda Zabel and Aram David, who have shared the journey with me from its very beginning. I dedicate this book to them.

Some of the material in this book appeared originally in the following articles and is used here with permission.

"Between Communal Survival and National Aspiration: Armenian Genocide Refugees, the League of Nations, and the Practices of Interwar Humanitarianism," *Humanity: An International Journal of Human Rights, Humanitarianism, and Development* 5, no. 2 (2014): 159–181.

"'Are There Any Children for Sale?': Genocide and the Transfer of Armenian Children (1915–1922)," *Journal of Human Rights* 12, no. 3 (2013): 283–295.

"The League of Nations' Rescue of Armenian Genocide Survivors and the Making of Modern Humanitarianism, 1920–1927," *American Historical Review* 115, no. 5 (2010): 1315–1339.

Davis, California
September 3, 2014

Note on Translation and Transliteration

Unless otherwise noted, all translations from Arabic, Turkish, Armenian, and French are my own.

In transliterating Arabic and Ottoman Turkish words, I have followed a simplified scheme based on that employed by the *International Journal of Middle East Studies*. In some cases, names of individuals are included as they themselves wrote their names in Western languages. For Armenian authors, I have included the more common spelling of their names according to the way those names would have been pronounced in Western Armenian, the language of the Armenians of the Ottoman Empire, but have also included the transliteration of their names according to the Library of Congress method, which uses the modern Armenian of the Republic of Armenian; hence Զաբէլ Եսայեան becomes Zabel Yesayan in the text, and then in the bibliographic note, Zapēl Esayean.

Abbreviations

ACRNE   American Committee for Relief in the Near East
AGBU   Armenian General Benevolent Union
AJC   American Jewish Committee
ARA   American Relief Administration
ARC   American Red Cross
AUB   American University in Beirut
ICRC   International Committee of the Red Cross
JDC   American Jewish Joint Distribution Committee
NEF   Near East Foundation
NER   Near East Relief

Map of the Eastern Mediterranean, 1914–1948.

CHAPTER I

The Beginnings of the Humanitarian Era in the Eastern Mediterranean

Those who were successful just as those who were poor,
those who went to cafés and night clubs just as those who
had nothing but hunger and homelessness, the war made
orphans of their children and widows of their wives.

—Ragib al-Tabbakh, 1923

Marash, Anatolia, February 9, 1920. As the Armenians of Marash fled their city in the face of civil war and the certainty of massacre, a twenty-three-year-old American Near East Relief (NER) official, Stanley E. Kerr, made the decision to stay behind in the organization's headquarters to care for the hundreds of children and elderly who could not travel. He was one of a tiny handful of Americans who remained in the war-torn city as other relief workers evacuated with the able-bodied and the retreating French army. "Tonight," Kerr wrote to his parents back home in Philadelphia, "the most bitter cold of all this winter.... Our orphans, old women and men will remain in our compounds.... Perhaps by remaining here we can protect the remaining Armenians from massacre.... We are in great danger, but not without hope.... No matter what happens remember that I am ready to make any sacrifice even death."[1] For the young American, this was his first real encounter with the full measure of the horrors facing the civilian population of the Eastern Mediterranean in the wake of the "war to end war." For the Armenians of Marash, the massacres, dispossession, and exile they faced that night came only at the end of a generation of war, communal violence, genocide, famine, and disease that had left a quarter of the

Ottoman state's subjects dead and millions displaced: in the Balkans and the Caucasus Muslim refugees fled advancing European armies; Ottoman Armenians who had survived state-sponsored efforts to destroy them as a people filled camps and shantytowns scattered along the outskirts of the major cities of the Levant; and Greeks and Turks on the "wrong" sides of new international borders would be "exchanged"— a euphemism for internationally sanctioned dispossession and forced migration—as nation-states emerged from the ashes of empire.[2]

Kerr's letter home on that terrible night provides a unique window into the state of mind of a young humanitarian worker in extremis, but also keenly aware of his professional responsibility. Equally, Kerr's presence in Marash, as an administrator of a network of orphanages, rehabilitation centers, and schools, is evidence that this violence and disaster, which had caused societal collapse, had prompted a modern— and massive—international humanitarian response that involved diverse aid and relief organizations including NER, the Red Cross and Red Crescent, Western and Middle Eastern civil society, colonial governments, and the nascent League of Nations. The juxtaposition of the evident inhumanity of war, civil conflict, and genocide, on the one hand, with the creation of forms of aid for the victims of violence, the establishment of institutions to resettle displaced peoples, and the elaboration of novel, international legal regimes for refugees, on the other, frames the questions raised here. This book traces the origins of modern humanitarianism, from the perspective of its implementation in the Eastern Mediterranean, as both practice and ideology, and connects it to the other dominant ideologies of the interwar period—nationalism and colonialism; it explores humanitarianism's role in the history of human rights and addresses how the concept of shared humanity informed bureaucratic, social, and legal humanitarian practices.

The Eastern Mediterranean was where much of modern humanitarianism was born. This fact tends to be missing from the dominant historiography of the region. Waves of displaced persons and new borders forced the international community embodied in the League of Nations to first define and then manage novel iterations of the "refugee" and the "minority." The sheer scale of interwar relief needs prompted the replacement of independent missionary-based charity with secular, professional, and bureaucratized intergovernmental forms of aid and development. And, finally, efforts to interdict trafficking in women and children mobilized nongovernmental humanitarian organizations and groups in Europe and the Americas to a degree not seen since the abolitionist movement of the nineteenth century. The region was also where troubling questions were increasingly being asked about what role the international community should play in helping nation-states rid themselves of unwanted religious and ethnic minority populations.

Where the systematic and critical study of human rights and humanitarianism is absent altogether from the corpus of the Eastern Mediterranean's twentieth-century historiography, the region is likewise largely missing from the literature on the global history of both.[3] Moreover, the prevailing narrative of the history of human rights mostly emphasizes the post–World War II era, the international reaction to the Holocaust, and the founding of the United Nations.[4] This project looks further back and locates an origin of contemporary human rights thinking in the practices and failures (including practical failures) of humanitarianism during the late interwar period. Bringing the theory and practice of humanitarianism into the history of human rights makes this project an important contribution to an emerging debate about human rights history and does so almost uniquely in the field from the perspective of the non-West.

Similarly, this book is built around a method that brings an understanding of the intellectual and social context of humanitarianism together with the lived reality of the places where the humanitarian act in its various forms took place. With this approach, I can write about humanitarianism in a comprehensive and transnational way and thus avoid an institutional history or an account that sees humanitarianism as a self-evident manifestation of liberalism, Protestantism, and social reform. This approach also allows me to disentangle—but not disconnect—humanitarianism from colonialism, in contrast to discussions derived from the techniques of colonial and postcolonial studies, which often see humanitarianism as solely a product of the colonial project. No less important is how this method restores a measure of agency to the objects of the Western humanitarian agenda.

I draw from archival sources, especially those of the League of Nations, the Nansen International Office for Refugees, American Near East Relief, the Rockefeller Foundation, and national archives in Turkey, France, Britain, and the United States. In addition, I employ contemporaneous literary and artistic responses, and memoirs and first-person accounts of victims, perpetrators, relief workers, and diplomats in European languages as well as Arabic, Turkish, and Armenian. This breadth of source material allows me to capture the inherent richness of humanitarianism as a problem of social and cultural history in a way that retains relevance to contemporary debates about the promotion of human rights, and the work of relief and development.

Finally, keeping in mind the work of Kerr and his professionalism and commitment in the face of real danger, I have written a history of humanitarianism that tells the story of a different kind of relationship between some Westerners—Americans in particular, but also others—and the peoples of the Eastern Mediterranean. In the first half of the twentieth century, that relationship unfolded in the universe of humanitarian assistance, relief, and teaching; undoubtedly, it was still informed by colonialism, paternalism, and ideas about ethnic and religious superiority, but it was also built around ending the suffering of others and providing safety, and even advanced and professional educational opportunities, to those whose lives had been utterly devastated by war and violence. It was a relationship in which forms of mutual respect, even friendship, could be established based on class and profession, but based on modern conceptions of shared humanity as well; and this sort of relationship was not just possible, but common.

TOWARD A THEORY OF MODERN HUMANITARIANISM

Compassion is a definitive element of the modern human experience. *Organized compassion*—the idea at the core of the concept of humanitarianism—is a phenomenon of even more recent origin, especially in the case of compassion for those who are distant and beyond borders. This book was written in part to better understand organized compassion as a historical phenomenon by elaborating a theoretical concept I call *modern humanitarianism*. The concept of modern humanitarianism is both a sign of a turn in the conceptualization of organized compassion and the linked phenomena of suffering, empathy, and sentiment; and a historical benchmark in the way the work of humanitarianism was structured, financed, organized, and implemented. Equally, modern humanitarianism is a phenomenon of late colonialism and its ideologies of race and nation.

In the eighteenth and nineteenth centuries, humanitarians sought to alleviate the suffering of others, which could mean early death, starvation, forms of exploitation, and disease; motivated by an ethic of sympathy and sustained by the sentimental narrative, this early humanitarianism was often made an instrument for conversion, especially to forms of Protestant Christianity.[5] Early humanitarianism was embedded in religiously driven and episodic forms of missionary activity, abolition, and attempts to regulate the treatment of soldiers during Europe-based conflicts, the chief example being the work of the International Committee of the Red Cross (1863). In the context of British, French, and American colonialism, humanitarianism featured in the "White Man's Burden" and the *mission civilisatrice* (civilizing mission)[6], and at the core of the military and diplomatic concept of *humanitarian intervention*[7], which the historian Samuel Moyn has wryly observed "often exported to foreign lands the savagery it purported to be banishing from them."[8]

While still possessing elements of its predecessor, modern humanitarianism was envisioned by its *participants* and *protagonists* as a permanent, transnational, institutional, neutral, and secular regime for understanding and addressing the *root causes* of human suffering.[9] It paralleled the evolution of philanthropy and was distinct in its reliance on social scientific approaches to the management of humanitarian problems—expanding late nineteenth-century notions of "scientific philanthropy" to a massive scale.[10] The participation by Western civil society and publics—and modern forms of advertising—in underwriting and agitating on behalf of humanitarian projects also distinguished this turn.[11] Further defining it was the emergence of a new and, to some extent, gendered practice—professional relief work—and the Western middle-class female relief worker; the general ambit of international humanitarianism derived in no small part from elite Western feminists' work on behalf of women's rights, suffrage, and social welfare. Critical, as well, was modern humanitarianism's explicit connection with international peacemaking as both a causative and preventative measure. A final element of modern humanitarianism was the anticipation that the international community—a concept with origins in the late nineteenth century as well—could, should, and would take action on behalf of humanitarian concerns.

By marking the historical turn implicit in the ideology and practices of modern humanitarianism, this work distinguishes the forms of relief, the creation of bureaucratic measures for civilian protection, refugee-based educational initiatives, and plans for social reform from earlier efforts in the region, primarily by missionaries, Islamic institutions, and the Ottoman state, to care for the poor and to settle migrants. Many of those earlier efforts resemble in some form the work of wartime and interwar humanitarians, but they were largely bereft of the ideological content and functional secularity of modern humanitarianism. The elaboration of the theory of modern humanitarianism also allows the humanitarian project in the interwar Eastern Mediterranean to be integrated into a larger global movement—of Western origin—of an attempted liberal ordering of the world. The political scientist Michael Barnett calls the work of humanitarians and others in this mode of reform and reordering "alchemical humanitarianism."[12] For Barnett, just as early modern alchemists sought to transfigure base elements into substances of value through science and magic, alchemical humanitarians bring scientific and social scientific methods and the "magic" of compassion, and also the magnetism of modernization and Western material culture, to effect reform and relief. And while Barnett's characterization is somewhat unfair, the spells of alchemists and the work of alchemical humanitarians have often had similar outcomes.

This critique aside, the global nature of modern humanitarianism, the consistency of its form and the style of its implementation, defines it as a universalizing ideology and a unique collection of practices that was in conversation with and nevertheless apart from other prevailing early twentieth-century universal ideologies of governance and social organization—nationalism and colonialism, in particular. In other words, modern humanitarianism stands on its own as an exceptional and little-understood element of that era. This is unfortunate, because in this period humanitarianism became among the chief vessels for the modern expression of compassion on a grand, even industrial, scale and a marker of the degree to which the concept of shared humanity of the peoples of the Eastern Mediterranean resonated with broad swaths of Western society. When historians and others study the dominant ideologies of nationalism and colonialism in the first half of the twentieth century, their eyes rightfully focus on the wanton brutality of the time; studying the humanitarianism of that same era is not a correction to that history but rather a way to understand an answer to its underlying inhumanity.

MODERN HUMANITARIANISM AND THE ENDS OF HUMANITARIAN INTERVENTION

A similar question about the evolution of the critical concept of shared humanity can be put to the so-called "humanitarian interventions" in the Ottoman state during the course of the nineteenth and early twentieth centuries. The major coercive violent military interventions of that era—the intervention on behalf of Greek independence in the 1820s, the British and French intervention in the communal crisis in Syria and Lebanon at midcentury, and the first and second interventions in

Crete—were mounted ostensibly "against massacre," to borrow a phrase from the title of historian Davide Rodogno's elegant study of the rise and decline of intervention. As Rodogno argues, clearly there was a putative "humanitarian" side of these interventions, inasmuch as they were conducted on behalf of strangers and others by states insisting—though not persuasively so—that their immediate interests were not at stake.[13] Nevertheless, the concert of European states undertaking those efforts did so with clear imperialist ends in mind, and with little concern for the broader social and political implications and repercussions of those efforts—and even less concern for the Christian minority communities on whose behalf those interventions took place.

The irony, of course, is that humanitarian intervention did not, and could not, prevent the terrible violence during the reign of Abdülhamid II (1890s); the counterrevolution of the Ottoman Second Constitutional period (1909), primarily in Adana; or, later, the mass deportations, rape, and massacres of the Armenian Genocide because of changes in the international system and the growing power and organizational capabilities of the Ottoman government and its military.[14] Nevertheless, the culture of intervention in the Ottoman state over the nineteenth century created in the public consciousness of intervening Western European states a collection of axiomatic truths about Ottoman state, society, and the treatment of non-Muslim minorities. The most important of these was that the Ottoman elite had become, for various reasons, exterior to "Europeanness" itself and that the "Ottoman Empire" was in its essence a barbaric entity beyond the fold of basic civilizational norms; that any domestic efforts at reform would always be inadequate to bringing Ottoman society into modernity; and moreover, that the Ottoman state's status as a Muslim empire would never allow for the real emancipation of non-Muslims. Critically, these cultural and political axioms and hierarchies played a role in conceptualizing the humanitarian mission during the interwar period. Equally, how previous interventions were understood later and characterized in Western public opinion shaped the way the larger meaning of the First World War would itself be explained. In this sense, the war and the postwar settlements and occupations drew for their humanitarian action on the repertoire of past humanitarian interventions.

The form and content of modern humanitarianism was an overlay both on the previous experience with humanitarian intervention and on the preexisting network of Islamic, Christian, and Jewish charitable institutions and modern Ottoman bureaucracies for care. Modern humanitarianism, despite the rhetoric of many of its proponents, did not occur in a social vacuum within the Ottoman state and its successors. Indeed, what is often missing from the historical discussion of humanitarianism is this interaction with local forces and institutions.

ISLAMIC CHARITY, OTTOMAN WELFARE POLITICS, AND THE NATURE OF SUFFERING AT THE END OF EMPIRE

This book posits the idea that modern humanitarianism is a specific ideology of organized compassion that originated in Western Europe and North America. That should not be interpreted as meaning that compassion was absent in Eastern Mediterranean society or that local or transnational forms of care and attempts to alleviate suffering did not also originate from places outside the West. Instead, those forms of caring operated by different ethics of sympathy, definitions of suffering, notions of human value, and basic organizational and funding techniques.

Addressing suffering, especially of the poor, orphans, and widows of one's own community, is a central tenet of Islam as well as a practice of the various Christian and Jewish communities that made up the Ottoman state. The particular elements of these practices varied over time. It is beyond the scope of this work to discuss the broader history of charity in Muslim societies. However, in the late nineteenth century, especially in the period after the broad process of state centralization and bureaucratization of the Tanzimat period (1839–1876), modern institutions designed to care for and manage the poor passed from the exclusive control of Muslim clerics as *waqf,* or holy endowment administrators, to a kind of semiprivate philanthropy. Increasingly, that species of care fell under the purview of the state. As described in the critical literature on this transitional period by historians Amy Singer, Mine Ener, and Nadir Özbek, the forms of institutional care in the Ottoman state and Khedival Egypt shifted from the realm of imperial patronage to state function in the last decades of the nineteenth century.[15] Similar to what was happening in other centralizing states in Europe and North America, the management of the poor, the creation of feeding centers, and the expansion of diverse elements of organized care became an aspect of the relationship between the state and *parts* of society. In the political thought of a handful of Ottoman and Egyptian social theorists of the time, this kind of care was even considered a definitive social contract–like responsibility of the state toward its citizens, particularly citizens who were Sunni Muslims.[16]

With that transition in mind, it is important to recall, however, that in this work I make a critical distinction between national or state-based efforts at public good and modern humanitarianism, which is transnational, nongovernmental, or intergovernmental in origin and implementation. This distinction is far from artificial and is important for several reasons. First, modern humanitarianism often functioned in the absence of the state and its institutions, or in the face of their collapse, as a consequence of either war or natural disaster. Second, when international nongovernmental or intergovernmental bodies mounted efforts to address suffering, they did so outside of the framework of actual governing. This last assertion is certainly contingent and, as I discuss throughout this work, humanitarian action can and often does play a part in establishing the groundwork for a postrevolutionary or postcolonial government; humanitarian programs have the potential to morph into governmentalized welfare and often possess the texture of governmentality, but simply put, humanitarian organizations are not governments. This distinction becomes even more important when considering the narrow range of action available to humanitarian organizations and intergovernmental bodies in the face of the political and legal needs of refugees, the stateless, and displaced peoples. Third, humanitarianism is driven neither by the same motives that impelled imperial patronage—piety or the creation and reinforcement of networks of clients or taxable citizens necessary for rule—nor by the state's need to enforce sovereignty and demonstrate its legitimacy. With the emergence of more modern forms of governance in mind, humanitarianism has no need to defend its legitimacy in the language of civil rights or by appeals to voters. Its legitimacy rests in a field that, by the reckoning of its protagonists, is *beyond the political* and is by its very nature legitimate because it explicitly responds to the problems of humanity and human suffering—suffering that is generally decontextualized from the politics that created it in the first place. Consequently, modern humanitarianism, driven by an ethic of neutrality, has often stood in mute witness to the politics and forms of injustice that cause mass suffering. As this work shows, the interwar period is an origin point for the systematic substitution of humanitarianism for the rights of citizens and human rights, politics, and, certainly, social justice, though not always consistently so.

Nevertheless, it is important to consider briefly two key Ottoman institutional forms that emerged in the nineteenth century that were in conversation with international humanitarianism: the Ottoman Red Crescent Society and the government institutions established to address the suffering of Caucasian and Balkan Muslim refugees fleeing nation-state formation and Russian imperialism. To fulfill international obligations it accepted in agreeing to the Treaty of Berlin, the Ottoman state established the Osmanlı Hilal-i Ahmer Cemiyeti, the Ottoman Red Crescent Society, as its analog of the Red Cross. Though it remained dormant through the reign of Abdülhamid II, the organization was revived by the Ottoman revolutionary elite, including the Ottoman feminist Halidé Edip Adıvar, at the time of the Balkan Wars, and it became an important expression of Ottoman modernity.[17] The resurgence of the Ottoman Red Crescent Society evidences the participation by elements at the highest echelons of the Ottoman state in emerging international humanitarian norms, or at least a degree of familiarity with those norms. Somewhat unique in the system anticipated by the Red Cross movement, the Ottoman state was also home to "subnational" non-state Red Cross affiliates, including that of the Armenian Red Cross.

The retreat of Ottoman power through the course of the nineteenth century led to massive population flows from southeastern Europe and the Black Sea littoral, which brought to Anatolia and the Levant a multiethnic population of primarily Muslim migrants, most of whom had been Ottoman subjects from territories that lay across new borders, but were also intellectuals and politicians on the wrong side of revolutionary and nationalist movements. In response, the Ottoman state promulgated the Muhacirin Kanunnamesi (Immigration Law) of 1857 and established the Idare-i Umumiye-i Muhacrirn Kommisyonu, the General Commission for the Administration of Immigration, which was folded into the reorganized Ottoman Ministry of the Interior in the 1870s, after the calamity of the Russo-Ottoman War.[18] The commission facilitated the flow of migrants into the territory of the state, granted citizenship, organized resettlement, and provided land grants and tax exemptions.

Migrants were distributed throughout the territory of the Ottoman state, but by the latter decades of the nineteenth century, the authorities increasingly pushed them to settle in restive border areas, or where they could confront and help control transhumance nomadic populations; in other places, particularly Inner Anatolia, their settlement was intended to alter demographics in favor of Muslim majorities in the countryside and small villages.[19] The logic of Ottoman immigrant settlement resembled that of other centralizing and colonial states in the same period that instrumentalized the migrant as a labor resource and a tool to create new loyal citizens or subjects in parts of the state where it was concerned about possible separatist movements or wanted to marginalize the original inhabitants.[20] Following the large-scale massacre of Armenians in the 1890s and again in 1909, Muslim migrants were resettled in areas once inhabited by Armenians.[21] Later, the fact that many Muslim refugees displaced by the Russian occupation of parts of Eastern Anatolia were hurriedly rushed into properties that Armenians were forced to evacuate during the 1915 genocide suggests that Ottoman efforts to ameliorate Muslim refugee suffering were among the motives for Armenian dispossession, extirpation, and extermination.[22] Exemplary of this process is a telegram from the Ottoman Interior Ministry's General Directorate of Tribal and Immigrant Affairs to the governorate of Aleppo in the winter of 1916, ordering that in the wake of mass deportations of Armenians from Southern Anatolia:

> One portion of the refugees who have fled from the war zones [i.e., from the Russian borderlands] to Diyarbekir shall be sent off to 'Ayntab, Marash and 'Urfa and settled there. Just as the abandoned [Armenian] houses will be used by the refugees in this manner, after the value has been estimated of abandoned property necessary for the provisioning and clothing of the refugees, the immigrants' share of the allocation is also to be calculated and can be delivered over to them as well.[23]

The alacrity with which Muslim refugees were resettled by the Ottoman state into homes only recently occupied by Armenians—whom that same state had forcibly displaced—reinforces the conclusion that the displacement of Armenians was far from a temporary measure of war—the explanation provided by the Ottomans—and rather had become a permanent regime of communal dispossession that accompanied mass killing. As discussed later in this work, the Ottoman Red Crescent was deeply complicit in the transfer of Armenian children, another element of that genocide. The late Ottoman experience with this multilayered transfer and resettlement project anticipates a critical engine of social and historical change. The unremitting frequency, throughout the interwar period and into the postcolonial era, of the displacement and dispossession of communities and populations for the benefit of other, but somehow preferred, displaced and dispossessed populations is evidence of organized compassion's most cruel possible logics: the suffering of one community is caused to alleviate that of another.

From the perspective of the history of modern humanitarianism, what is most important about the larger context of the Ottoman state's project of settling and supporting displaced Muslims is the historical memory produced by the Turkish state that the community of contemporary Western humanitarians exhibited little concern for Muslim suffering relative to the immense attention paid to that of Anatolian non-Muslims in the same period. Indeed, the response to the suffering of Muslim migrants during the half century preceding the end of Ottoman rule has no analog in the form and content of the way Armenian, Balkan Christian, and Greek suffering had been woven into Western political discourse and public opinion. Explaining the way in which suffering is drawn into the *humanitarian imagination*—or is left out—and then calls into being a humanitarian response is a key concern of this book. The evident lack of response to Muslim suffering by Western humanitarians, or even the acknowledgment of Muslim suffering, colored the way modern humanitarianism was encountered in the late Ottoman period and into the interwar era in Muslim majority states. Moreover, that belief has shaped humanitarianism's contemporary historiography in the post-Ottoman milieu, including how it features in forms of Turkish nationalist discourse and the outsized role it plays in the corrosive modern practice of genocide denial, in which Western indifference to Muslim suffering is a common trope in both popular and academic literature.[24]

Nevertheless, it is critical to remember that the leadership and beneficiaries of the work of the migrant resettlement administration were primarily and purposefully Sunni Muslim subject-citizens of the empire—and in particular those whose ethnicity and origin was deemed most useful to the state—highlighting the fact that the function of organized compassion at the level of the Ottoman state tended to follow sectarian, and sometimes ethnic, lines; the state tended to accept responsibility for its Muslim subjects alongside the general if unstated expectation that needy non-Muslims would be cared for by their own communal institutions. The segregation of state assistance extended to which communities received food and medical aid from it and which did not during the war. With the onset of the Armenian Genocide in 1915, the Ottoman state made the equivalent of war on a subset of its own citizens, placing that subset in a state of exception and denying to it the basic civil protections, rights, and care that it extended to other communities. In concluding his discussion of both the close attention paid by Ottoman authorities to the outbreak of disease in Muslim refugee populations—and the assistance provided to those groups—and the utter lack of assistance provided to Armenian deportees at the same time, historian Taner Akçam writes of the state's archives:

In contrast to the enormous amount of energy, concern and resources that went into the care and resettlement of Muslim refugees and immigrants, one will search the archives in vain for *any* such messages throughout the entire period of the deportations [1915–1917] that reflect anything close to this level of concern for the care and protection of the Armenian deportees, much less for detailed lists of instructions and resource allocations.[25]

Armenians and other non-Muslim communities like the Assyrians were placed beyond the circle of care that the Ottoman state drew around its own Muslim majorities—albeit imperfectly so. That systematic and structural denial of care and violation of rights continued into the 1920s, most notably as the successor state of modern Turkey denationalized refugee Armenians outside its borders, prevented the return of others, and implemented fierce discriminatory policies toward the tiny minority that remained.

Modern humanitarianism in the Eastern Mediterranean took shape in the delineated regimes of caring and exception, as well as in the face of the Ottoman state's largely effective efforts at mass extermination of a minority group. Hence, despite the universalist impulse of modern humanitarianism, as it was put in practice during and after World War I, its objects tended to be non-Muslims—with notable exceptions. To cite only a few examples among many: American faculty at Beirut's Syrian Protestant College sent field hospitals to care for wounded Ottoman soldiers in the Beersheba and Gallipoli theaters of war in 1915; they also established soup kitchens that fed needy Muslims and Christians throughout Lebanon. Perhaps the most sustained cooperation between international humanitarianism and Ottoman institutions took place in the capital, Istanbul. In the first two years of the conflict, the Ottoman Red Crescent Society engaged in joint operations with the War Relief Board of the Rockefeller Foundation (RF) in general relief work, primarily through soup kitchens and orphanages that fed and cared for Muslims, Christians, and Jews in and around the city. However, that cooperation had ended by 1916. The break was explained by the RF's Istanbul representative, Edward R. Stoerer, as a result of a feeling on the part of the Ottoman political elite "that it was undignified to receive active help from the outside and an inclination to resent the suggestion that it was necessary. Though at all times money given outright to them to be administered by their own agents would have been acceptable."[26] After the war, NER hospitals in places like Marash and Ismit were open to all sick and wounded.[27] More important, distinguishing the Ottoman state's concerns about the way accepting foreign humanitarian assistance might undermine its legitimacy or sovereignty (or indeed how the ruling Young Turk military junta believed that aid could help real or imagined enemies of the state), from a prevailing contemporary narrative of Turkish national victimization is critical to understanding how choices were made by both Western humanitarians and the Ottoman state about which groups received assistance and why.

Doubtless, early twentieth-century ideas about race and religious preference informed the choices international humanitarians made in the aftermath of the Great War. However, their efforts were directed toward the Armenians rather than toward Turkish-speaking and other Muslim victims of the war because of the practical reality that the former had faced genocide and dispossession, were living in refugee camps in Egypt, Syria, Greece, and the Soviet Union, and were being prevented by the Republic of Turkey from going home. They were stateless, had no legal standing under international law, and were wholly reliant on Western humanitarian institutions and organizations for their mere survival. They had become *homo sacer,* in the sense used by philosopher Giorgio Agamben; the Ottoman state and its agents had stripped them of the attributes of humanity, including civic belonging, and those that were not killed outright became possessors merely of "bare life" [Gk. ζωή: *zoê*].[28] Western observers at the time, like the RF's Stoerer, echoed the unprecedented quality of this loss among the Ottoman Armenians, writing in his confidential 1917 report that "the desert south of Aleppo was filled with the struggling mass who had seen the foundations of all possible living destroyed in such a way that their initiative and resistance had disappeared."[29] Critically, the concept of *homo sacer* describes the way that the hegemonic and sovereign power reduces human beings to bare life and then exposes them to persisting structural violence. Hence, that violence was directed not just against the bodies of the sufferers, by exposing them to starvation, disease, rape, and murder, but also against the political and social community that victims had inhabited—all of which was compounded by the act of displacement and concentration: the victims were put out of place and into exile in unfamiliar lands, where they were at the mercy of the very institutions and agents of the state that had dispossessed them.

Beginning in the postgenocide period, Armenian intellectuals and relief workers—against that view from the perspective of perpetrator—began to employ the Western Armenian word խլեակ (*khleak*), which originally meant "wreck," as in shipwreck, to distinguish human beings in that distinct state of existence from victims of previous episodes of communal violence or other forms of internal displacement. The title of

Dr. M. Salbi's 1919 description of the work of the Egyptian Armenian Red Cross and British relief workers at the Armenian refugee camp in Port Said, *Aleakner ew khleakner—Waves and Wrecks*—is evocative of the notion of humans nearly drowned and washed up on shore with nothing remaining but their emaciated and barely sensate being—a being whose survival was possible only with the help of others beyond their own community. Armenian refugees from the mountains near Antakya in the Ottoman province of Alexandretta are the subjects of *Waves and Wrecks*. That community had violently resisted a deportation order in 1915. In the face of massacre, a French naval vessel evacuated survivors, who were brought by sea to British-controlled Egypt. The rescued were placed in what was among the first examples of an organized refugee camp, complete with ordered ranks of identical factory-made tents, barbed-wire fences, and militarized security.[30] The word *khleak* conveys further the meaning of the remnant of a thing uprooted, destroyed, and fragmented, and indeed by the 1970s had become the way Western Armenian speakers, including those living in exile in Lebanon and Syria, but also in the Americas, denoted the survivors of the genocide.

A central theoretical contribution of this book is the argument that modern genocide's stripping away of the political, social, and moral tendons that connected Ottoman Armenians to their own individual human being, human communities, and then broader humanity—in other words, the process that made Armenian citizens of the Ottoman state into *khleakner*—prompted a specific and equally modern form of humanitarianism. That humanitarianism addressed more than just a response to their bodily suffering; it embodied a bureaucratically organized and expert knowledge–driven effort to repair their human being, reconnect them to their communities, and restore them to humanity.

Ottoman Muslims had suffered terribly in the war and its aftermath, especially during the Greco-Turkish War of 1919–1922, but the political, cultural, and social elements of that suffering were different; Ottoman Muslims had not faced massive and systematic governmental persecution, dispossession, and denationalization. The multiethnic communities in Anatolia and Istanbul that were recast as Turks as the project of modern Turkish nationalism unfolded would be their nation's definitive and preeminent ethnicity, hold onto religious prerogatives as Sunni Muslims, and enjoy a modicum of rights, including to property and nationality; they had a state and all that it entailed. The very nature of Armenian suffering distinguishes it from the suffering of the late Ottoman state's preferred citizens; that difference does not deny the

FIGURE 1.1. Ottoman Armenian refugees from Musa Dağı at the Port Said refugee camp, ca. 1916. The men are being marched out of the camp by British military officials to a nearby work site. Note the ranks of mass-produced tents. Glen Russell Carrier, United States, photographer, Near East Relief. Courtesy of Special Collections, Fine Arts Library, Harvard University, NERC.484, AKP061.

suffering of any, but rather helps explain the humanitarian reason for humanitarianism's imperfect universality (figure 1.1).

Again, like Agamben and others—particularly Zygmunt Bauman, who sees in the death camps of the Holocaust the synedochic *nomos of modernity*—my own sense is that the deportation caravans, which delivered Armenian victims of organized state violence and extirpation to the deserts of Mesopotamia, are equally definitive of the rules of that modernity and are not the exception to those rules.[31] Perhaps uniquely, in the case of the destruction of the Armenians of Anatolia, other durable rules that imposed ethnic and religious subordination on non-Muslims seemingly outside of the modern were also in play, evidence of the potential oscillation between modern and nonmodern in the commission of genocide.

Those rules have cast long shadows across the history and practice of modern humanitarianism.

MISSIONARIES, HUMANITARIANISM, AND SECULAR EVANGELICALISM

A key argument of this book is that modern humanitarianism represents a significant shift away from the work of Protestant Christian missions and missionaries in the non-West. By the last decades of the nineteenth century and in the lead-up to World War I, the Ottoman state's absence from the sphere of care for non-Muslims—orphans, hospitals, education—was filled not just by local Christian communal institutions but also with a collection of Protestant missionaries from Scandinavia, Germany, Great Britain, and the United States. The study of Protestant missions and missionaries in the Ottoman Eastern Mediterranean (but less so in Ottoman Anatolia) has attracted a great deal of attention—both a function of the ready availability of source material in Western languages and the somewhat unique position missionaries had as representatives of the West, but not necessarily, as in the case of American and Scandinavia missionaries, Western colonizing powers in the Eastern Mediterranean. Pioneering work in the field by historians Inger Marie Okkenhaug, Ussama Makdisi, Ellen Fleischman, Heather Sharkey, and Nazan Maksudyan, among others, paints a historical picture of the remarkably complex relationships that emerged in the late nineteenth century between Western missionaries and local Christian communities.[32] These historians emphasize how the initial intent of the Western missionary presence in the Middle East—the conversion of Jews and Muslims to Protestant Christianity—failed. In the face of that failure Western missionaries turned instead to the transformation of resident Christians—primarily Coptic, Apostolic Armenian, and Eastern Orthodox Christians, who spoke a variety of languages, including Arabic and Greek—into Protestants. It became a question less of converting non-Christians to Christianity than of replacing what the missionaries saw as "primitive Christianity"—replete with what they considered superstitions, Oriental trappings, and theological inadequacy—with a modern Christianity that embraced an individuated relationship with Christ, literacy, moral hygiene, and technological progress. As a consequence, missionaries became increasingly involved in the education, health care, and social development of the growing community of once "primitive" Christians who were now Armenian Presbyterians or Palestinian Anglicans.

A commitment to the care and moral uplift of that community was central to the institutional evolution of the Syrian Protestant College, which in the interwar period was renamed the American University of Beirut.[33] The humanitarian contribution of the college, its faculty, and its students, as well as those of similar institutions in inner Anatolia and the Ottoman capital, plays a large role in this book. As described by Makdisi, the college through the second half of the nineteenth century slowly deemphasized its mission to convert and instead began to position itself in the region as a conduit through which modernity itself would be instituted. The belief in conversion was not abandoned entirely. Instead, conversion, it was believed, would be realized in the fullness of time as a consequence of the moral reordering of the region. The semisecularization of the missionary project likewise allowed the foreign faculty of the college and similar institutions to interact more freely with broader changes in Ottoman society, including engaging young Muslim men and women in Western-style secondary and higher education.

While many of the individuals in the theater of humanitarian action had their origins in the region as missionaries, as did most of the organizers of the humanitarian project of NER, collectively they stood at the culmination of a secularizing movement in the missionary project, in which the goals and methods of evangelism gave way almost entirely to addressing the suffering of human beings and developing institutions for their care, social development, and education. That process of secularization is again outside the framework of this book, but is more broadly reflective of changing trans-Atlantic ideas about religion, the relationship between national culture and religious authenticity, and, as discussed above, the emergence of the practice of "scientific philanthropy," in particular by the Rockefeller Foundation, which shifted resources toward the secular project and away from the traditional missionary one.

What I argue with this work, however, is that the shift toward a secular humanitarianism refocused the impulse that motivated missionaries from conversion to addressing the bodily, and, in many cases, the root causes, of the political and social suffering of the *objects of humanitarianism* (the victims of war, rape, famine, disease). In other words, the concept of faith driving the missionary's work was replaced with a distinctly secular kind of moral reasoning: *humanitarian reason.* Reacting to a concept proposed by anthropologist Didier Fassin, I envision the *problem of humanity* facing the object of humanitarianism as a problem for humanity of the *subject of humanitarianism* (the professional relief worker, the donor, the international institutional bureaucrat, the former missionary). Moreover, that reasoning was based on a confidence in the efficacy of *professionalism,* buttressed by social science, advanced medicine, and public health, to address those problems. In Fassin's use, the concept of humanitarian reason has become the moral economy and part of the social imaginary of modern Western society itself.[34] Here my use is much more limited to humanitarian subjects and the immediate political and social environments they inhabited, but it is still suggestive of a historical point of origin for the idea itself. More important, employing this conceptual framework of humanitarian reason, I can challenge the notion that the reason of humanitarianism is simply, after Hannah Arendt, the transfer of modern human compassion—as opposed to pity—to the generic stranger.[35] The history of modern humanitarianism tells us that at the center of humanitarian reason is a project of *unstrangering* the object of humanitarianism, a process whereby the humanitarian subjects' actions are less about assisting those who are strange and different, and more about helping those found to be knowable, similar, and deserving. As discussed throughout this work, humanitarian reason employs a vast box of linguistic, historiographical, and representational tools, literary and moral archetypes of gender, class, and race, and narratives of civilization to effectively unstranger the humanitarian object and make its problems into a *problem for humanity*.

MODERN HUMANITARIANISM
AS A HISTORICAL PROBLEM

This book is in part a response to the need to provide the practice of humanitarianism, in its dual modes of emergency relief and development, with a historical and intellectual genealogy that disentangles, but also explains, its connections with other kinds of aspirational idealism—in particular human rights. Such a project helps clarify humanitarianism's further entanglements—in the past, with colonialism, and in the present, with neoliberalism and the corporatization and militarization of humanitarian action. Theorists and practitioners have a growing sense that humanitarianism, in the form of humanitarian governance, is being called on to expand its range of action into fields of human activity that have been entirely neglected (the protection of the rights of sexual minorities or the challenge to rights posed by anthropogenic environmental degradation, for example) or just generally considered the purview of the state.[36] Practitioner groups, in particular, have been increasingly interested in the history of humanitarianism. Beyond just the quasi-military bureaucratic formulation of "lessons learned," these groups have expressed the importance of introducing disciplinary historical thinking into the standard reflective practice of aid workers and development officials.[37]

This need also arises from the broader intellectual project of human rights history and the history of human rights. Human rights and modern humanitarianism have an intertwined history, but, as this book shows, it is often difficult to identify how human rights thinking influenced humanitarianism or vice versa. What is clear, however, is that the two concepts have moments of intense historical intersection, especially in the morass of humanitarian failure that preceded World War II and in the violent sorting out of populations and partitions that immediately followed.[38] Exploring questions about the early relationship between the two can inform contemporary debates about rights-based development, and about the interest of governmental and intergovernmental humanitarian organizations in human rights.[39] In these debates, it is critical to show how concepts like neutrality, selectivity, and nongovernmentality became elemental features of the practice of humanitarianism, as well as how rights abuse (civil, human, or national) figures in the historical conceptualization of human suffering. Humanitarianism's contemporary focus on neutrality—regardless of whether or not it is actually achieved—was part of the interwar historical experience, but so too were concerns about what would today be called restorative justice, rehabilitation, and communal and cultural survival. Equally, modern humanitarianism, like human rights, is a potentially totalizing, even utopian, ideology that aspires to be beyond the political, while at the same time being driven by some very powerful social engines and very political politics.

The debate over the genealogical relationship between humanitarianism and human rights has most recently been taken up in *The Great War and the Origins of Humanitarianism, 1918–1924* (2014), by a leading historian of modern France, Bruno Cabanes. He contends that humanitarianism in the aftermath of the Great War was built around the concept he calls *humanitarian rights,* which were invoked and defended by the various humanitarian projects of the League of Nations and international organizations like Save the Children and Near East Relief. In Cabanes's formulation, these humanitarian rights were understood as collective in the case of minority rights, or individual in those that belong to children and women *as victims;* these humanitarian rights are distinct from human rights, as the latter evolved in the period after World War II. Part of Cabanes's evidence comes from the fact that there was a great deal of overlap among the members of activist organizations, especially those advocating women's suffrage and early advocacy for the interdiction of the trafficking of women and children.

Cabanes places the European historian Mark Mazower, and presumably Samuel Moyn and me, in the category of scholars who "claim that there is neither progression nor continuity between the era of humanitarian rights and the modern era of human rights."[40] Cabanes's characterization of my work is correct insofar as it confirms my sense of the lack of gradual linear evolution connecting modern humanitarianism to the legal and cultural formulation of modern individual human rights. However, Cabanes's assertion of humanitarian rights raises significant questions, and from my understanding of the work of humanitarian organizations and individuals in the Eastern Mediterranean, I see little evidence that such a concept was at work in any meaningful way. This is not just a simple definitional distinction: explaining the motivations and values of humanitarian subjects as a manifestation of their own rights thinking about humanitarian objects is deeply problematic. As I discuss throughout this work, the simple fact is that humanitarianism was often used as a substitution for rights and politics, especially those associated with citizenship and national belonging, and was certainly not a parallel rights regime that stands in the genealogy of human rights.[41] It is the case that relief workers and others from Western democracies brought their own conceptions of citizenship rights and personal histories of activism to the Eastern Mediterranean, but they did not translate those concepts into humanitarian practice. Rather, the reason of humanitarianism pivoted not on the rights of the victim of war or genocide, but on the humanity of those providing assistance and, to a lesser extent, the humanity of those receiving it. This holds true as well for the linked concept of human dignity, which is very much a religiously influenced doctrine and not a right. And while the "right to have rights," as described by Hannah Arendt—an idea that germinated in the failure of the interwar minority rights regimes—is related to the notion of shared humanity (but more so to the kinds of political communities neither empires nor humanitarian organizations can form), shared humanity itself does not constitute a rights formula.

Historian Michelle Tusan, whose primary focus is the relationship between British imperialism and the politics of liberalism in the Middle East, argues in a similar vein that "humanitarianism and human rights should not be considered separate, unrelated subjects of study. In the case of the Armenian Genocide, this means reading 'crimes against humanity' as an early category of human rights justice with its basis in humanitarian ideals and imperial institutions that defined premeditated massacres against civilians as a morally reprehensible and prosecutable offense."[42] Ultimately, Tusan conflates the rhetoric used to justify "humanitarian intervention" with human rights. It is difficult to draw a connection between British diplomatic posturing on the treatment of Armenians, postwar war crimes trials against some of the Young Turk perpetrators of the Armenian Genocide (especially as the accused were exchanged for British prisoners of war), and legal and ethical human rights regime. This is not a critique of the evidence Tusan marshals to show that British policy makers, under immense domestic pressure, mounted modest efforts on behalf of the Armenian minority of the Ottoman state as part of its self-declared "humanitarian empire." However, her claim that these efforts constitute human rights prosecutions and interventions layers unjustifiably violent humanitarian intervention with human rights. The same evidence indicates that British action was motivated not by a universal notion of human rights, but rather by a transient identification of the utility of Armenians to geopolitical ends and as an act of Christian solidarity for a Christian "nation" at risk. Tusan's evidence, drawn primarily from statements and writings by representatives of the British Empire itself, can just as easily be used to show that the empire engaged in what political theorist Jeanne Morefield describes as the "politics of deflection"—that is, employing a nostalgic narrative of imagined liberal imperialism to defend a cynical and illiberal foreign policy.[43] As Tusan shows in her own article, and as I discuss in the penultimate chapter of this work, the collapse of Britain's war crime process and abandonment of Armenian national aspirations, both accomplished so easily in the face of a resurgent Kemalist Turkey, calls into real doubt the level of commitment to human rights, let alone humanitarian ideals, of this "humanitarian empire," even for a population with such immense public support in Britain as the Armenians.

Yet the ideas, practices, and historical participants in human rights and humanitarianism are intertwined in the sense that where humanitarianism failed, it created a space in which human rights thinking and innovation was one of several possible alternatives. Still, simply envisioning humanitarianism as a proto human rights system, or a teleological human rights in practice without a historically evident human rights in theory, is quite simply anachronistic and has the impact of obscuring some of the reasons, practices, outcomes, and failures of modern humanitarianism.

These contested histories of human rights, and the possible overlap of human rights with other ideologies, forms of governance, and social movements, are passing through a stage reminiscent of the discussions about nationalism in the 1980s occasioned by its critical revisions by Ernest Gellner in his *Nations and Nationalism* (1983) and Benedict Anderson in his *Imagined Communities* (1983.)[44] Though an imperfect analogy, the need to ascribe an antiquity to human rights—as nationalists do for nationalism's nations—flows from a desire to confirm human rights' genuineness and authenticity that might be lacking were its relative novelty confirmed. Human rights as a basis for action, social justice, and a more humane international legal and social order does not require a lengthy history. On the contrary, a deep history of human rights seems of little concern to contemporary international legal scholars, activists, and practitioners; only when the concept is abstracted from practice by historians does a "long tale" for human rights emerge. But a history that misreads human rights in any moment of expressed humanity or compassion, the public justification for the "humanitarian" machinations of empires, or the assertion of other kinds of civic or communal rights undermines the fact that the modern formation of human rights as a culture and tool for justice exists in the setting of the recent past and was the product of the collective ingenuity of men and women who had lived through (and survived) the mid-twentieth century's humanitarian failures. In sum, the application of a history of modern humanitarianism to the practical understanding of the origins of human rights, especially its experience outside of Western Europe, is among the motivations of this work—even if that history emphasizes the moments of disjuncture, rather than just the intersection, between the two.

Driving it as well is a broader and related historiographical question that populates the tensions inherent to contemporary social history of the colonial and postcolonial non-West: how can we use Western state, intergovernmental, and foundation archives to write about humanitarianism in a way that does more than repackage a kind of diplomatic or institutional history in which the history of non-Western people is retold from a Eurocentric perspective? That question is raised by the fact that the amount of source material produced by humanitarian organizations and intergovernmental bodies is truly immense, and dwarfs that produced by the objects of humanitarianism themselves. This is certainly the case for those records held by the League of Nations at the United Nations archive in Geneva, which are readily accessible and in European languages. That archive, despite its origins in an international organization, is still very much a colonial archive. As a colonial archive it tends to flatten the historical experience of the peoples in the Eastern Mediterranean toward whom its programs and policies were directed. Often, studies of the League and its work in the region, as a consequence of a failure to employ local sources—Turkish, Armenian, Arabic, and Kurdish—also fail to grasp how the League functioned to facilitate European domination of the non-West. This approach ignores the League's sometimes overt and sometimes subtle paternalism, and the role it played in legitimizing and perpetuating colonialism and later nationalism. Critically, as a history of the League of Nations and its humanitarianism emerges, it should interrogate—and, where necessary, reverse altogether—the way in which the archive constructed its own reality. In addition, as the League's archive is vast, better preserved, and much more accessible than other "indigenous" archives (as a function in part of colonialism, but also, as in the case of Syria and Iraq, civil war), we should be conscious of how that might skew the way we formulate basic historical questions. Moreover, among the functions of the colonial archive is to deny the objects of humanitarianism as colonial subjects access to authoritative speech or the right to control their own representation.

The NER's archival record, located at the Rockefeller Archive Center in upstate New York, is more fragmentary as a consequence of institutional indifference, but it too is vast and is only now beginning to be fully cataloged.[45] The close relationship between NER, the US State Department, and the various foundations affiliated with the Rockefeller family means possible lacunae in the organization's own archives can been filled with correspondences, reports, and communications with those other bodies. Nevertheless, the temptation with these sources is to adopt their narrative form and reproduce stories of proposals and projects as they were initiated at the center and then implemented in the field. The result is a kind of antiquarianism and overly repetitive "laundry lists" of the activities of relief workers and descriptions of refugee camps, feeding centers, and resettlement programs that do little to explain modern humanitarianism as an ideology and practice. Such a history cannot explain the moment of encounter between humanitarianism's subjects and objects, or the effects on its objects after the subjects go home. Moreover, the very nature of the historical study of humanitarianism tends to cloud from view the objects of the humanitarian act, rendering them silent and at the same time magnifying the role of the subject. Chiefly this is because the history that humanitarianism produces about itself is a catalog of its institutional features, the projects and motives of the relief workers and others involved in making it work.[46] What I have sought to do in this work, instead, is focus on the point of juncture where policies, personnel, and programs meet, and where the intentions, expectations, and prejudices of the center often crumble in the face of the realities of the periphery.

More to the point, the practice of humanitarianism itself disallows for the inherent complexity of the individual objects of humanitarianism, reducing their history and experience into a single universal title or type: the sufferer, the refugee, the orphan. It is as though to sustain the individual and her unique human being, that being must first become a not-quite-human or perhaps deformed item in a bureaucratic taxonomy.[47] The history of humanitarianism at its best must not reproduce this reduction to blank categories; a real burden is placed, therefore, on the historian to show how humanitarianism changes and transforms its objects and subjects, much like the trauma that precipitated it in the first place. Most important, he must not lose sight of their humanity and listen where he can to their voices. As I have argued elsewhere, this is the way the historian can unleash as a tool of method his empathetic imagination and retain the *humanity* of his work (and himself) when confronted with so much hate, violence, loss, and *inhumanity*.[48]

Building from a new social history of World War I in the Ottoman Eastern Mediterranean, the body of this book does not begin with a humanitarian act, but rather with a decision *not* to help.[49] The first year of World War I in the Eastern Mediterranean was accompanied by late fall rains and the multiyear appearance of swarming locust. The environment compounded the effects of requisitioning, conscription, and the end of any semblance of civilian rule. It was a period marked by food shortages, loss of export markets, and the internment of foreign nationals. As I describe in the next chapter, rains that created the conditions for the locusts also caused the Tigris River to rise above its banks, flooding the Ottoman provincial capital of Baghdad. Though American diplomats asked the American Red Cross (ARC) and the American Jewish Committee (AJC) to help, no help was forthcoming. However, at the same time, large amounts of aid were being raised by a vast network of humanitarian subjects in the United States and the region to help ease the effects of the war and locusts on communities in Jerusalem and Beirut. Comparing and contrasting the different responses, chapter 2 explores how the humanitarian imagination is formed, especially through the process of "unstrangering" the humanitarian object, and then enjoins action. In this case, the cause of Beirut and Jerusalem, enlarged into humanitarian thinking as the Holy Land, helped build a coalition of Progressives, Zionists, Protestant missionaries, liberal intellectuals, extraordinarily wealthy men, and Arab and Armenian immigrant groups, who formed political organizations and philanthropic foundations centered in New York City. From that coalition emerged the practices, media strategies, idealism, and ethics—the repertoire—of American modern humanitarianism in what those Americans saw as the "Near East." Much more so than the American experience with war relief in Europe, the work of American committees and organizations, including the AJC and the forerunners to NER, embraced modes of colonialism— most importantly a civilizing mission—without possessing a colony, and consequently without the attendant brutality.

The repertoire of Western humanitarianism in the Eastern Mediterranean and elsewhere was buttressed by the emergence of a new genre of writing about suffering. Epitomized by the work of Roger Casement, the Anglo-Irish diplomat who penned a 1905 report critical of the European management of the Congo, this new style of writing created humanitarian knowledge that was foundational to the project of modern humanitarianism itself. Central to that creation of humanitarian knowledge was a movement away from the sentimental narrative generally, and, in the Eastern Mediterranean, missionary accounts in particular. Both forms had been deeply important to mobilizing support for abolition and nineteenth-century "humanitarian interventions." Instead, the humanitarian report adopted a forensic, evidence-based, and ethnographic method, and in the years before World War I, even a legalistic approach. Critically, the report could document the systemic (that is, root) causes of human suffering and then build a portfolio of solutions.

This kind of report looms large in the history of humanitarianism in the Eastern Mediterranean. In chapter 3, I show how reports across the era—intended to intervene in European, American, and Ottoman public spheres—shaped perceptions about Ottoman state-society relations and defined the specific meaning of neutrality in the practice of humanitarianism in the years before World War I. Moreover, the format of the report made it possible for observers of the region to understand *as it was happening* that Ottoman Armenians faced genocide. The cumulative effect of that knowledge populated the humanitarian imagination, and indeed aspects of it were used to generate financial and political support for humanitarian efforts; they became the controlling narrative in the way the Near East was constructed as a discrete unit and perceived by humanitarians for the remainder of the interwar period. The report also became important to the presumed objects of humanitarianism: in this period, Armenians and other groups who had fallen victim to atrocity began to generate humanitarian knowledge for use within their own communities and in support of domestic, international, and diasporic relief efforts.

The end of World War I and the occupation of the Eastern Mediterranean by European forces created conditions under which the limited American humanitarian effort was expanded into a massive relief and development program directed by NER. In part, that program sought to use the humanitarian presence as a means to an end of the social, political, and moral reordering of the region—a project I call *American humanitarian exceptionalism.* Chapter 4 explores the limits of that exceptionalism through the historical experience of professional relief workers like Stanley E. Kerr and the physician Mabel Evelyn Elliott. It places their work in the context of NER's greatest failure: the attempt to recreate postgenocide Armenian communities in south-central Anatolia (1919–1923). Focusing on the professional development of the relief workers, I use the events of the disaster to explore why humanitarians were prepared, as Kerr was, to risk their own lives in the aid of others. In the wake of the failure, NER changed its focus to children and the work of establishing an Armenian community in refuge and exile. A few of the children—the objects of humanitarianism—served by NER left evidence of their encounters with this humanitarian project. Chapter 4 continues by bringing those voices into conversation with the relief workers and the broader project of "Americanization" to begin an argument for how American humanitarianism contributed to the form of the Armenian diaspora.

That diasporic community was also formed by the historical experience of the recovery first by Armenian exile philanthropic groups and NER and later the League of Nations—the rescue movement—of thousands of young people who had been trafficked or transferred from their families during the genocide. Reflecting on the particular form of suffering that was endured by children, young adults, and their families, chapter 5 examines the intersection of the form of humanitarianism envisioned by the League and the collapse of Ottoman sovereignty and beginning of European colonial rule. That humanitarian response was built, in part, on an expanding definition of what constituted suffering. Beyond bodily suffering, the League's actions indicate that many in the emerging international community felt that other forms of suffering should elicit a humanitarian response. Focusing on the work of the Rescue Home in Aleppo and the Neutral House in Istanbul, chapter 5 explores the way rescue transgressed social norms and was in fact resisted by the Turkish-speaking Ottoman elite—as well as Sunni Arabs—who saw in the humanitarian project a threat to forms of social dominance. The chapter concludes with a discussion of the implications of that situation for modern humanitarianism itself, in which the humanitarian act is seen as evidence of colonialism and subversion, rather than an act derivative of shared humanity, and is constitutive of resistance, rather than cooperation.

With the collapse of efforts to create a state for Armenians in the face of that resistance, the League of Nations elaborated a humanitarian response to the various forms of Armenian suffering, including statelessness, but also the loss of communal and cultural integrity that accompanied exile. Chapter 6 examines how the international community, in the form of the League, first created the Armenians as the "most deserving" objects of humanitarianism only to abandon support for their national aspirations in the face of a resurgent Republic of Turkey. I use this chapter to discuss the formation of the interwar international humanitarian regime for refugees, and the limited efforts to help those refugees settle, but not assimilate—especially when the distinctive nature of their community was useful to European colonialism. The emergence of this regime for refugees also forced humanitarians to imagine possible legal remedies that brought them into conversations about human rights and their possible utility, or inaccessibility, in the years before the Second World War.

The book concludes with a discussion of the end of the massive modern humanitarian effort of the interwar period and the attempts to translate the humanitarian presence into a permanent regime for development, education, and reform. In chapter 7, I follow historical and policy threads into the post–World War II era, and in particular the Cold War–era US development "Point Four Program" in the region, while also examining the legacy of humanitarian population transfer and its relationship to the theory of genocide and the origins of its canonization as the "crime of crimes" in international human rights law.

As I have written this book and thought about the nature of the archives and the kinds of sources I have used—and reflected on my own emotional responses to the individual stories of loss, cruelty, survival, and resilience, especially of children—I find myself feeling what it must be like to be a curator of a great museum, where only a small portion of what is held in storage can ever be shared and explained. This may be among the first books examining modern humanitarianism and its reach in the Eastern Mediterranean, but it certainly will not be the last, nor should it be. I hope, instead, that it will be considered a starting point to a historical conversation that better connects history, historians, and humanitarians to vital questions about what it means to be human, to suffer, and to have compassion.

CHAPTER 2

The Humanitarian Imagination and the Year of the Locust

International Relief in the Wartime Eastern Mediterranean, 1914–1918

As the Ottoman state stumbled into the global conflagration of World War I, uncommonly late fall rains watered the high steppe and desert at the edges of the settled regions of the Eastern Mediterranean. Those rains set the stage for the metamorphosis of the indigenous grasshopper into swarming locusts the following year.

Remembering the coming of the locusts in his diary, Ihsan Turjman, a Palestinian serving in the Ottoman military, wrote: "Monday, March 29, 1915. . . . Heavy rain fell on Jerusalem today, which we needed badly. Locusts are attacking all over the country. The locust invasion started seven days ago. Today it took the locust cloud two hours to pass over the city. God protect us from the three plagues war, locusts and disease, for these are spreading through the country. Pity the poor."[1] A few months after the end of the war, Bayard Dodge, at the time a professor at the Syrian Protestant College, recalled to his father, Cleveland H. Dodge, one of New York City's wealthiest men,

> In the Spring of 1915 a new misfortune came upon the country and added to the hunger and distress of the people. One day a great cloud appeared in the southern sky. As it approached the terrible fact impressed itself upon the people of the land that a huge plague of locusts had descended upon them. Swarms of flying insects covered the ground and filled the air. . . . It was in July, when the young worms were hatched, that we found out what a plague of locusts could mean. . . . Everywhere they covered the ground and ate everything green with an unbelievable rapacity . . . in fact everything green was eaten by the locusts. When they had eaten up everything which they

could find, they disappeared as mysteriously as they had come but their work of destruction had been accomplished and accomplished thoroughly.[2]

The year 1915 is remembered throughout the region as the 'Am al-Jarrad—the Year of the Locust. Locust plagues are not uncommon in the Eastern Mediterranean and occur at roughly ten- to fifteen-year intervals. This particular plague lasted from March through October of that year and recurred again in 1916. Despite concerted efforts by the Ottoman authorities to control and exterminate the insects—including requiring all able-bodied teenagers and men in the affected major cities to collect kilos of locust eggs per day or face a hefty fine—the locusts ate field crops, destroyed nut, fruit, and citrus orchards, consumed grape vineyards, and devoured olive trees. The loss of food and fodder helped push some communities already on the edge of food scarcity—because of the rise in prices and military requisitioning—into starvation.[3]

However, the impact of the locusts was only one part of the larger economic dislocations caused by the war; indeed, in Beirut starvation among the city's poor had begun before the plague. Bayard Dodge and others remembered seeing starving women attacking shipments of flour in the streets of Beirut, pulling the sacks off the wagons to take a few handfuls home to their children—a reminder that famine can be less about natural food scarcity, and instead about access to food and the way military and government policies often put that access out of reach of the poor and, in the case of Beirut, even the emerging middle classes.[4] There was a causal relationship between the locust plague and suffering, but previous plagues in the region had not led to half a million extra deaths in the civilian population (a conservative estimate of the casualties in Greater Syria between 1915 and 1918.)[5] Perhaps the reason the locusts were held responsible for so much suffering in retrospect is that information about the distribution of food throughout the country was strictly curtailed by Ottoman newspaper censorship and security measures that made criticism of the state and its officials dangerous; the locusts could be safely blamed in a way their human counterparts could not.

For the civilians of the Eastern Mediterranean, the onset of World War I came at the end of almost a generation of on-again, off-again conflict between the Ottoman state, breakaway regions in the Balkans and the Arabian peninsula, and European states. The Great War was different from those more limited wars in terms of the immense burden it placed on the peoples of the region, and not just in terms of the loss of men to mass conscription, but also through the seizure of property and food. More so, the war meant that the region's once-major trading partners—Britain and France—were now enemies, and even commerce with neutral states was difficult in the face of naval blockades in the Eastern Mediterranean. This affected the importation of food and had a devastating impact on nascent industry and the export of commodities from citrus fruits to tobacco, cotton, and silk. Perhaps the greatest difference however, was that the Ottoman state was willing to make the equivalent of war on segments of its own population, either through neglect or the mechanisms of mass extermination. Though the outcome of the war would redraw the political map of the region as the Ottoman state was replaced by nation-states and colonial occupations, the conflict's social impact served as the impetus for new kinds of international humanitarian action. That action supplanted older forms of Western missionary-based charity, on one hand, and was interlaced with more secular but no less zealous missions to address suffering and instigate specific kinds of deep social and institutional change, on the other. More often than not, the end product of that desired change was implicated in various forms of the European colonial project and specific modes of American paternalism.

The history of the various forms of relief and humanitarian action during the war reveals that the topography of observable suffering—the kinds of suffering and categories of victims—informed a specific consciousness of the "humanitarian emergency," to borrow a contemporary concept. In turn, this consciousness, what I term the *humanitarian imagination,* structured the choices and strategies adopted by ad hoc relief groups and emerging international institutions, including Near East Relief (NER) and the American Red Cross, about whether or not to help and what form that help would take. Put quite simply, during the Great War in the Middle East, some humanitarian emergencies prompted a humanitarian response. Some did not.

Modern-day humanitarians would argue that the possibilities for humanitarian action are limited and attribute the reason for choosing to help or withholding assistance to a broad spectrum of factors, including the physical location of the emergency (is it hard to get there?), interference by local governments, and even the danger posed to aid workers by militias and rebel groups. These conditions equally applied to humanitarianism in the Eastern Mediterranean during World War I and its aftermath and were complicated by fears that civilian aid might make its way into the hands of belligerents. These worries were voiced early in the conflict by the French and British, who believed that American food aid could be diverted to assist the Ottoman military. Similar concerns were raised in the European theater of war and contributed to the style of humanitarian assistance that is evidenced in the work of the British-based Save the Children Fund, which sought to provide food aid to children in occupied Western Europe, as well as to the children of Britain's enemies in Germany and Austria-Hungary.[6]

Still, these objective and even material explanations fall short of accounting for why some groups, even those in similarly difficult relief environments, received assistance during the war years, while others did not. Clearly, who was helped was as much about how the groups and individuals could be constructed as deserving *objects of humanitarianism* as it was about logistics or safety. Creating or perhaps becoming an object of humanitarianism was an accretive act that derived not just from the severity of need but also from the way groups and individuals in need became inscribed in the humanitarian imagination. In this sense, the humanitarian imagination is the organizing principle of *organized compassion:* it is defined by historical encounters between the subjects and objects of humanitarianism; by the existence of constituencies, advocacy groups, and diasporas; by the prevailing logics of civilizational narratives; and by how successfully empathy is created and then sustained. The humanitarian imagination is additionally shaped by how the salvation of those in danger meets the political and moral needs of the humanitarian subject, and whether or not those helped are gauged to be *deserving* of that help. The most critical feature of the humanitarian imagination, however, is how the emergency is formulated and then understood as a *problem for humanity* because it is a *problem of humanity.*

Reflecting on the history Save the Children, David Reiff asks us to imagine how different it might have been if the organization had been named "Save the People." "The agency's mandate of 'helping children in emergencies' may be morally uncomplicated. But relief is not. It was morally ambiguous in the heyday of nineteenth-century European colonialism, it was morally ambiguous in 1919, it was morally ambiguous in Biafra in 1967, and it has been just as morally ambiguous in the aftermath of the Cold War."[7] This chapter examines the ambiguity inherent in the way natural disasters, famine, massacre, and displacement have (or have not) been organized into a problem of humanity that became then a problem for humanity to address. These problems of humanity formed the basis for the international humanitarian response—or lack thereof—during the First World War in Baghdad, as well as in Jerusalem, Beirut, and their hinterlands.

Implicit in the broad comparison of the humanitarian imagination at work in these three cities is a challenge to the assumption that the creation of sentiment through narration is critical to helping "the stranger." What the historical experience of humanitarianism during the first years of World War I in the Eastern Mediterranean shows is that the ultimate decision to engage in humanitarian assistance derives instead from a modern project of "unstrangering" the object of humanitarianism that is beyond the nominal concept of empathy. Put another way, while it may be still a form of empathy, it is an emotional and intellectual response that is built on more than an acknowledgment of the humanity of the object, but is formed through narrative, photographic imagery, and formal identification in an act of class, social, or religious solidarity. The work of humanitarianism is predicated on the closing of the distance between the humanitarian subject and the humanitarian object, so that the latter is rendered not so strange after all, but rather, in the imagination of the humanitarian subject, knowable, even to the point of being envisioned as an extension of the self or community of that subject.[8]

BAGHDAD: DECEMBER 1, 1914

Red Cross does not feel justified attempting Bagdad flood
relief at present.

—William Jennings Bryan (Washington, DC) to Henry
Morgenthau (Constantinople), December 31, 1914

The same late-fall rains that triggered the locusts in the Levant to emerge also fell on the Iraqi highlands and caused the Tigris and Euphrates Rivers to flood. Until the recent advent of the system of dams along the length of Mesopotamia, river floods occurred frequently, most often in spring, as the snow melted from the slopes of Anatolia's Taurus Mountains. But despite telegrammed warnings from the governor of the northern city of Mosul of the river's dangerous rise, the municipal authorities of Baghdad did little to prepare for the inundation.

Over the course of the nineteenth century, Ottoman reform and municipal planning projects had walled Baghdad from flooding. Bringing wild rivers to heel behind dams and levees was a chief concern of the Ottomans in their Mesopotamian provinces, as it was for other modernizing states. As the river flooded in late 1914, the land around Baghdad was transformed into a shallow inland sea and refugees poured into the city, seeking shelter on the low levees surrounding the provincial capital. Crops that would have been harvested in anticipation of the spring flood were lost, as was livestock. The innermost half-circular dike that was the last line of the city's defense had fallen into a state of disrepair, and on the first night of December, it failed. The river washed into the city, destroying in its wake entire neighborhoods, especially those of the city's poor; stored food stocks of wheat and sugar and animal fodder were ruined. Resident foreigners estimated the number left homeless at twelve thousand. More important, these accounts concluded that the local authorities were incapable or unwilling to address the suffering of Baghdad's civilian inhabitants—in part because of the flood's overwhelming nature, but also because of a general indifference in the face of the Ottoman army's need to secure food and matériel for the war effort.[9]

Alongside a detailed description of the flood from his consul in Baghdad, the American ambassador in Istanbul, Henry Morgenthau, sent an appeal for assistance to Secretary of State William Jennings Bryan and asked him to share it with the American Jewish Committee (AJC) and the American Red Cross (ARC), the two leading US-based humanitarian organizations that had begun to do some work in Europe and the Eastern Mediterranean on behalf of refugees and displaced populations. The appeal to the AJC was not coincidental; rather, it was a recognition of a fact well-known to Morgenthau, though perhaps not to the community of American Jews, that fully a third of Baghdad's population at the time were Arabic-speaking Jews. Indeed Baghdad, like Salonica (Thessaloniki), now in Greece, and to a lesser extent Aleppo, in today's Syria, was a city central to Ottoman Jewish life. Jews dominated much of Baghdad's economy and participated vigorously in its intellectual and cultural scene.[10]

Nevertheless, the reply from the chairman of the ARC, which had an office in Istanbul (established a few years earlier to extend American assistance to Ottoman Armenian survivors of the series of state-sponsored massacres during the 1890s) carries the sense that the situation in Baghdad was *beyond* the reach of humanitarianism:

> The Red Cross funds at our disposal for relief are all designated by the givers for European war relief. No doubt the suffering at Bagdad is acute, but so it is on a colossal scale in the seven European nations at war. We are bending all our energies to meet the immeasurable demands for assistance that come to us from those countries and we know that our help, considerable though it may be in the aggregate, goes but a short way in effective relief of the misery. . . . We do not feel that we would be justified in attempting Bagdad flood relief, which would mean the assumption of another burden at a time when we know that the tasks already assumed are greater than our resources.[11]

The ARC did authorize Morgenthau to use some funds already in his own care from the organization if he saw fit. The archives are silent as to any further American assistance to the people of Baghdad. The floods that year were followed by a cholera outbreak that added to the suffering caused by the mass conscription of eligible men and the requisition of food and supplies by the Ottoman military. Repairs on the levees that protected the city from the annual flood did not take place until after the British occupation and the onset of interwar colonialism in March 1917.

Baghdad looms large in our own contemporary vision, but why did it fall so far beyond or outside of the humanitarian imagination in that moment, when equally devastating economic dislocation, famine, and starvation did spur humanitarian action in the Eastern Mediterranean? Even then, Baghdad was a major provincial capital with commercial connections to global trade networks; news of its devastation by flood and Morgenthau's appeal appeared in the pages of the *New York Times*—but only once and then never again. The utter lack of compassion for its people is striking in retrospect. In part, it may have been just as indicated: the major donors to the ARC were committed to the war effort in Western Europe. But there was no empathetic connection between the twelve thousand homeless and soon starving and sick inhabitants of Baghdad and possible humanitarian subjects in the West. That link did not and could not exist in the absence of the complex lattice of history, commercial and philanthropic relationships, and the essentializing effects of racial and religious thinking that focused the humanitarian imagination and brought it to bear on other emergencies at hand. Perhaps also the fact that the flooding of the city was not an unforeseen act, and indeed was a by-product of what would have been confirmation of dominant attitudes about Ottoman ineptitude and corruption, made the inhabitants of Baghdad, in the view of some, responsible for their own destitution and thus less deserving of humanity's help.

JERUSALEM: DECEMBER 7, 1914

I would say that the Red Cross would be glad to cooperate in meeting the needs in Palestine as described by Consul Glazebrook.

—J. W. Davis (Washington, DC) to Secretary of State (Washington, DC), December 7, 1914

Referring to your telegram of yesterday, the American Jewish Committee is considering the advisability of sending a ship with provisions for the relief of the destitute of Palestine, but before it can act advisedly on the subject it is important to know whether the cargo will be requisitioned by the Turkish Government if it is delivered in Palestine and whether any of the belligerent nations would intercept the ship or prevent the cargo from being landed if these possible obstacles are obviated; I believe that arrangements for the sending of the ship could be perfected.

—Louis Marshall (New York) to Secretary of State (Washington, DC), December 4, 1914

As the Ottoman state officially entered the First World War in November 1914, poor harvests, combined with mass requisitioning of food and livestock by the Ottoman military authorities, had pushed the inhabitants of Jerusalem perilously close to starvation. This was exacerbated by the fact that much of the Palestinian economy was centered on the export of agricultural commodities—like the famed Jaffa orange—to European markets now closed due to the war. Unlike word of the Baghdad flood, which percolated slowly from the Ottoman provinces to the capital and then to New York, information about the conditions in Ottoman Palestine reached the West through multiple contacts and organizations, and with tremendous speed: one Rabbi B. Abramovic of St. Louis sent a communication to the US State Department in late October, claiming, "Received today cablegram from Central Committee of Jewish population of Palestine, that they are starving."[12]

Similar telegrams inundated the offices of the US Secretary of State. Within three weeks of the first indications of starvation (mid-November 1915), and at the urging of Stephen Samuel Wise (1874–1949), the activist rabbi of New York's Temple B'nai Jeshurun, several Jewish humanitarian organizations, in particular the Provisional Executive Committee for General Zionist Affairs and the American Jewish Relief Committee (which became the AJC), had begun to work with the US government to secure safe passage of a ship or even ships to relieve Jewish suffering in Palestine. Wise, among the founders of the National Association for the Advancement of Colored People (NAACP), was a leader of Progressive-era American Zionism and, alongside other major Jewish figures of the day, including the jurist Louis Brandeis, went on to work with various foundations to establish the outlines of the broader American humanitarian relief project in the Eastern Mediterranean.

To the extent that relief supplies and money were allowed by Ottoman, French, and British authorities to enter Palestine, these efforts were successful. By March 1915, the AJC had secured the support of the US government to dispatch relief supplies on an American naval vessel, *Vulcan*. The secretary of the Federated Jewish Charities of Baltimore, Louis Levin, was appointed to oversee the transfer and distribution of those supplies; *Vulcan* departed Philadelphia on March 14, 1915, and arrived in Alexandria, Egypt, three weeks later. Once there, Levin purchased several tons of supplies, including six hundred pounds of tea.

Through intense negotiations, the customs fees at the Jaffa port of entry were waived, but Levin faced the added difficulty of transporting the goods via camel and donkey, as the Jaffa–Jerusalem railway was out of service. In Jerusalem, a local committee to distribute the aid had been organized along sectarian lines; still, though, Jews received 55 percent of the total allotment, with the remainder being divided among Muslims and Christians.[13] And while Levin noted in his final report that conditions in Jerusalem were not so desperate, "The country is not without food, though some of the necessaries of life are very high . . . had food not advanced at all, there would have been great distress nevertheless."[14] He also observed that business and trade had come to a halt and that medicine and fuel oil had to be imported. Locusts had arrived that spring as well, though the full implications of that plague would not be felt for several months. Seemingly exhausted by this mission, Levin concluded his report with the advice that sending money to Palestine would be a better idea.[15]

Why Jerusalem and not Baghdad? Recognizing the inherent difficulties in juxtaposing the distinct forms of disaster in each of these communities, the stark contrast in response is definitive, nonetheless, of how the humanitarian imagination worked. Compassion was extended to the Jews (and others) of Palestine and not the Jews (and others) of Baghdad because the problems of the former could more easily be understood and explained by Wise and American subjects of humanitarianism as one affecting humanity. This link to a particular view of humanity is an outcome of not only the demographic origins of many of the inhabitants of 1914 Jerusalem but also the larger meaning of the Jewish presence in Palestine for American Jews and others in that historical moment.

By the outbreak of the war, the Jewish population of Ottoman Jerusalem had risen to over forty-five thousand, up from some twenty-eight thousand in the period before the Second 'Aliya.[16] Much of the total population was foreign in origin, and thousands of Jews had immigrated to Jerusalem or other parts of Palestine to establish colonies for various reasons, including escaping pogroms in Eastern and Central Europe or as an expression of Zionism; some European and American Christians had created small "colonies" there as a manifestation of their millennial thinking. By the outbreak of the war, Palestine had attracted Christian colonists from the United States and Europe, a fact reflected in residual place and institution names like Hamoshava Hagermanit, the German Colony neighborhood founded by Evangelical Lutherans in Haifa or the American Colony Hotel north of Jerusalem's old city. In this sense, the victims of hunger were not so different from those promoting and providing humanitarian assistance, or at least not as different as those in Baghdad. The occasional identification of the objects of humanitarianism using the first person ("ours, us, we") in letters to the US State Department is itself a reminder of the reality of the level of cross-identification.

At the root of the alacrity and depth of assistance offered to the communities in Palestine was also the *closeness*—or affinity, as it were—of Ottoman Palestine as the Holy Land to the United States, at least in the broader conceptualization by donors and organizations in the United States constructing an understanding of the humanitarian emergency. The intimacy of Americans with both an imagined Biblical Holy Land and an actual Palestine has been the subject of a great deal of scholarly attention.[17] Formed by everything from the advent of higher criticism and Biblical archeology to travel literature—Mark Twain's *Innocents Abroad* being the most notable in this genre—this association is seen as both a prefiguration of post-1948 American support for the creation of the state of Israel and a manifestation of the way nineteenth-century Americans understood their own historical experience with settler colonialism, especially in the American West. By the end of the nineteenth century, this literary and religious closeness was augmented by the relative ease by which Americans could travel abroad. Before the war, many Americans had been to Palestine; larger numbers knew of it from their Bibles and Sunday school classes, in which photographs and paintings of religious sites and scenes of daily life were common. Jerusalem was a presence in their lives and consciousness that a flooded Baghdad just was not.

Beyond the fact of this closeness and the forms of empathy it could engender, the Jewish colonists of Palestine also occupied a position in larger Progressive-era American Zionism's vision of social reform and modernization, which saw in that movement a central act in the "recovery" of Israel, and also a very particular kind of civilizing mission. Stephen Wise, the liberal rabbi who played such a prominent role in advocating for sending relief to the Jewish communities, and also for Armenian relief, himself had traveled to Jerusalem via Egypt for the first time in the months before the outbreak of World War I. His autobiography, written thirty-five years after his first visit and seen through the lens of his two later trips to Palestine under the British Mandate, documents how this consciousness of closeness was formed and in turn buttressed a unique sense of mission. Wise's account is replete with stories typical of American travel writing on Palestine and its generally pejorative view of Palestine's Arab inhabitants. These stories include a discussion of a mother's rejection of unsolicited health advice from Mrs. Louise Wise, who had accompanied her husband to swat flies away from the child's eyes because "it is the will of God"; a description of the beating of a local Arab peasant by an Ottoman official for failing to deliver grain; stories of avaricious officials and complaints about demands for tips in Egypt; and an account of a man who would not let his wife ride a donkey he himself was riding, because he would be "forever disgraced." Indeed, for Wise, "The Palestine of the immediate prewar year, 1913, was for the most part, save for spots where there were Jewish beginnings, a land of misery, disease, poverty, lawlessness, and ignorance."[18]

The decadence of the Holy Land, which Wise called the "old Turkish-dominated, Turkish-corrupted and Arab-neglected Palestine," would be redeemed through Jewish settlement (which he refers to as "re-settlement"). Still, Wise was critical of what he saw as the larger negligence of Europe and America's Jews toward the Zionist project:

> What little there was in Palestine had been begun and developed before the rise of Zionism, and the little added was a testimony of dishonor to the Jewish people. Whether because of lack of imagination or because of morally searing fear, these had committed and were for a time destined to continue to commit the sin of leavening the thin line of Jewish outposts without those reinforcements which it was the part of collective decency, irrespective of theory, to bring to their heroic brothers.[19]

At stake in the wartime suffering of Jews in Palestine was the utter failure of the entire Zionist project. The loss of this community's integrity to starvation and impoverishment was a threat to the advent of modernity in Palestine that their very being there represented to Wise, and thus, that threat had universal implications for civilization, and a capacious meaning that burdened humanity itself with added responsibility. As a consequence, that potential loss defined the problem of humanity that produced the humanitarian emergency of that moment.

Wise returned to the United States from his 1913 trip intent on raising awareness of the Zionist cause. Through his friendship with both

Ambassador Morgenthau and President Woodrow Wilson he attempted to organize a return visit to Ottoman Palestine at the head of the investigative commission to assess the needs of the Jewish communities. The outbreak of the war forestalled such efforts, and Wise instead undertook the kind of relief work that culminated in the sailing of *Vulcan*. In the early months of the war, he had secured a loan of fifty thousand dollars from donors in West Coast American cities including Seattle and Los Angeles to aid Jewish orange growers. Building on the relative success of that campaign, he organized the American Provisional Committee for Zionist Affairs (APCZA). The committee's "first task . . . was to save as much as possible of what had been planted in the twenty or more colonies in Palestine, the work of the *chalutzim*—the pioneers."[20] The committee fell under the umbrella of the AJC, which became the major Jewish civil society interlocutor with the US government during the war and its aftermath, and would also attract financial support from American luminaries, including the department store magnate Nathan Straus.

For Wise, the fact that the AJC's humanitarianism was able to bring prominent American Jews to the larger Zionist cause marked that organization's manifold importance. Among the organization's new supporters was the jurist Louis Brandeis, who became the committee's chair in 1914. Wise believed that the relief work of the committee had brought Brandeis back to involvement with the Jewish community, and "he came, after a number of intervening years, to give a goodly part of his life, almost the best part, to the Zionist cause, as if in reparation for the years of neglect of the Jewish problem and the terrible needs it involved."[21] Relief of needy Jews in wartime Palestine was a cause that American Jews who had been reluctant to involve themselves in Zionism could embrace. Transforming the wartime suffering of Jewish colonists into a humanitarian emergency framed their condition as a cause worthy of attention; it was about humanity itself and not mere politics. Essential questions about the role of Zionism in an era of broader Jewish assimilation and even nascent concerns among some Progressive-era Americans about involvement in overseas colonialism could be set aside in the face of the humanitarian nature of the problem. As such, it was a problem *beyond the political* that simultaneously ennobled the humanitarian subject and alleviated the suffering of a knowable, modern, and empathetic humanitarian object. Nevertheless, as Wise concludes of Brandeis's leadership of the AJC, which ended with his appointment to the US Supreme Court in 1916, "His leadership in the early years of the war made possible the fulfillment of our major task—the political one."[22] Wise attributed much of Woodrow Wilson's later support for the Balfour Declaration (1916) and the continuing support for Zionist aspirations in British-occupied Palestine to his relationship with Brandeis. However, Wilson's support was also predicated on the belief that Zionism could be used to channel European Jewish radicalism away from support for Leftist ideologies, and that Palestine, rather than the United States, would be a place where Eastern European Jewish migrants could go.[23]

This overlap of the American Jewish humanitarian project in the Eastern Mediterranean with a domestic political project, including those devoted to forms of moral uplift, is a recurring historical theme in this period. In this instance, however, not only were Jews who had distanced themselves from Wise's vision of American liberal Judaism brought back into the fold, but the restoration of the Land of Israel through modern humanitarian development also became a feature on America's providential horizons. The politics of national redemption would become a part of the work of NER as well—Wise himself was one of its founding board members. As discussed later in this book, NER's mission evolved over the course of the war and its aftermath, but at the center of its activities was providing assistance to Ottoman Armenians and other Christian minorities, who were imagined as definitive American protégés.

Wise's affiliation with NER at this early stage was an expression of his sympathy for the cause of the Armenian inhabitants of the Ottoman state in the face of growing evidence of genocide. It also shows that Wise, like others in a widening circle of philanthropists, educators, religious leaders, and politicians in New York and elsewhere, had begun to conceptualize the human impact of the war in the Eastern Mediterranean as a series of humanitarian emergencies, distinct from the way the war in Europe and its humanitarian needs would come to be seen. Indeed, what is critical about the early experience of modern humanitarianism in Ottoman Palestine is how it shows the emergence of a uniquely American *civilizing mission* in the region, in which relief work both had a semidivine meaning and functioned to demonstrate the transferability of American-style modernity to what Wise and others saw as a decrepit and decayed land.

At the same time, the empathy implicit in Wise's support for Armenian relief is evidence of how his sense of shared humanity extended well beyond his own coreligionists. In fact, Wise faced disapproval for this support (and its implicit criticism of the Ottoman state) because it might

endanger the Jews of Palestine. The circle of shared humanity had motivated Wise to advocate in the United States on behalf of civil rights for
African Americans, union rights for industrial workers, and a host of
other Progressive causes; for him, Jewish identity itself was demonstrated
by the act of caring for others. His sustained devotion to these causes
throughout his lifetime proves the depth of his conviction. Nevertheless,
that empathy had clear boundaries: it did not extend, for example, to the
Arab agriculturalists removed from land their families had farmed for
generations as it was sold to Jewish colonists, nor to local non-Jewish
laborers who were barred from working in Jewish-owned agriculture or
in factories: "The hurt to the Arab laborers was un-designed. It was
bound, too, to bring about a larger development of the land, which, after
years, made it possible to employ the services of large numbers of Arab
laborers—that is, after the first, hard, grinding pioneering work had been
done by the Jewish colonists."[24] The indifference to Arab suffering or
willingness to excuse it, perhaps only in the short term, is indicative of
how the practice of modern humanitarian could at once appeal to the
universality of shared humanity and still functionally exclude portions of
that humanity by adopting a narrow field of action. In retrospect, Wise's
decisions, though understandable in his particular context, seem all the
more cruel in the face of a biography deep with concern for the oppressed.

That selectivity and evidence of the intent to civilize is present in the
other early postwar accounts of modern humanitarian efforts mounted
by transnational Jewish relief organizations. The British occupation of
Ottoman Palestine in the fall and early winter of 1917 reduced many of
the obstacles to the transfer of money and delivery of direct food aid
that had so stymied American relief efforts. Moreover, it meant that
nationals of formerly belligerent states, most notably Great Britain and
to a lesser extent France, could participate in that work. Established in
Cairo, the Special Committee for the Relief of Jews in Palestine operated as the main agency for relief until 1918, when such work was
transferred to the Relief Department of the Zionist Commission. The
transfer of operations to the Zionist Commission was heralded as a
major step forward in the form of relief in Palestine, representing
"progress from mere alms-giving to relief of a constructive character
. . . for productive purposes, and not merely to secure the hand-to-
mouth existence of the indigent."[25] That constructive character translated to a fourteen-point plan for social improvement and the creation
of permanent institutions for health care, education, and moral discipline.

In this sense, modern humanitarianism's emphasis on addressing the root causes of human suffering with the intent to eliminate those causes altogether provided the blueprint for "humanitarian governance," in which relief and humanitarianism evolved into the social service and education wings of a quasi-sovereign Zionist proto-state in Palestine. In the early months of the Western occupation of Palestine, the British had ceded to the Zionist movement almost exclusive control of the humanitarian efforts directed toward the Jewish population. That relief was intended solely for Jews indicates again the outline of the polity to be governed. Indeed, among the "services" the new agency provided were traditional poor relief and the distribution of food. It also distributed religious items and books; established hospitals, institutions for the aged, and orphanages; provided job training and workshops, primarily for women; offered agricultural loans; and prohibited prostitution and some wine sales.[26] While the Zionists could not exert complete agency over all the fields of government, in this one sphere (humanitarianism-cum-social welfare) they had exclusive control, could act like a state, and could demonstrate their competency to be one. The provision of humanitarian assistance to the Jewish communities of Palestine—including not just the immigrant colonies but also European merchants in Jaffa and the impoverished inhabitants of Jerusalem—allowed the Zionist Commission to operate with a degree of political freedom it lacked during the Ottoman period; the working of humanitarian assistance allowed as well for the practical imagining of the Yishuv as a modern sovereign nation-state.

This connection between humanitarianism and subnational, perhaps even insurgent, governance has recurred in the face of colonialism, authoritarian rule, and even civil war. The emphasis that the Muslim Brotherhood in Egypt, during its period of political marginalization in the 1980s to the early 2000s, placed on the provision of humanitarian assistance (for example, during the 1992 Cairo earthquake) demonstrated its ability to provide relief—and popular legitimacy—where the Egyptian state proved unwilling or unable to. Similarly, Hezbollah in Lebanon exerts much of its state-within-a-state power through humanitarian assistance and social welfare programs. In another parallel, during the Algerian War of Independence (1954–1962), Algerian nationalists formed the Algerian Red Crescent Society in the model of contemporaneous Red Crescent organizations in other Arab countries. This was a direct challenge to the French colonial state's monopoly on connections with international humanitarian assistance. The relative success of the Algerian Red Crescent Society in the field, and its ability to address suffering, provide medical assistance in a way that comported with international standards, and garner international aid, proved, as it were, the modernity of the Algerian nation and its right to rule itself.[27] This example demonstrates again how humanitarianism can operate as a carapace over otherwise unpopular or problematic political currents.

As Wise observed on his return trips to the Holy Land—now Palestine, under a League of Nations mandate—the success of the humanitarian missions of the war and postwar period illustrated both to fellow Jews and to the world community the achievement of tokens of governance and of something of equal importance, a vital and self-confident moral and political community. Still, the universal appeal to humanity that underscored Wise's efforts betrays this blind spot in the practical vision of the modern humanitarian. And while the modest food aid that did reach Palestine in the first shipment on *Vulcan* was shared to some extent by all the needy in Jerusalem (though not proportionately), later efforts during the war and the years following the British occupation made plain that the focus would be not just relieving the immediate suffering of Jews in Palestine, but using the mechanism of relief to embark on bold development projects that would address the roots of their suffering as a *people*. As Wise concludes, "The business of the dwellers in and restorers of Palestine was to build a future, to make that future conform to the best in the Jewish past and create . . . a new nobleness in the Jewish future."[28] Modern humanitarianism had provided an opportunity to make the "new nobleness" a communal response to the threat to humanity posed by the depredations of the war years. It was more than an end unto itself, but rather an end couched in terms of rebirth and renewal that bore, nonetheless, many of the hallmarks of interwar colonialism.

BEIRUT: APRIL 21, 1915

For months the pitiful cry of beggars has been echoing in our ears and the streets of Beirut have been lined with poor wretches, whose lives have been flickering out from weakness and fever. Even more terrible than the starvation of these poor wretches on the streets of the city, has been the hidden suffering of thousands of families, who have been too proud to beg and yet too poor to live. Attempts to find work have failed and day after day, day after day, they have sunk deeper and deeper into the depths of despair, with nothing but hope to live upon. War is a terrible thing and nothing can be more awful than the battlefield, unless perhaps it is the neglected home in the horrors of war.

—Bayard Dodge, "Relief Work in Syria during the Period of the War"

Historians liken wartime Beirut to a city under siege.[29] Its physical location at the foot of a coastal mountain range made it dependent on imported food, either shipped in from Egypt or Bulgaria, or brought over land from inland Syria and the grain-growing regions of the Orontes River valley and the Hawran. Beirut's emergence over the course of the nineteenth century as a major cultural and economic center of Greater Syria, with a population of some 150,000, was a product of its integration into these larger regional trade networks—and with the collapse of those networks, the city faced a terrible crisis.

With the beginning of the war, the port of Beirut was blockaded by the French and British navies, which contributed to the shortages of food, but the diversion of what the locusts did not eat to the Ottoman military effort and unregulated food speculation played a much more important role. Indeed, this was how the causes of the food shortages were understood by American diplomats in Beirut at the time, who attributed the starving of the city's poor less to the effects of locusts than to a "coal famine."[30] A lack of fuel prevented grain shipments by rail altogether from the interior; as Beirut starved, wheat was still widely available in Aleppo and Damascus. In the spring of 1915, there was even some hope of diverting the collier *Vulcan* after she delivered food to Palestine, so that she could then bring coal to Beirut.[31] Regardless of its origins, the famine caused unprecedented forms of misery and destitution, reportedly accompanied even by the eating of human flesh. The social dislocation of the famine had far-reaching effects on the city's social and domestic spheres.[32]

Yet what distinguished Beirut from other hard-hit cities in the region was that it attracted international humanitarian assistance. It was the site of large-scale relief work organized first by resident Americans, and later in coordination with local Muslim and non-Muslim members of the city's wealthy and upper-middle class; the city later received massive support from philanthropic organizations in the United States as well. How the crisis in Beirut was understood, and the form of response to it, shaped the American humanitarian enterprise in the Eastern Mediterranean for the remainder of the interwar period and, to some extent, well into the 1940s. Driven by many of the same forces that transformed the cause of Palestinian Jews into a cause of humanity, wartime relief in Beirut is broadly definitive of the way organized compassion is the outcome of institutional and individual closeness, and also how certain kinds of suffering and sufferers may come to matter more than others.

Posing the question of why Beirut and not Baghdad is complicated by the fact that the emergency in Beirut unfolded over the course of almost the entire war—unlike Baghdad's emergency, which was acute in nature. But the cosmopolitan city on the Mediterranean shore possessed historical, ideological, and commercial connections with the centers of humanitarian organization that the city on the Tigris did not. Not only was Beirut home to a major American institution in the form of the Syrian Protestant College (SPC), which was renamed the American University in Beirut after the war, and the creation of French Mandate Lebanon, it was also linked to the American presence in the region through education and missionary work in a way that was unrivaled in the rest of the Ottoman state, even in Istanbul. That presence extended as far back as the 1840s, and generations of Ivy League–educated Americans had worked in mission schools and formed the faculty of the SPC. By the advent of the war, the college and its foreign faculty were woven deeply into the social and intellectual life of the city.[33]

What Beirut and Lebanon had as well was the massive Syro-Lebanese diaspora, which had settled primarily in the United States but also in Egypt, Western Europe, and South America. This diaspora population was in a position not just to help through transferring funds back "home," as it were, to their extended families, lessening somewhat the economic impact of the Year of the Locust, but also to advocate on behalf of Beirut and its hinterland with governments and aid organizations. Critically, this advocacy took on an Arab nationalist dimension, in which the suffering of the Lebanese at the hands of the Turks was as much about food shortages as it was about the fact that they were not Turks, but rather Arabs and Christians with long-standing ties to the West.

Finally, unlike Baghdad, Beirut was also home to a branch of the American Red Cross (ARC). The Beirut chapter was established in 1909 and was managed locally by US consular officials, college faculty and their wives, and employees of the American Presbyterian Mission Press, known locally as the American Press. The press, which published in both Arabic and English, was a holdover from the days when the Syrian Protestant College was at the center of a larger American missionary effort to convert Muslims and Jews in the Holy Lands to Christianity.

In the years immediately before the outbreak of the war, the ARC in the United States was undergoing reform following the forced ouster of its founder, Clara Barton. By 1914, the ARC had been transformed into a prototypical modern humanitarian organization, embracing both the

Progressive-era reform agenda and a social science research–based approach to addressing suffering. The description of the ARC's work in Beirut shows some evidence that the changes that had taken place in the United States had had an impact on the way the organization operated. This is especially apparent in the way the group developed programs in coordination with research faculty at the SPC, its scrupulous neutrality and nonsectarianism, and its fostering of programs that encouraged economic development rather than just charity. That said, the work of the ARC was still very much an effort mounted by a small expatriate community that focused on the city and the immediate countryside around it. Memoirs and letters by faculty and employees of the American Press convey a sense of deep paternalistic obligation to the City and the Mountain, as Beirut and its hinterland is often called. Nonetheless, while there certainly was a sense that the locusts, famine, and economic dislocation caused by the war affected other communities in the Levant, only later, after information about the genocide of the Ottoman Armenians and the certainty of a British and French victory reached them, did the "amateur" humanitarians of Beirut begin to imagine positioning themselves in a broader humanitarianism-centered reform project for the entirety of the Arab Eastern Mediterranean.

The ARC's relief work unfolded in Beirut and Lebanon in several stages and was aided by the fact of American neutrality in the global war. Nonetheless, the organization was hampered by political intrigue between the political leadership of the city of Beirut and that which controlled the hinterland in the mountains behind it. Among the ARC's earliest efforts was to send a field hospital to Palestine that was staffed by faculty and students from the SPC's medical school and German missionary nurses to care for those wounded from fighting between Ottoman and British forces at the Suez Canal (February 1915). A similar mission was undertaken at the time of the British attack at Gallipoli, after which medical students and faculty again traveled on *Vulcan* to administer medical assistance to Ottoman forces. Operating field hospitals was one of the established responsibilities of the ARC; however, the choice of the Beirut chapter to participate in treating the wounded also demonstrated fidelity to the Ottoman state at a time when the depth of the expatriate community's commitment could have been questioned. For the Americans in Beirut, the neutral act of ministering to the wounded had the anticipated effect of gaining the support of Cemal Pasha, the Ottoman military governor of Syria and one-third of the Young Turks' ruling junta. While the ARC did not mount any other

FIGURE 2.1. Suq al-Gharb soup kitchen, ca. 1916. Source: Howard Bliss Collection 1902–1920, Folder AA:2.3.3.18.3, American University of Beirut/Library Archives.

medical missions, many of its medical college alumni did serve in the Ottoman military's medical corps.

The bulk of the ARC's other early activities in and around Beirut took the form of soup kitchens and food distribution centers (figure 2.1). Early in the war, the Syrian Protestant College faculty had developed a systematic application process that enrolled some fifteen hundred people per month and allowed for a more efficient network of feeding centers and a way to quantify the depth of need. Alongside its work facilitating food distribution, the ARC organized the city into subunits overseen by Western, usually female, volunteers, and provided employment to men and boys to repair roads and remove trash; women were put to work tatting or doing needlework. And while the coming of the locusts exacerbated the emergency, accounts from SPC faculty and the local ARC workers indicate that, for much of 1916, the worst effects of starvation were kept at bay in the city and nearby communities.[34]

Nevertheless, as the ARC worked in Beirut, the *cause* of the starving of the City and the Mountain was gaining increasing attention in the United States through a unique coalition that brought together various diaspora civil society organizations with some of America's most elite philanthropists and reformers. Similar to news of the crisis in Jerusalem, information about the humanitarian situation in Beirut traveled along religious and ethnic networks, and quickly. For example, in May 1916, Michel Lutfallah, a leading Arab nationalist, and one Shuqayr Pasha, both wealthy expatriates living in Cairo, approached the US consul alongside several other leaders of the Syrian community in Egypt to express their deep concerns about the conditions in Beirut and elsewhere. The appeal to humanity is striking in the petition they handed him: "We have no doubt that the U.S. Government who, thanks to their privileged position as neutrals and as custodians of the laws of humanity, have so nobly contributed to the alleviation of the miseries of other people whose sad lot it was to suffer keenly from the War, will not hesitate, in the view of the urgent need for relief to render another such service in the cause of suffering humanity."[35]

At the same time, the poet Gibran Khalil Gibran (1883–1931), who served as secretary-general of the New York–based Syrian-Mount Lebanon Relief Committee, wrote to the recently appointed US secretary of state, Robert Lansing, "The people of Syria and Mt. Lebanon, Sir, are actually dying of starvation and the diseases resulting from lack of nourishment. Their distress is appalling, and they are to-day a helpless people doomed to extinction. . . . We appeal to you, Sir, we the Syrians of this country, thousands of whom are American citizens, in behalf of our stricken country and our starving people." The letter indicates that the Syrian-Mount Lebanon Relief Committee was "working in cooperation with the American Committee and we hope to raise enough funds soon to be able to send a shipload of food supplies . . . to ward off, if possible the effects of the impending famine that threatens the extinction of a whole race."[36] Gibran's letter was accompanied by translations of anonymous firsthand accounts of the effects of the famine.

Responding to information from Beirut, the newly formed American Committee for Armenian and Syrian Relief, what Gibran called the "American Committee," adopted the cause of the starving in Lebanon in addition to its increasing concern about the condition of Armenians in Anatolia. Chaired by James L. Barton, foreign secretary of the American Board of Commissioners for Foreign Missions, who had extensive experience in the Ottoman state, the organization included in its leadership and board members eminent religious and educational figures, such as Harvard University's Charles W. Elliott, Rabbi Stephen Wise, the diplomat Oscar Straus, the publisher George A. Plimpton, and the philanthropist Cleveland H. Dodge, who was at the same time one of Woodrow Wilson's major campaign donors and father of Bayard Dodge.

The American Committee evolved into Near East Relief, which, as discussed in later chapters, became the preeminent modern humanitarian institution in the Eastern Mediterranean. However, at that moment, the committee was also taking shape to fill the vacuum left by the US-based ARC as the latter organization shifted its focus almost exclusively to the war in Europe. In the summer of 1916, NER began raising funds to supply a "Christmas Ship" to bring supplies to Beirut on the model of *Vulcan* (figure 2.2). The campaign, which attracted tremendous support among the American public, demonstrated to its organizers the efficacy of modern advertising for humanitarian fundraising, something that they replicated as the organization evolved to assist Armenian Genocide survivors during and after the war. The ship, again an American collier, *Caesar,* was loaded with seven hundred thousand dollars' worth of food and supplies but never reached Beirut. It languished for months at a dock in Alexandria awaiting permission to disembark from the Ottoman authorities; eventually, its cargo was sold and the funds were slated for use in Lebanon. For the American relief workers, the loss of the Christmas Ship was deeply demoralizing and, indeed, in the months that followed, the rate of Lebanese death increased.[37]

The entrance of the United States into the war against Germany in April 1917 further hampered foreign relief efforts, and the local ARC chapter temporarily ceased operations in the summer. Relief projects, soup kitchens, and make-work programs were continued on an ad hoc basis or shifted to the college's faculty, who were able to distribute direct grants to needy families and assist in the management of a large orphanage at Brummana, in the mountains to the east of the city, which was established to take in the increasing number of destitute children. Ottoman officials in Beirut and Mt. Lebanon implemented similar relief measures with far less success; local civil society groups that were generally organized along sectarian lines participated in relief work.[38]

In the last year of the war, the former chairman of the ARC and director of the American Press, Charles Dana, was interned in Istanbul with his wife and his niece, Margaret McGilvary, who had served as the organization's secretary. Shortly after the war, Dana and McGilvary returned to Beirut. McGilvary's 1920 memoir, *The Dawn of a New Era in Syria,* is the most compelling first-person account of the work of the Beirut chapter of the ARC, and it also documents the intensity of connection the Americans in the city felt toward its inhabitants. Beyond

FIGURE 2.2. Cover of American Committee for Armenian and Syrian Relief pamphlet promoting the "Christmas Ship," ca. 1917. Source: RAC-RF 1:100, International Projects, box 77, folder 724. © Rockefeller Archive Center.

detailing the scope of the Beirut-based relief work, the book reconstructs the humanitarian problem in Beirut and Lebanon not just as one of food distribution, but rather as an outcome of alien rule and lack of social cohesion. According to McGilvary, the purpose of relief had been not only to feed the poor but also to help the Beiruti middle class to remain intact and usher in the "new era" of her book's title. Upon her homecoming, she observed:

The population at large was absolutely destitute, and, for the first time during the war utterly without resources. It was no longer the habitually indigent who were now suffering. That class had been exterminated early in the
siege. It was the middle-class, who had been . . . accustomed to modest comfort and decent living . . . [who were now] depending on charity for their
very existence. . . . The most discouraging feature, from the philanthropic
standpoint, was the fact that during this year many families that had been
partially supported by relief-funds died. A terrible reminder of the apparent
waste and futility of investing money in so feeble a security as human life.[39]

"That class," the middle class, had been the constituency of society
to which the SPC faculty had looked to implement the kinds of reforms
that could successfully translate modernity from America to the Eastern
Mediterranean. Preserving that class, whom the Americans in Beirut
related to in personal and paternalistic terms and as evidence of the
modernizing impact they were having, was the imperative and thus the
problem of humanity at the center of their collective humanitarian
imagination. Equally, the collapse of Ottoman rule had created an
opportunity to address not just immediate suffering but suffering's root
causes; in other words, the work of the ARC and NER had laid the
groundwork for a broader modern humanitarian enterprise. For McGilvary, the success of that project was at risk, and she advocated not just
continued relief for the poor, but also a focus on economic reconstruction that would aid the middle class and put Syria more firmly on the
path to modernization and regional leadership:

Syria has hardly begun to recover from the effects of the war and she still
needs all the sympathy cooperation and philanthropy which have been
accorded her during the past four years. The most striking illustration of
serious need which occurs to me is a simile that someone used recently in a
discussion of this very problem. He was pleading for continued American
relief support and he said "as soon as a child learns to take his first step do
we expect that it will henceforth be able to walk alone without further assistance from parents or nurse?"[40]

In McGilvary's estimation, beyond continued assistance, understood
here in the most paternalistic of terms, soup kitchens and orphanages
were just the opening act in the broader humanitarian *and* political
engagement of the United States with Beirut, Lebanon, and Syria that
would be completed by placing the new state under direct American
administration as a consequence of the postwar settlement.[41] For her,
the optimal situation would see the limited relief work of the war years
translate into an American humanitarian government in Syria that

would not just aid in reconstruction but help develop it as a *modern nation-state*. This would mean creating a Syrian nationalism, embracing a nonsectarian Syrian identity, and defeating any efforts to divide the country along religious lines.[42] Bayard Dodge's own assessment echoes McGilvary's in its paternalistic vision of an American role in rebuilding Syria. In comparing the late Ottoman period and the war years with the present moment, Bayard Dodge told his father, "Liberty, reconstruction, and public service have replaced despotism, demoralization and misappropriation."[43] What was needed to continue this work was "sympathy":

> But the stern sympathy of a teacher rather than that of an indulgent parent. The work cannot be accomplished in a year or even in ten years. The hundreds of orphans must be guided along the path of life. The thousands of poor people must be uplifted. Perhaps the Red Cross can never complete or even half complete its work, but it ought not to build up temporary structures, which will later on be uprooted and torn down. Whatever little can be done should be accomplished with reconstruction in view. It should be a well-laid foundation to be handed over to more permanent agencies, rather than a quickly built framework, which will fall to pieces as soon as the Red Cross workers return home.[44]

For Bayard Dodge and the faculty of the SPC, their experience of relief had provided them an opportunity to transform their broader mission into a permanent expression of American benevolence, rather than traditional evangelism. Indeed, the humanitarian disaster of the war allowed for the university to fully transition away from a missionary-based enterprise and embrace a more modern and secular vision of education and development. Nevertheless, this humanitarianism took shape as any hope of American political presence faded in the face of French colonialism, which established Lebanon and Syria as separate republics. Still, the faculty of the college and their friends and relatives in New York played an equally critical role in defining the emergency for Americans and bringing it into the larger circle of philanthropy emerging from institutions led by the Rockefeller Foundation (RF).

The transition that ad hoc relief underwent during the war—from addressing the immediate needs of starving populations to a complex comprehensive program for identifying and then addressing the root causes of human suffering—is the historical trajectory of the preeminent humanitarian projects embarked on in Palestine and Beirut. Broadly conceived, these projects were part of a movement in the United States to meet the global humanitarian challenges of world war. Writing about the American historical experience with that movement, historian Branden Little concludes that:

> Humanitarian aid therefore functioned as a vehicle by which Americans could directly participate in the war during the period of US neutrality from 1914 to 1917 and beyond. Through publicity and fund-raising campaigns the [Commission for Relief in Belgium, the RF, and the ARC] alerted the American public [to] the horrors of war and through a nationally coordinated network of state and local chapters provided mechanisms to assist Europeans. Most Americans had few qualms about feeding the "deserving poor" as they perceived the Belgians but opinions about sufferers [in] other regions varied considerably. Some saw relief work as a way of striking a blow against German barbarism and as a desirable prelude to US military intervention; others opposed to the war and to US military intervention viewed relief as a means to check the worst aspects of the conflagration.[45]

The American humanitarian project in the Eastern Mediterranean was similarly motivated and employed many of the same organizational techniques for fundraising and distribution. For some Americans, supporting relief in Europe was analogous to going to war itself—its "moral equivalent," if such a correspondence were in fact possible. The sense of mobilization and urgency that made humanitarianism resemble war presents itself in the work of the AJC and the SPC faculty, but the ideological underpinnings and social and political goals of relief in the Eastern Mediterranean distinguished it from the European experience, and indeed it was constructed in the humanitarian imagination quite differently. The problem in the Eastern Mediterranean was imagined within the framework of its holy geography, of the suffering of Christians at the hands of Muslims, of noble pioneers holding civilization's line against barbarism. Ultimately, in the humanitarian imagination, the suffering of the peoples of the region demanded a different kind of American humanitarian presence.

The ultimate separation of the major relief organizations into those that served the Eastern Mediterranean rather than Europe, in particular the way the American Relief Administration (ARA) was tasked with Europe and Russia, was in part an administrative one, but also reflects how the emergency in the Eastern Mediterranean was understood and suggests that, in unraveling the history of modern humanitarianism, the location of relief has as much a probative value as the institutions involved. That said, while the humanitarian subjects imagined the "Near East" differently from "the Orient," Russia, or Europe, they could still categorize those problems for humanity in universalist terms and invoke a general appeal to shared humanity. In that sense, the historical experience of relief in the Eastern Mediterranean still maps onto the larger formulation of modern humanitarianism. In practice, while this early project of relief embraced the semblance of neutrality and universal need, it was still located in identifiable forms of the civilizing mission that informed the character of colonialism, even if it was not accompanied by a colonial occupation. For the Americans—mostly Protestants and liberal Jews—modern humanitarianism functioned as an ethical and moral vessel in which to place the politics of an American presence in the region and to distinguish that presence from other colonialisms practiced by European imperialists and "Oriental" despots: Ottoman, French, and British. For the diaspora of Levantine Arabs in the United States and elsewhere, advocating for relief produced a venue from which to advocate for Arab independence from Ottoman rule—that rule being, in their estimation, the *cause* of suffering as much as the locusts were.

Humanitarianism allowed for an expression of an American colonial paternalism without the brutality of foreign rule; it also presaged the emergence of a philanthropic coalition that brought Progressive-era social scientific reformers together with old-school missionaries; the former had been searching for a way to expand idealism abroad while the latter sought a way to remain relevant in an environment in which the evangelical project was impractical, but a secular and educational role was not. These early relief efforts were dwarfed by the programs, and need, that followed the end of the war.

CHAPTER 3

The Form and Content of Suffering

Humanitarian Knowledge, Mass Publics,
and the Report, 1885–1927

In 1904, Roger Casement, an Anglo-Irish diplomat, penned a report documenting the massive institutional exploitation, population transfer, murder, and torture that had come to be part of everyday life in the Congo Free State's rubber trade. Prepared for the British Parliament, the report contributed to the end of Belgium's King Leopold II's personal rule of much of central Africa. In the two decades since the Berlin Conference (1886) had awarded the Congo to Leopold on the condition that he open the region to international commerce and improve the lives of its inhabitants, first-person accounts from Christian missionaries and journalists had trickled out about mass atrocities and massacres. These accounts often included photographs of mutilated children and whip-scarred backs as a powerful tool authenticating the written text. Despite the photographic evidence, Leopold and his supporters dismissed the stories as the ravings of missionaries, Leftist ideologues, and anticolonialists. Indeed, the king himself employed an army of journalists, travel writers, and, in the case of the University of Chicago anthropologist Frederick Starr, an academic to make his case that his critics' claims were exaggerated and to assert the benevolent and humanitarian nature of his rule.[1]

Though it relied on those previous accounts, the Casement Report was different in its tenor, use of evidence, and affect. It employed a careful reporting style that bore the hallmarks of professional disciplinary forms of analysis—political economy, ethnography, history, and anthropology. To readers today, it feels modern in ways that the overblown

rhetoric and "sad and sentimental tales" of missionaries and abolition-
ists of the nineteenth and early twentieth centuries do not. Consider
Casement's discussion of his visit to the Lake Mantumba region. He
writes:

> A careful investigation of the conditions of native life around [Lake Man-
> tumba] confirmed the truth of the statements made to me by M. Wauters, the
> local American missionary, and many natives, that the great decrease in pop-
> ulation, the dirty and ill-kept towns, and the complete absence of goats,
> sheep, or fowls—once very plentiful in this country—were to be attributed
> above all else to the continued effort made during many years to compel the
> natives to work india-rubber. Large bodies of native troops had formerly been
> quartered in the district, and the punitive measures undertaken to this end
> had endured for a considerable period. During the course of these operations
> there had been much loss of life, accompanied, I fear, by a somewhat general
> mutilation of the dead, as proof that the soldiers had done their duty.[2]

The forensic nature of the report—accompanied by photographs, first-
person testimony from Europeans *and* Congolese, including refugees,
and records kept by company officials documenting the company's own
policies—was both dispassionate and persuasive, and it ultimately led
to international parliamentary action. Yet Casement's report also provided an intellectual underpinning to a popular transatlantic movement
that included literary and political luminaries of the Gilded Age like
Samuel Clemens and Arthur Conan Doyle, both of whom wrote extensively on the Congo. Moreover, it is possible to identify other reports of
the era that are similar in style and effect on domestic causes. The foreign humanitarian report should be understood as an element of a larger
body of Progressive-era literature on such diverse fields as child labor,
female emancipation, and public health.

Still, this particular report held the actions of Europeans in the Congo
up against what Casement and some of his readers had begun to consider universal norms of civilized behavior. These norms, which were
conceived at times as a legal framework and at others as a moral code,
were built from the humanity (and liberal being) of Leopold's victims
and the inhumanity of what was happening to them. Less important in
the story Casement tells—though still present—is the need to create
empathy for victims as the basis for the reader's moral obligation;
rather, his appeal enjoins a distinctively modern and rational form of
humanitarian action that is different from sentimental empathy. The
Casement Report is novel in the way it brings into focus the actions of
Europeans and a European monarch. Moreover, it is possible to read it

as a larger indictment of European colonialism, though the European states that ultimately brought Leopold's rule to an end still maintained vast colonies throughout the globe where the denial of basic human rights and violence against colonial subjects were routine.

Casement's work on the Congo and later reports on the treatment of the indigenous Putamayo in Brazil, who were also victims of rapacious rubber barons, represent a watershed in the origins of what is now considered human rights reporting.[3] The form and content of those reports evidence the evolution of a specific way of creating an understanding of and knowledge about the *problems of humanity* that populate and form the modern humanitarian imagination as they become *problems for humanity,* and thus prompt humanitarian action. The emergence of modern humanitarianism is, in part, a product of the rise of that narrative form. The content of the reporting intersects with the political and social expectations of the Western middle-class public sphere and its technocratic, disciplinary knowledge–driven—and sometimes rights-based—response to humanitarian need. And while it is certainly the case that "sad and sentimental tales" were (and are) used to open wallets, the definitive and sustained humanitarian projects of the early twentieth century in the Middle East and elsewhere were built from this new form of knowledge.

More succinctly, modern humanitarianism required the kinds of knowledge that a simple empathy-evoking story could not provide. The advent of modern humanitarianism did not extinguish what, for lack of a better term, could be labeled the "sentimental missionary narrative" that, especially in the Middle East, adopted a religious vernacular to describe the suffering of non-Muslim minorities. Rather, the sentimental narrative persisted through the war years and often overlapped with the modern narrative. But by 1914 it was going out of style and was being replaced not just by the humanitarian report, but also by memoirs of professionals, including those involved in public health and higher education.

At the core of the reports of this era are four elements that mark them as both a key component of modern humanitarianism and distinctive from nineteenth-century styles of writing about humanity and suffering: First, such reports employ a capacious definition of suffering—one that goes beyond starvation or massacre to include forms of social, legal, political, and what in modern parlance would be called cultural suffering. Second, they use history and social science to categorize the victims and perpetrators of suffering in ethnic, class, racial, and religious terms that are not necessarily asserted as essential or natural, but sometimes as historically contingent. Third, they blend—even interchange—concepts of civilization and humanity and equate an ecumenical (though in practice Protestant) Christianity with civilization. And fourth, they use the parlance of reform, here in both political and social senses, and what at the time would have been called "scientific philanthropy," to address suffering and often a reflective and even self-critical stance toward the implementation of that assistance.

The form and content of the report parallels the diminishing role of conversion narratives and a reductive understanding of Ottoman society, in particular, as touchstones in writing about suffering, and their replacement with secular narratives of race, nations and nationalism, and civilizations and civilizing missions. The secularization of the narrative is especially critical to the historical experience of humanitarianism in the Eastern Mediterranean, as putative religious conflict was reinterpreted against a backdrop of nations and peoples astride a great cleft in civilization, in which victims of inhumanity and humanitarian subjects were arrayed on one side and perpetrators, again often understood as peoples and nations, were on the other. This secular move to the format of the report also helped humanitarian organizations assert neutrality in the way they dealt with Muslims and non-Muslims, even when humanitarian practice emphasized aid to Christians and Jews.

The end of the nineteenth and first decades of the twentieth century was the golden age of the humanitarian report in its various formats in the Ottoman and post-Ottoman Eastern Mediterranean. These reports focused primarily on the suffering of non-Muslim subjects of the Ottoman state as a *problem for humanity* with solutions exterior to military intervention. Bracketing that period are two key reports. Among the earliest humanitarian organization reports is Clara Barton's *America's Relief Expedition to Asia Minor under the Red Cross* (1896). Barton, the founding president of the American Red Cross (ARC), led a relief mission in Anatolia in the wake of a series of state-sanctioned massacres of Ottoman Armenians that caused as many as two hundred thousand deaths.[4] At the other end of the period is Fridtjof Nansen's *Armenians and the Near East* (1927). Nansen, who served as the League of Nations' high commissioner for refugees, hoped with his report to lay the foundations for a permanent solution to the problems caused by the humanitarian disasters of the war years and the failure of the international community to formulate an adequate political solution to the mass displacement and denationalization of the Ottoman Armenians. Across those intervening three decades, a body of *humanitarian knowledge* was created about Armenian suffering as well as about the history, culture, and society of the Ottoman state. This knowledge had implications beyond the immediate forms of humanitarian action; it influenced popular opinion in Europe and North America about the region for much of the remainder of the twentieth century as it shaped forms of colonial and postcolonial politics.

This chapter follows the evolution of humanitarian knowledge as it formed from the reports of the era and around the treatment of non-Muslims in the Ottoman state during World War I. That knowledge had been shaped by moments of massacre as early as the Greek war for independence, but had accelerated after the last major European intervention in the Levant (1860) and would be utterly transformed by the 1880s. What is crucially distinctive about the content of the humanitarian knowledge created by the reports of this era, however, is how it organized the Ottoman state's efforts to destroy the community of Ottoman Armenians during World War I into a cohesive narrative with a history, precedents, and global implications. That narrative transcended older ways of thinking and writing about mass killing, starvation, and displacement and instead insisted that what was happening, in the title of the most influential report of the era, was nothing less than the "Murder of a Nation."

Equally important is understanding how that humanitarian knowledge was shaped and reshaped in ways that enjoined action. These reports were not written for a limited audience, with some exceptions. Rather, they were prepared in a way that assumed the mass circulation of the stories and ideas each employed. Indeed, reports of the period were often printed by some of the leading publishers of the day. That "mass marketing" brought this particular problem of humanity to an ever-widening circle of organizations, community groups, and individuals, who, through activism and financial support, could participate as humanitarian subjects. It is not just the way the narrative of what historians since the 1960s have called the Armenian Genocide instigated a project for humanitarian assistance in the years after 1915 that marks the broader importance of humanitarian knowledge. What is also important is understanding that that knowledge generated an international consciousness that what had happened to the Armenians had been a "crime against humanity," which in turn galvanized calls for *justice*. That said, as the history of mass atrocity and genocide in the Ottoman state and its successor became an established fact, especially in the wake of the war, in international forums like the League of Nations, it generated *antihumanitarian narratives* that sought to minimize the horror or deny altogether the truth of the humanitarian problem.

The emergence of the humanitarian report and the evolution of humanitarian knowledge about the Armenian Genocide rest in a broader framework than simply the genocide's relationship with the origins of relief organizations like Near East Relief (NER) or how it informed British parliamentary discussions on the "Eastern Question." Part of explaining the process of emergence is understanding how the object of humanitarianism—Armenians themselves—as both survivors and members of a global diaspora played a role in the accumulation of the humanitarian knowledge of their own suffering. The potential agency of the humanitarian object in the formation of humanitarian knowledge is a historical fact that often goes unnoticed in histories of humanitarianism, and is difficult to account for in the face of humanitarianism's inherent paternalism. The historical record indicates that the voices of the humanitarian object risked silencing by paternalistic humanitarians as they sought to placate antagonistic national governments or to reinforce claims to neutrality. But they are there nonetheless, and, as an effort to understand and address Armenian suffering began in humanitarian circles, Armenians themselves sought to comprehend the enormity of the Medz Yeghern, the "Great Crime," and what it meant to them as individuals, families, refugees, and a political and social community. This process of comprehension was autochthonous in the way it shaped an Armenian consciousness and built a postgenocide Armenian identity, and in dialogue with modern humanitarianism as the material and political needs of the community grew more acute.

ASSESSING SUFFERING'S CAUSE: DEFINING
HUMANITARIAN NEUTRALITY AND THE
HAMIDIAN MASSACRES

The quick, glad cry of welcome of a city [Zeytun] that had known
but terror, sorrow and neglect for months—a little rest, help given,
and over the mountains deep in snow, wear and worn their caravans
go, toiling on towards fever and death. . . . This is the work of
America's people abroad. My message, through you, to her people at
home—not to her small and poor, but to her rich and powerful
people is, remember this picture and be not weary in well doing.

—Clara Barton (Istanbul) to Frances Willard (New York),
1895 (from *Report*)

Like the cause of the Congo, the state-sponsored massacre of Ottoman Armenians from 1894 to 1896, often characterized as the Hamidian massacres, attracted a great deal of attention from major figures of late nineteenth-century political and social reform in Europe and the United States. It even brought the British statesman W.E. Gladstone out of retirement to advocate for the cause of the Armenians.[5] Building on a generation of stories of atrocity against non-Muslim minorities of the Ottoman state, primarily in the Balkans, the reports of massacre and forced displacement transmitted to the West via Protestant missionaries, journalists, and diplomats—and despite efforts by the Ottoman state to block news of the extent of the massacres—generated public support and concern. While in Britain the response to the Hamidian massacres was a key moment in the emergence in liberal thought of a humanitarian and international register within which to put the Eastern Question, in the United States the response figured prominently in the origins of modern humanitarianism; moreover, it established the way the relationship between the Ottoman state, its Muslim majorities, and its Armenian minority would be conceptualized there into the interwar period.[6]

From the perspective of late Ottoman history, despite a relative wealth of documentation, the Hamidian massacres remain inadequately understood, both in terms of causes and broader social impact, beyond the sense that they were related to Ottoman anxiety about the loss of territorial integrity and the collapsing certainty of Sunni Muslim political and social dominance.[7] In general, the massacres were authorized by the Ottoman sultan to reinforce the subordinate status of Armenians in the face of Armenian demands for greater political autonomy and citizenship rights. They were also related to the process of Ottoman state centralization and its economic dislocation in the face of modernization. The civilian massacres occurred in spasms of incredible violence, often involving Kurdish irregulars and the Ottoman Army.[8] Some of the fiercest massacres were mounted as reprisals for Armenian calls for Western political or military intervention, the most notable being the response to the seizure of the Ottoman Bank (1896) in the heart of Istanbul's commercial district by members of the newly founded Armenian nationalist organization, the Armenian Revolutionary Federation. Far from leading to help for the West, seizure of the bank prompted attacks on Armenian civilians and institutions in the capital. As historian Donald Bloxham concludes, "The massacres of 1894–1896 were a means of putting the Armenians in their place—an extremely violent measure of ethnic dominance rather than, yet, exclusivity—and of warning them against future appeals to the Christian powers."[9] The massacres had been accompanied by the destruction of Armenian farms and agricultural infrastructure, and, consequently, rural communities throughout Inner Anatolia faced periodic, but severe, famine.

Addressing the material needs of the postmassacre Armenians held great purchase among many of the leading figures of fin-de-siècle reform movements in the United States, and committees to raise money for Armenian relief were established in most major cities. The author and recipient of the letter quoted above even brought together the founder of the ARC, Clara Barton, and the suffragist and founder of the Women's Christian Temperance Union, Frances Willard (1839–1898). The letter had been reprinted in Barton's *Report: America's Relief Expedition to Asia Minor under the Red Cross* and had been used to illustrate the form and extent of the suffering her colleagues found in the Inner Anatolian cities of Marash, Aintab, and Zeytun. It had the added feature of celebrating the American contribution to that relief effort and, by the same token, enjoining more assistance for the ARC.

Before the massacres, the ARC had gained international experience in feeding programs in Russia following the 1891–1892 famine. However, Clara Barton's expedition to Anatolia marked the entrance of international relief into the Eastern Mediterranean; the scope and style of that relief placed her team's efforts firmly in the ambit of modern humanitarianism itself. Barton's report, written immediately after her return from Istanbul, documents the ARC's work in painstaking detail, yet it eschews identifying the *cause* of the humanitarian emergency, either as sectarian oppression or something else. Her rejection was unique at that moment, in which public opinion—driven by missionary accounts—overwhelming understood the events in Anatolia as one of rapacious Muslim Turks killing innocent Armenian Christians. This is not to say that Barton herself did not perceive the events in a similar light, but at least publically, she positioned her organization as *neutral* as well as nongovernmental to surmount potential Ottoman interference with her work.

Barton illustrated what that neutrality meant in her recollection of a three-way conversation with the Ottoman minister of state, Ahmed Tevfik Pasha (1845–1936), and American minister plenipotentiary Alexander Watkins Terrell (1827–1912) before her team's departure from Istanbul. Barton paraphrased what Terrell, a former Confederate officer and political appointee, had said in the report: he explained that the ARC's "objects were purely humanitarian, having neither political, racial or religious bearing as such; that as the head of the organization thus represented I [Barton] *could* have no other ideas, and it was the privilege of putting these ideas into practice" that had brought them to Istanbul. Barton further explained why she was there:

> Recent events had aroused the sympathy of the entire American people until they asked, almost to the extent of a demand, that assistance from them should be allowed to go directly to these sufferers, hundreds of whom had friends and relatives in America—a fact which naturally strengthened both the interest and the demand; that it was at the request of our people, *en masse*, that I and a few assistants had come; that our object would be to use the funds ourselves among the people needing them wherever they were found, in helping them to resume their former positions and avocations thus relieving them from continued distress, the State from the burden of providing for them, and other nations and people from a torrent of sympathy which was both hard to endure and unwholesome in its effects.[10]

And in providing this assistance, "There would be no respecting of persons; humanity alone would be their guide. 'We have,' I added, 'brought only ourselves, no correspondent has accompanied us and we shall have none, and shall not go home to write a book on Turkey.'"[11] Neutrality was instrumental to noninterference and even to military protection for relief workers and their projects. It is a testament to Barton's diplomacy, as well, that she understood how sensitive the Ottoman state was, even at that date, to external criticism of its treatment of minorities. "Neutrality in this case," concludes Marion Moser Jones in her recent history of the ARC, "seemed to entail purposeful inattention to the obvious political dimensions of the problem, in order to secure safety and access to people in need."[12] Whether Barton's adoption of the position of neutrality was simply a pragmatic choice or part of a larger elaboration of principles is unclear. Nonetheless, she anticipated that the ARC and other groups associated with it would need to continue their engagement, and that hard-won Ottoman government cooperation would be critical to the long-term success of their project.

More important, Barton's report does provide evidence of how the *idea* of nominal Red Cross–style battlefield neutrality was being transferred to civilian relief (but not to civilian protection). As conceived in the First Geneva Convention (1864), *neutrality* was the reason belligerent *states* were prevented from interfering with the humanitarian work of the International Committee of the Red Cross (ICRC) or other neutral organizations. Barton often invoked the Geneva Convention and the fact that the Ottoman state was a signatory to the accord in her attempts to facilitate her operations. Critically, however, the historical context of the Hamidian massacres was not an instance of interstate warfare, but rather of state violence against its own people. What neutrality meant in the specific field of the Ottoman state's relationship with its own population was more that the Ottoman state and its subject victims were imagined in both political and religious terms as discrete participants in a conflict in which the ARC took no sides. This despite the fact that the aid was intended only for one of those sides; neutrality was demonstrated by neither commenting on the social superstructure and immediate political context of suffering nor addressing forms of hate and discrimination that fostered that suffering.

The enactment of neutrality came in other forms—Barton refused to take Armenian American professionals with her into the field and opted to hire Greek doctors to help in medical programs. As word reached America of her commitment to aid on the basis of need rather than community (though in practice this was not the case) it nearly led to the collapse of the project, as local committees were enraged that their monies could go to support non-Armenians and possibly even perpetrators. Indeed, Barton's report is bereft of Armenian voices, with the exception of a medical report by the American-trained medical doctor Hagop Hintlian on conditions in the city of Arapkır.

Even Barton herself recognized how deeply problematic her report's failure to address the political and social causes of Armenian suffering were, and she tried to preempt objections to her report's shortcomings:

> Reports are always tedious. If some reader, having persevered thus far . . . shall find himself or herself saying with . . . disappointment, "But this does not give the information expected, it does not recommend any specific course to be pursued, whether emigration for the Armenians, and if so, where, and how; or Autonomy, and if so how to be secured. . . . We had expected some light on these questions." . . . We must remind our . . . anxious readers and friends . . . that we have never been required to do this.[13]

Nevertheless, Barton's conceptualization of her organization's neutrality as not taking sides in a situation of violence by a state against its own civilians has endured in the way some humanitarian actors continue to understand or assert the neutrality of their organizations and activities. This stance is at the root of a broader critique of humanitarianism: that neutrality in some situations is functionally and knowingly the same as siding with the state, perpetrator group, or colonial power. Médecins Sans Frontières, for example, was founded by former French doctors associated with the French Red Cross who were critical of how neutrality in Nigeria's civil war (1967–1970) harmed the very civilians they had come to help. In the Eastern Mediterranean, this supposed neutrality took on the additional dimension of not taking sides between Christians and Muslims. This form of neutrality persists as an underlying tension in the way relief need is assessed and provided, and balance between two inherently unequal groups is asserted as the sign of the neutral. Still, in Barton's writing, neutrality—here meaning putting the "politics" of the Eastern Question aside—to ameliorate the suffering of "the Armenian race, [that is] existing under the ordinances of, at least, semi-civilization, and professing the religion of Jesus Christ," is at the center of the moral obligation imposed on the reader.[14] Barton's report is among perhaps the earliest examples of the substitution of humanitarianism for politics, in which calls for reform or even justice are seen to interfere with the moral purpose at hand. The fact that the mission saved lives through food distribution and medical assistance, and that the ARC had a continuing presence in the Ottoman state until 1917, would seem to validate her approach.

Johannes Lepsius's 1897 book *Armenien und Europa: Eine Anklageschrift wider die christlichen Grossmächte und ein Aufruf an das christliche Deutschland* (Armenia and Europe: An indictment of the Christian great powers and a call to a Christian Germany), which addresses the same episode of violence, shares Barton's detailed account of the scope of the humanitarian disaster, but dissents from her formulation of neutrality and instead identifies a complex matrix of social, legal, and political causes for Armenian suffering. This work anticipates Casement's *Heart of Darkness*–style investigative humanitarian reporting much more than the dry rendering of relief activities by Barton. Like Casement, Lepsius blends a travelogue that describes his journey into the killing fields of Anatolia with a forensic, even prosecutorial, intervention. Lepsius is unique in arguing about the larger social impact of massacre as contributing to an ongoing humanitarian disaster and in his warning of the future consequences of a failure to address not just suffering but, in a formulation critical to modern humanitarianism, the root causes of that suffering.

Lepsius (1858–1926) was a German Lutheran public intellectual and missionary who became the leading advocate for Armenian relief in Wilhelmine Germany. The larger thrust of his work was the reconciliation of German Protestant missionary efforts in the Ottoman Empire, the Orientmission, with German imperial interests in the region, the Orientpolitik. This meant engaging German public support for the humanitarian needs of Armenians, while avoiding any conflict with German government efforts to build cultural, political, and economic alliances with the Ottoman Muslim state elite.[15] But Lepsius also saw himself as part of a larger community of Protestant missionaries and educators engaged in a social gospel approach to the needs of Christian communities in the Middle East.[16] The political and religious nature of Lepsius's training and outlook meant that answering the question "*What is the outcome?*" of the massacres was as central to the humanitarian project as ignoring it was to Barton's work.

In Lepsius's conceptualization, the massacres would have the effect of the "complete agricultural ruin of the whole of the eastern part of Asia Minor and of the north of Mesopotamia, while naturally Western Asia Minor and Syria suffer also" (140). And that agricultural devastation would not only have an impact on Armenian survivors but also "make the collapse of Turkey inevitable."[17] Moreover, the massacres and social dislocation had caused a "general agricultural depression," the effects of which were damaging to both Christians and the Muslim majority population. In a revealing insight, Lepsius also identifies as a root cause a political change in elite Muslim attitudes toward non-Muslims.[18]

> The worst result, however, of the destructive policy of the Porte is the rekindled fanaticism of the Mohammedans [*sic*], who have learnt from the events of the last few months that they can steep themselves in Christian blood, and that Christian Europe takes about as much notice of a persecution of Christians in the East, as of a change of the moon. The Turk knows now that the . . . hearts of diplomatists are no longer stirred by romantic sentiments. . . . It is impossible for any one to have travelled of late in the East, and to have gained an insight into the disposition of the Mohammedan population, without being convinced that their arrogance now knows no bounds, and that they hope shortly to rid themselves of all Christians living under Mohammedan rules.[19]

Thus, for Lepsius, the impunity extended to perpetrators prompted the rise of a novel form of sectarian hatred, which is at the root of the humanitarian disaster, and for which Lepsius also blames Western diplomacy. Nevertheless, for Lepsius, solving this particular problem of humanity had three parts, which cumulatively formed the basis for the way Armenians as humanitarian objects were conceived; it constitutes the lasting impact of the humanitarian reports of the era. First, the Ottoman state as then constituted was incapable of and unwilling to implement an adequate program of political and social reform. In other words, changes in the political and legal systems that the Ottoman state might acquiesce to in a diplomatic setting would not be implemented and basic Armenian civil and political rights would continue to be violated.[20] Second, the West had a responsibility to provide assistance to the survivors of the massacres, not out of empathy, but because of its role in fomenting Armenian national aspirations, in part as a cudgel in its anti-Ottoman policies, but also as a response to the civilized and Christian identity of the Armenians. And third, that direct "European supervision" was crucial to the effective restoration of the religious and cultural bases of the Armenian community, including the reversal of the mass forced conversion to Islam that had figured as a side effect of the Hamidian massacres. The conclusions underlying Lepsius's prescription were: (a) that the Ottoman state was inherently unable to effect reform; (b) that the West had a responsibility to Armenians; and (c) that "on-the-ground" European administration and direction of assistance and protection would be the filter through which later massacres and ultimately the wholesale destruction of the Armenian community would be understood, public opinion mobilized, and humanitarian action staged.

Finally, and again unlike Barton, Lepsius relied heavily on first-person accounts of the massacres to illustrate the human cost of state violence. Noting that he had collected over three hundred case studies and a limited amount of photographic evidence, he cataloged province by province, documenting where massacres took place, occurrences of sexual violence, the expropriation of property, and the desecration of holy places in addition to extrajudicial murder. As he detailed the extent of the violence, Lepsius uses the word "crime" to describe the events. He notes, in the universalizing terms critical to the elaboration of modern humanitarianism, "Such are the things for which we are responsible."[21] The universalization of responsibility, alongside the use of a language of justice, indicates how at least Lepsius, and perhaps others at the time, had begun to conceptualize the root causes of Armenian suffering within something akin to an international humanitarian legal framework, in which the actions of a state and the response of the "international community" were measured against a standard of humanity and civilized behavior.

OTTOMAN REVOLUTION, FAILED DREAMS OF CITIZENSHIP, AND INDIGENOUS HUMANITARIANISM

It is not possible to understand and feel the horrible reality all at once. It remains beyond the ability of human imagination. Those who have lived it are not able to narrate it in its entirety.

—Zabel Yesayan

The worst fears of Lepsius and others, who had seen in the events of 1894 to 1896 a prologue rather than a culmination of violence against the Armenians of the Ottoman state, were realized as conservative forces mounted a counterrevolution against the modernizing and reforming government of the Committee of Union and Progress (CUP) in early 1909. The CUP had come to power following the Revolution of 1908, which reinitiated Ottoman constitutional rule and asserted political and legal equality for all citizens, regardless of religion or ethnicity. In the course of the counterrevolution, civilian Armenians and other non-Muslims were targeted by members of the majority community for some of the same reasons as in 1894 to 1896. In 1909, the late Ottoman social and ethnic anxiety about Muslim dominance was exacerbated by the revolution, which insisted on the secularity of Ottoman citizenship.[22] The rebellion was eventually put down by the CUP government, but not before some twenty thousand had been murdered. Several thousand died in an outbreak of dysentery that followed and nearly one hundred thousand were internally displaced. The violence was especially pronounced in and around the provincial capital of Adana, which was partly destroyed by fire and became a magnet for those displaced from the surrounding countryside, as seen in historic photographs of the time (figure 3.1).

Like the Hamidian massacres, the events of 1909 attracted international attention, and, indeed, the ARC became involved in relief. However, the new revolutionary setting, in which non-Muslim primarily middle-class participation in government and civil society was tolerated, opened a space for elite Armenians to act as humanitarian subjects in league with international organizations and established Armenian communal institutions. In the period of the Hamidian massacres, the degree of state involvement in the events prevented any such Armenian involvement. The new humanitarian field—a space still largely dominated by international relief organizations with origins in Western Europe and the United States—created an opportunity for Armenians to produce humanitarian knowledge themselves as they sought to understand and quantify the events of 1909 and to explain what had happened to members of their community and larger Ottoman society. The process of making the events knowable brings into focus how humanitarianism was being conceptualized outside of its place of origin among a population with some connection to the victims of violence themselves, a population that had become the object of the international humanitarian imagination. Yet it also indicates increasing Armenian anxieties about the culturally effacing effects of international

FIGURE 3.1. Informal camp of Armenians displaced during the Adana massacres, 1909.
Courtesy of the Ernst Jäckh collection at the Columbia University Archive.

humanitarianism and suggests that Armenians themselves resisted elements of it, while at the same time seeking to use the tools of humanitarianism to confront the Ottoman state.

The events of 1909 were critical in the emergence of a literature of
witness among Armenians. The relative freedom of expression that
accompanied the brief period of constitutional rule between 1909 and
the onset of World War I, without the crushing official censorship
regime of the previous decade, created an environment in which Armenian poets, writers, and journalists could reflect on the periodic massacre of other Armenians, primarily in the Inner Anatolian provinces, and
their emerging status as citizens in the new order. Chief among those for
whom the Adana massacres prompted a literary response were the
author and poet Atom Yarjanian (1878–1915), known by the pen name
Siamanto, whose 1909 *Karmir Lurer Barekames* (*Bloody News from
My Friend*) is a wrenching collection of poetic meditations on the meaning of massacre and the sense of loss, and Zabel Yesayan (1878–1943),
one of the most important Armenian intellectuals of the late Ottoman
period, whose 1911 *Averagnerun Mech* (Among the ruins) is considered
by some Armenian literary critics as "one of the greatest works of Western Armenian literature."[23]

In May 1909 a coalition of Armenian political and religious leaders, representatives of the empire's Greek community, and Ottoman Turkish officials convened an international relief committee that dispatched a fact-finding mission to Adana. It was led by Yesayan in her capacity as a member of the Armenian Red Cross Society. She had published widely in Armenian, French, and Ottoman Turkish before being appointed to head the Adana mission. Among those accompanying her were two other Armenian female writers, Saténik Ohandjanian and Archakouhi Téotik (1875–1922), the former also from the Red Cross and the latter a representative of the Armenian Ladies Association for the Promotion of the Nation (Azganuer Hayuheats Enkerutiwm) and author of the 1910 report *Amis mě i Kilikia: Kts'ktur nōt'er* (A month in Cilicia: Some notes). The fact that women were selected to lead the mission is evidence of the increasingly gendered performance of humanitarianism and the marking of the space of humanitarian action, with its emphasis on female survivors and orphans, as feminine. Yesayan had also authored a report for the Armenian ecclesiastical leadership and the Armenian Red Cross; although the report itself may no longer exist, elements of it survive in letters, in articles, and in *Among the Ruins*.

Yesayan traveled from Istanbul to Adana by ship in the summer of 1909, just after the massacres, and remained there until the fall, whereupon she returned to the capital in part because she feared for her own safety. Her memoir is a complex work, and her thoughts on relief, the humanity of victims and perpetrators, and the question of the legitimacy of violent resistance are woven into an account of her visit to the killing fields around Adana. In many critical ways, the work transcends the standard humanitarian narrative of the era; however, it does document the workings of Ottoman Armenian relief efforts, the way those efforts were understood at the time, and how they interacted with state authorities and international bodies. More important for Yesayan, the two issues at the core of the humanitarian problem were, first, what the massacres and then the political and humanitarian measures mounted in their wake said about the question of Armenian citizenship and equality in the postrevolutionary Ottoman state; and, second, and more pragmatically, how best to meet the needs of the orphaned child survivors of the massacre.

Like many other members of the Ottoman Armenian elite, Yesayan had come to believe that the Revolution of 1908 and the restoration of the Ottoman Constitution had made it possible for Armenians to enjoy meaningful citizenship in the Ottoman political community. For her, not only did the massacres show the incomplete nature of that revolution as a political project, but the humanitarian response also further tested the limits of the revolution's rhetoric of political freedom and tolerance. In her introduction, Yesayan positions herself within the context of postrevolutionary Ottoman citizenship as a liberal subject who had witnessed inhumanity that should move all of Ottoman society. Noting that Armenians and Turks had fought together to bring about the return of constitutional rule, she writes:

> I want to explain the state of mind in which this book was written. I want the reader to know that my impressions are not prejudiced by a particular political direction, they are not embittered by nationalism, [nor] traditional feelings of revenge or any return of racial hatred. . . . I would like the reader to forget even the nationality of the author, in order to recall that in these pages speak only pain, sometimes indignation, and sometimes despair, motivated by human feelings . . . What I saw . . . has the status to disturb the basis of the entire state. [I write this] as a free citizen, as the child of this land, endowed with equal rights and equal duties. . . . These pages should not be considered, the result of the impressions of an Armenian woman, but rather the spontaneous and sincere impressions of any human creature."[24]

What follows are first-person testimonies and vivid descriptions that transformed the numbers of dead into a cause that sought, in part, to locate Armenian suffering within the context of citizenship and national belonging. Armenian suffering remained, of course, a problem of humanity, but also a problem for fulfilling the promise of revolution. In this sense, relief was a burden that fell not just on the shoulders of Armenians but also on the larger Ottoman polity, or at least that portion of the polity that had embraced the revolution. To make this argument, Yesayan drew on a recurring trope in CUP political thought that all the peoples of the Ottoman Empire had suffered under the tyranny of the Ottoman sultan, Abdülhamid II. The persecution of the Armenians in Adana was an unfortunate return to that past. Armenian suffering—or, rather, addressing its root causes—became imperative to securing the revolution for all.

Weighing heavily on Yesayan's mind as she visited Adana was the memory of the Hamidian massacres and the fact that they had created as many as sixty thousand orphans. Many of those orphans had been absorbed into Muslim households and converted to Islam, but still others were placed in orphanages run by foreign missionaries. The orphanages were administered by a collection of groups and religious orders that ranged from the German Kaiserswerth deaconesses to American Presbyterians.

Among some members of the Armenian elite, the housing and education of children in these institutions was experienced as a loss to the Armenian community as a whole. As an example, Téotik, in her report, tells of an encounter with the American missionary Mary G. Webb, who had brought a group of orphaned Armenian girls to an Adana photographer in the wake of the massacres. Webb told Téotik that she was planning to send images of the orphans to the United States to raise money in support of her work in the Armenian village of Hajin. Téotik noticed that among themselves the girls spoke Armenian, but Webb spoke to them in Turkish. While Téotik was impressed with Webb's efforts and was certain that the girls were well cared for, healthy, and being educated, she wrote in an aside, as though in the voice of Webb addressing the girls: "Bizim duamizi yapacaksinis, bisim dilimizi ogrenecksiniz?"—"You will do our prayers, you will learn our language."[25] There was also a sense of communal humiliation, in that Armenians could not provide for the education and upkeep of their own children. "When the [1909] massacres happened," historian Raymond Kévorkian explains, "these painful memories were still very active, and were all the more easily revived in that they recalled too well the tragedies that the Armenians had experienced under the Hamidian regime."[26] By Yesayan's own admission, *Among the Ruins* does not address fully the issue of orphan care, in part because it was an ongoing project and she may have thought that calling attention to it could undermine it. The question of the treatment of orphans brought to the surface other complex feelings that Yesayan, as an advocate of an emerging "indigenous" humanitarianism, encountered with great difficulty. Contrasting the work of Armenians with that of international humanitarians, she acknowledges:

> The foreigners approached the afflicted with smiles, and songs, and particularly with filled hands [material assistance], [while] we [approached them] only with tears. . . . On our faces, they could only see the reflection of their true sufferings. We resolved so many times to appear rock-solid to them . . . to wipe away the tears that burned our eyes, to appear smiling and impassible to the afflicted, so they could find confidence and hope in our calm . . . but we were not successful, and were never successful.[27]

The humanitarian emergency of the 1909 massacres extended beyond the mass killing; it became increasingly about preventing the loss of surviving Armenian children to assimilation into the dominant Ottoman Turkish society through its state orphanage system, as well as through the work of the foreign missionaries. Yesayan was beginning to weave the idea of "national," or communal, suffering into the definition of the humanitarian emergency, anticipating the postwar formulation in which humanitarian work sought to address the suffering of nations, rather than just individual victims. In this regard, her work departs from the humanitarian report's tendency to universalize suffering as a generic problem. Here the condition of the postmassacre Armenian children was still a problem of humanity in general, but also a specific problem for the Armenian community—a conclusion suggestive of a defining element of any indigenous humanitarian movement.[28]

This communalizing of suffering also had to confront issues of class and distance. Vast differences of profession and levels of education and wealth separated elite members of the Istanbul Armenian middle class—Yesayan's intended readers—from the victims of the violence in the province of Adana, who tended to be the rural and urban poor who were illiterate in Western Armenian. Among her hopes was that supporting the orphans and providing relief in and of itself would mobilize a kind of political and social connection—solidarity—that otherwise would not have been present between the diverse Armenian communities of Ottoman Anatolia.

There are echoes of this imagination of community through the workings of humanitarianism present in the historical experience of American Jewish relief projects in World War I–era Ottoman Palestine. Yesayan's advocacy bears a striking similarity to Stephen Wise's hopes of building into the disparate community of American Jews a consciousness about Jewish suffering and a sense of not just religious solidarity, but also political consensus. In her articles and essays, Yesayan entreated Armenians in Istanbul and elsewhere to see in the threat to the welfare of Armenian children—even those of poor peasant farmers in far-off Anatolia—an existential threat to the community of Ottoman Armenians themselves.

But more important, Yesayan's writing, which on the one hand mourns the loss of Armenian life, on the other hand celebrates the instances of Armenian resistance to massacre as evidence of engaged citizenship and the agency of a free people. Modern humanitarianism tends to exhibit an ambivalence, perhaps even an antipathy, to accounts of resistance by humanitarian objects. This derives in part from the elite paternalism of the humanitarian subject, in which resistance may complicate the understood causes of suffering and raise the possibility that victims could have independent agency, become killers, and cause the further suffering of others.

In the end, Yesayan herself was not immune from the suffering she witnessed in Adana. In 1915, she was the only woman among dozens of

Armenian intellectuals, journalists, politicians, and religious leaders who were arrested, deported, and for the most part executed by the Young Turk government at the outset of the destruction of the Ottoman Armenians. Managing to escape via Bulgaria, Yesayan would never return to Istanbul, but rather resumed her literary work in the Caucasus, where she published an early first-person account of surviving the genocide.

NAMING A CRIME AGAINST HUMANITY: THE HUMANITARIAN REPORT AND THE ONSET OF GENOCIDE

Yet even if the statistics were more abundant and more eloquent still, they might fail to convey to our imagination the actuality of what has happened. A nation blotted out!

—Arnold Toynbee, 1915

Knowledge of the destruction of the Ottoman Armenians began to seep into the imagination of Western humanitarians as they developed a better understanding of the extent of suffering during the Year of the Locust in the Levant. Even as that news brought to mind the events of 1894 to 1896 and again 1909, those generating knowledge in 1915 were confronted by the fact that, unlike the previous paroxysms of violence against Ottoman Armenians, this was different in scale and intent. Beyond just drawing a distinct line between the humanitarian action needed to address the starvation and social dislocations of the wartime famine and massacre of the population at large, the reports of that time conceived of and elaborated a new conceptual framework with which to describe and assess the destruction of an entire ethnic community by the war machine and bureaucracy of a modern state. The formation of that narrative framework drew strands of thought about Armenians, minorities in the Ottoman state, and the history of violence there into a coherent narrative that was colored both by dominant ideas about nations and nationalism and by the needs of wartime propaganda. The possibility of mass extermination had become a constant in the body of knowledge that had emerged over the previous twenty years about the Ottoman state and society. Indeed, Lepsius and the American newspaperman George Hepworth had both warned of the likelihood of extermination, Hepworth even going so far as to make the prescient prediction that it would occur within twenty years of his 1895 research visit to Anatolia.

Much of that "real-time" knowledge was produced for the first time in a systematic way by humanitarian philanthropy itself. The Rockefeller Foundation (RF), in order to manage its understanding of the extent of war relief needs and facilitate the work of its War Relief Commission, dispatched research teams to Europe and the Ottoman state in the first months of the war. Rather than rely on information from those requesting aid alone, the RF's creation of knowledge fell firmly within the repertoire of the emerging practice of scientific philanthropy. The team arrived in Istanbul in the summer of 1915. This report, unlike earlier reports, was not intended for public dissemination, but rather to inform the actions of the institution. The team's assessments have the texture of reports, but also include an intelligence briefing, which considers the proper role of the institution and guarantees the confidentiality of its sources.[29] The first of the RF reports discussed the impact of the war on the population at large, primarily through an analysis of the agricultural problems caused by the draft of so many young men into the Ottoman army. It also considered the impact of the Russian advance in Eastern Anatolia, which had initiated a wave of refugees, and while the commission thought that providing relief for that population was warranted, it observed that the Ottoman state would not, at the time, even acknowledge that any of its territory had been lost, let alone allow foreigners to mount a relief effort.[30]

More important, the War Relief Commission report divided the general food insecurity and suffering in the Ottoman state from what it called the "Armenian Situation"—confirming even at that early date that the treatment of the Ottoman Armenians was understood to be distinct from wartime conditions affecting other parts of Ottoman society. Noting that the war had created an opportunity for impunity—"it is many years since the Turks have had such an opportunity to deal with the Armenians without the possibility of interference from other European powers"—the report acknowledged how difficult it was to achieve a complete picture of the extent of suffering because of efforts by the "Turks to prevent knowledge of what is going on in the interior from reaching the outside world until it is too late."[31]

Despite the difficulty of obtaining firsthand confirmation, the report concluded, from the consistency of accounts it had collected from US diplomats and Protestant missionaries who had fled Inner Anatolia for Istanbul, that a "policy" existed, "consisting partly of massacre; partly of wholesale deportation of Armenians to inaccessible places where it is doubtful whether they will be able to care for themselves; and partly of forcible Mohammedanization [*sic*]."[32] Building a generic account of this policy's implementation on the basis of witness statements from Trabzon, Zeytun (now Süleymanlı), Haçin (now Saimbeyli), Marash (now Kahramanmaraş), and Tarsus, the report explained:

> It appears that in some instances entire Armenian communities have been deported and forced to abandon their homes and places for business, the Turks permitting them to carry only such goods as they are able to put on their back or into a small wagon. They were then marched to far distant parts of the country and left to get on as best they could. . . . In other places the men appear to have been separated from the women, deported and the women given to the Turks; and in still other places there appears to have been a considerable massacre of men, and in all places an attempt at forcible [conversion to Islam].[33]

Describing the situation as "acute," the report concluded that relief to the interior of Anatolia would not be possible at that moment, but rather, "We were told that in the course of the next month or two relief work might be [able to] commence quietly and while it might be resented by the Turks the missionaries are confident it could be carried on without serious interference, as the Turks will feel that the Armenian communities have been broken up so thoroughly that *temporary relief cannot repair the damage.*"[34] The cold and clinical reasoning of that final sentence resonates with the larger critique of humanitarianism's inability to prevent, let alone address, suffering in the face of a modern state's willingness to commit genocide; indeed, it signals how the modern state can even welcome the modes of humanitarian action as an adjunct to the act of genocide itself. RF reports from following years included among the first maps showing the deportation routes and centers of concentration (figures 3.2 and 3.3).

The conclusion that the Ottoman state had used the exigency of World War I to embark on the destruction of Ottoman Armenians was also shared by British historian Arnold Toynbee's *Armenian Atrocities: The Murder of a Nation* (1915), which was expanded into a British parliamentary report, *The Treatment of Armenians in the Ottoman Empire, 1915–1916* (the so-called "Blue Book"), as well as by the 1919 memoir of American diplomat Henry Morgenthau, who had been the US ambassador in Istanbul for much of the war.[35] These reports were the most influential on the *public* humanitarian imagination of the era, at once shaping a consciousness of genocide and engendering a sui generis humanitarian response. They provide evidence of a growing stream of thought among modern humanitarians that addressing organ-

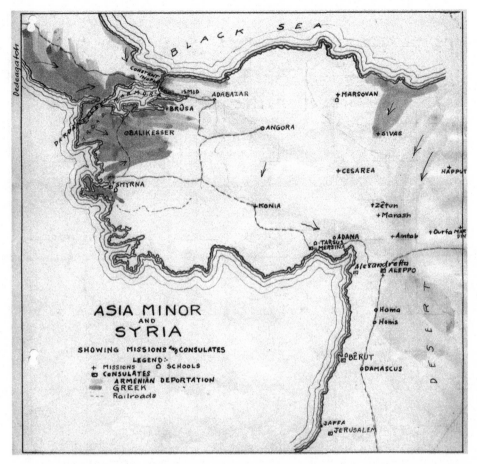

FIGURE 3.2. Map of missions and consulates in Asia Minor and Syria. Rockefeller Foundation War Relief Commission map of centers of displacement and concentration of Armenians, ca. 1917. Source: RAC-RF, "Report of the War Relief Commission to the Rockefeller Foundation on Conditions in Turkey" (1917). © Rockefeller Archive Center.

ized violence by colonial and modernizing states against their own populations was within the purview of humanitarianism, extending humanitarianism's reach into questions of justice and rehabilitation, even in the face of claims of national sovereignty and national self-determination. The way those questions were made most manifest at the time was by imagining an independent Armenian homeland, with the separation of Armenians and Turks—understood as both an outcome of the Ottoman state's participation in the war and a humanitarian solution to an intractable conflict. That said, it is unclear if either Toynbee or

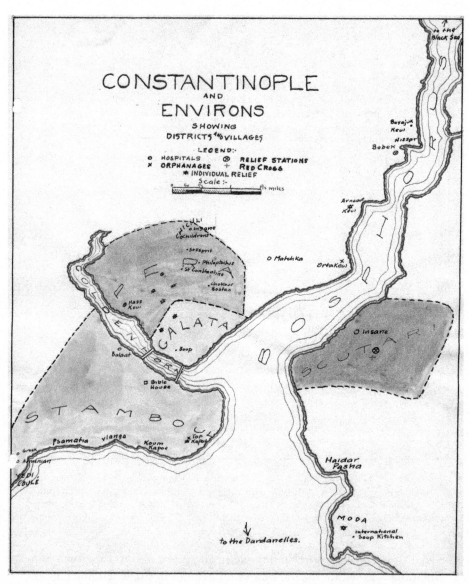

FIGURE 3.3. Map of districts and villages in Constantinople and environs. Rockefeller Foundation War Relief Commission map of centers of displacement and concentration of Armenians, ca. 1917. Source: RAC-RF, "Report of the War Relief Commission to the Rockefeller Foundation on Conditions in Turkey" (1917). © Rockefeller Archive Center.

Morgenthau ever saw the destruction of the Armenians in the Ottoman Empire as akin to late nineteenth-century genocides in the Western Hemisphere or those in the British Empire's Antipodean colonies.

Toynbee's 1915 report was built from a compilation of documentary evidence developed by the American Committee on Armenian Atrocities. Again, that committee, which would evolve into the American Committee for Relief in the Near East (ACRNE), and later Near East Relief, included among its membership such elite Progressive-era religious leaders and philanthropists as Stephen Wise, Oscar Straus, and Cleveland H. Dodge, and was led by James L. Barton and Samuel Dutton. The committee had become the main US clearinghouse for information about the Armenians in the Ottoman state. Moreover, as Toynbee was publishing this work, the committee had begun a massive effort in American civil society to raise awareness and funds for relief. Dutton rather than Barton was the primary driver in this movement, and he built an organization that included chapters in most major US cities and involved women's groups and Armenian organizations. The report, which wove disparate US State Department diplomatic dispatches; communication with American, German, and British medical and educational missionaries; and translations of accounts in the Armenian diasporic press into a historical narrative, is a mirror of the way that NER conceptualized the humanitarian emergency. The clear link between Toynbee's account and wartime and postwar understandings of the Armenian Genocide among American humanitarians and the later League of Nations marks the broader significance of his writing. Equally, Toynbee is exemplary of Western intellectuals who had come of age in the period of the Hamidian massacres and World War I and would later apply their own experience with genocide in World War I to the historical framing of the Holocaust. Writing in the 1960s, Toynbee recalled, "This was the CUP's crime; and my study of it left an impression on my mind that was not effaced by the still more cold-blooded genocide, on a far larger scale, that was committed during the Second World War by the Nazi."[36]

Toynbee, like Lepsius twenty years earlier, adopted a prosecutorial attitude toward the Ottoman state and its imperial German ally: "The evidence in hand has been sufficiently indicated, and it will be better to set forth the whole series of crime from their beginning."[37] As he built his case, recurring tropes of early humanitarian reports appear: the antiquity of Armenian Christianity, the failure of the Ottoman state to rule effectively, and the fact that despite the rhetoric of revolution, the

Young Turks did not extend equality and protection to the Ottoman Armenians. "The crime," Toynbee argued, "was concerted very systematically, for there is evidence of identical procedure from over fifty places. . . . They are too numerous to be detailed."[38] What follows in Toynbee's account is among the earliest public narratives of genocide. Critically, he synthesized the various reports of massacre and deportation into a generic but dramatic story that emphasized the intentionality and systemic nature of the state's actions. "On any given day the streets of whatever town it might be were occupied by the local gendarmerie," he begins,

> all able-bodied men of Armenian race that had been exempted from military draft to present themselves . . . these were all marched out of the town by the gendarmes. They had not far to go, for the gendarmerie had been reinforced for the purpose from the gaols, and the brigands and Kurds at large were waiting in the hills. They were waiting to murder the prisoners. The first secluded valley witnessed their wholesale massacre. . . . This was the first act. It precluded the pitiful possibility of resistance to the second, which was of a more ingenious and far reaching kind.[39]

The unique element of the Young Turks' plan followed: the forced migration, known at the time as the deportation of urban Armenians, who were

> not savages like the Red Indians [sic] who retired before the White Man across the American continent. They were not nomadic shepherds like their barbarous neighbours the Kurds. They were people living the same like as ourselves, townspeople established in the town for generations and the chief authors of its local prosperity. They were sedentary people, doctors and lawyers and teachers, businessmen and artisans and shopkeepers, and they raised solid monuments to their intelligence and industry, costly churches and well-appointed schools. In fact they were in the closest personal touch with Western civilisation.[40]

Deported into the high deserts of Mesopotamia, displaced Armenians faced further depredation, rape, enslavement, and death from exposure, starvation, and disease. In this passage, Toynbee introduces the critical notion that Armenians were deserving of help not just because of their putative Christianity, but because they are "like ourselves," and not just in terms of "our" shared humanity with the "stranger." Rather, the Armenians had achieved a level of civilization that made them, like the Zionist settlers and Beiruti middle class during the Year of the Locust, knowable and "unstrangered." Compassion and action on behalf of the Armenians, therefore, was predicated not merely on the fact that they are suffering humans, but also on the fact that suffering is made more acute and more of a *problem for humanity* because Armenians are civilized (and not the aboriginal inhabitants of the Americas) with a burgeoning middle class and educational and commercial ties with the West. Seeing in the massacres and deportations the destruction of people "like ourselves" is what translates the genocide into a problem of humanity. It is striking as well that, parallel to Stephen Wise's own account of the period, Toynbee somehow sees the destruction of the native peoples of North America—presumably because they lacked the requisite level of civilization—as not falling into the same category as the Medz Yeghern, but rather as an acceptable form of genocide.

Turning from the assault on the social fabric of the Armenians as a modernizing and civilized community in the Ottoman state, Toynbee uses the treatment of deported women and children to put the Ottoman state elite on the other side of a civilizational divide. Detailing child transfer, mass rape, the enslavement of women who were "as civilised and refined as women of Western Europe," and the theft of Armenian property, he concludes by comparing the actions of the Ottomans to those of the Assyrians in ancient Mesopotamia: "The Assyrian's crime was not so fiendish as the Turk's. 'Organised and effective massacre'— that is what such a deportation means, and that must always have been its implication."[41]

In retrospect, despite the occasional inflammatory language and exclamation points, the historical claims made in Toynbee's *Armenian Atrocities* and the Blue Book have largely been borne out by the historical research on the Armenian Genocide in the hundred years since it occurred. Both works are analogous to Raphaël Lemkin's monumental work on the destruction of European Jewry and other communities during World War II, *Axis Rule in Occupied Europe* (1944), in which Lemkin elaborated the historic-legal concept of genocide. All these works were written from reports and witness statements from the killing fields and convey an imperfect though accurately inferred understanding of the intent of the perpetrators. It is sometimes easy to name genocide in retrospect, but in this case Toynbee, taking his cue from his American interlocutors, constructed a narrative of an ongoing genocide. More to the point, the fact that the humanitarian narrative emphasized genocide imposed a moral obligation on its readers under which what was at stake was not just individual Armenians and their suffering, but rather the Armenian nation and its suffering. Toynbee's reporting also promoted what became the overarching topos of the humanitarian emergency—the deracinated female and child survivor—rather than destroyed urban communities and social structures, broken families, and murdered men.

The basic narrative framework established by Toynbee and others remained a constant in the promotional materials that NER produced from the fall of 1915 through the end of the war. These were intended to raise awareness among the American public about the destruction of the Ottoman Armenians and to generate funds to be distributed by a network of Protestant missionaries residing in Anatolia and Syria. The public donations would supplement the RF's philanthropic support.[42]

The campaign mounted by the NER on behalf of Armenian suffering was unprecedented in size and relied heavily on emerging advertising and marketing techniques for its success. NER sought nothing less than the total democratization of humanitarian knowledge. An early example is a pamphlet that NER produced in 1916, entitled *The Cry of a Million: Exiled Destitute Dying*. The pamphlet was intended to supplement public speeches and sermons on the weekend of October 21 and 22, 1916, which President Woodrow Wilson had declared Armenian-Syrian Relief Day. Using a large font and evocative photographs, the text of the pamphlet, which reads at times as sentimental appeal and at others as carefully crafted Madison Avenue advertising copy, employed a précis of Toynbee's broader argument and the RF's assessment:

> Amid all the terrible accompaniments of the European War there is none more heartrending than this. According to the most reliable reports about 750,000 have perished by massacre, disease and hardship. A million survivors, each with a story tragic enough to break the hardest heart, are in dire distress. They are remote from their homes, without shelter, clothing or food, their hearts filled with despair. America is the only nation that can meet their need. Extraordinary financial prosperity, impossible but for the war, abounds here. Shall this nation fatten because of Europe's demand for our goods and forget the sorrows in the war zones? The suffering cry out in their anguish. Will we hear and heed their appeal?[43]

The pamphlet narrates a "tragic history" in which "only yesterday they [the Armenians] were the best educated, most skillful, most industrious, and most valuable people in the Turkish Empire." "'Only yesterday,'" it continues, "Those are fateful words! Modern History began on August 1, 1914, when Europe and Asia caught fire."[44] The pamphlet proceeds to describe the mass killing of Armenian men, followed by the forced migration and death of Armenian women and children. Special note is made, through euphemism, of the rape and enslavement of girls. A before photograph of anonymous well-dressed dancing Armenian schoolgirls is juxtaposed with one of sitting and passive orphans dressed in rags at a feeding station. What is missing is any concrete discussion of cause except that the Armenians have faced historical persecution; also missing is any discussion of the Christianity of the Armenians or the fact that the perpetrators were Muslims. Most Americans would have known that Armenians were Christians, and indeed records provided to Congregationalist ministers to prepare their sermons for Armenian Syrian Relief Day indicate that what was at stake was the obliteration of "a Christian race." Replacing the older calls for religious solidarity that was more typical of the period of the Hamidian massacres, this campaign was an appeal on behalf of a deserving people, who were industrious, hardworking, and, again, "like us." Clearly the Armenians' Christianity was a component of that unstrangering process, but American missionary activity throughout Anatolia in the preceding generation, in particular the network of schools that had played such a role in raising the level of "civilization" of the Armenians, had been a form of investment, and thus supporting Armenian relief was a way to protect that investment.

"Do we hear the cry?" the pamphlet concludes as it asks Americans to "yield to benevolent impulses and pour out relief for the suffering and needy. America is a comfortable and rich country. In contrast with the peace and quiet which are ours let us think of the terror and the strife in Armenia. We have safe homes. . . . Their homes are in ruins. . . . The moan of a race moves out across the heart of a stricken world."[45] The juxtaposition of American prosperity with the destitution of the Armenians expands the ambit of the implicit moral obligation: the wealth and peace of American society impose an added responsibility to manifest compassion and promote justice for Armenians as individuals and as a nation. The exceptional nature of American responsibility to Armenians—a specific problem of humanity—emerged from this moment and shaped the next decade of relief and rehabilitation efforts. What is clear from the content of NER's understanding of this problem of humanity was that Americans' obligation did not end with feeding the hungry, but rather constituted an extended commitment to the restoration and rebuilding of the Armenian community in some form. As the pamphlet explained, "Until the war ends thousands must be fed. After the war multitudes must be given assistance in reestablishing their homes, stocking their farms and securing implements and seeds for their fields."[46]

The success of the late 1916 project emboldened NER to seek to raise thirty million dollars for that postwar relief. Perhaps the most evocative

dimension of that campaign was a series of posters that visually embodied the nature of the problem, primarily through variations on the
theme of helpless female and child survivors. Designed by some of
the leading graphic artists of the time, including Władysław T. Benda,
the posters are often quite beautiful. Usually employing the slogan "Lest
We Perish" or "Give or We Perish," the posters were displayed in city
libraries, churches, and other public spaces and formed part of a larger
graphic lexicon of wartime relief and domestic propaganda posters.
Most displayed a generic girl (figure 3.4) or a woman and her child
among ruins. A poster portraying a neoclassical Columbia with a sword
protecting a waifish child dressed in rags (figure 3.5), presumably an
Armenian child, is emblematic of an emerging idea that the relief of
Armenian suffering had become a specifically American obligation—
and one that only Americans were capable of accomplishing. It also
implicitly asserts a sort of national heroism; the invocation of pity is
confirmation of the potential power of appeals to sentiment even as that
style of appeal was going out of favor. The design of the poster is a
reminder of the persisting nature of the "sad and sentimental" tales in
humanitarian discourse even as established funding organizations
and quasi-governmental institutions demanded levels of truth in reporting and relief plans that would lead to self-sufficiency or rehabilitation.
By any measure, the fundraising appeals of the NER were a success.
As discussed later in this book, NER raised and spent over one hundred
million dollars by the mid-1920s and was at one time responsible
for the care and feeding of half a million, primarily female and child
survivors.

THE LEAGUE OF NATIONS' REPORT AND
FORGETTING A PROBLEM FOR HUMANITY

We recognize with deep regret that it is impossible now to fulfill our
pledges to the Armenians; for these pledges involved political and territorial rearrangements now beyond our power to achieve.

—Fridtjof Nansen, 1925

The humanitarian reports on the condition of Armenians from the
Hamidian period forward argued that chief among the root causes of
Armenians' suffering was their subordinate status in the Ottoman state.
That status left them vulnerable to exploitation, violence, and genocide.
This need for protection manifested in the fact that, beyond addressing
immediate relief needs, most of the reports prior to World War I argued

FIGURE 3.4. "Give or We Perish." Poster by Władysław T. Benda, ca. 1917. Based on photographs, posters such as this one, which emphasized the vulnerability of Armenian women and children, were employed by Western humanitarian organizations to generate political and monetary support for relief programs. Source: LC-USZC4–10121 DLC (color film copy transparency), Library of Congress Prints and Photographs Division, Washington, DC.

FIGURE 3.5. "They Shall Not Perish: Campaign for $30,000,000."
Poster by Douglas Volk, ca. 1918. Source: LC-USZC4–3173 (color
film copy transparency), Library of Congress Prints and Photographs
Division, Washington, DC.

for Armenian political autonomy within the Ottoman state, rather than
independence. A recurring idea in some of these earlier reports was that
the call for Armenian revolution was having a damaging effect on the
general Armenian population. With the advent of the war itself, humanitarian thought embraced Wilsonian notions of self-determination for
Armenians as a basis for addressing that suffering, and the creation of

an Armenian national home became a central feature of humanitarian advocacy. As discussed later in this work, the alliance between humanitarianism and interwar politics of national self-determination failed in the face of a resurgent Republic of Turkey and a postrevolutionary Soviet Union. Consequently, the Armenian cause was increasingly forgotten—rather a forgettable problem of humanity—and became more a problem for the skeletal humanitarian bureaucracy of the League of Nations. The reasons for this are manifold and have as much to do with what today would be termed "donor fatigue" as with American isolationism and British and French colonial politics in the Levant.

Nevertheless, the failure of diplomacy and politics is reflected in the last major humanitarian report on the era, which documented the work of the polar explorer-turned-humanitarian Fridtjof Nansen (1861–1930) and his adjutant Vidkun Quisling on behalf of the League of Nations' refugee resettlement projects. Nansen's role in developing a refugee travel document—the Nansen passport—is discussed in a subsequent chapter; however, in 1925, his main concern was "repatriating," or rather relocating, Armenians to the Soviet Republic of Armenia. The majority of those slated for settlement in the tiny Soviet entity were not natives of that part of the Caucasus, but rather were from Anatolia. Regardless, the failure to find a political solution to the Armenian Question, as the search for a solution to the problems caused by the genocide was euphemistically called, was of particular concern to Nansen and others affiliated with the League of Nations who saw it as a defining element of a new humanitarian order. "It is not within the scope of this Introduction to describe the events which occurred soon after the end of the Great War," the report begins: "The offer to the United States of America of a mandate for Armenia, the invitation to President Wilson to define certain boundaries of the proposed Armenian State, and the provisions of the Treaty of Sèvres are all matters of common knowledge. When the Treaty of Sèvres was definitely put on one side, other proposals were made to help the Armenians by international means."[47]

Where the report, primarily in the voice of Nansen's presentations to the Fifth Committee of the League of Nations, which was dedicated to the Armenian issue, speaks to the need of the international body to keep the promises made to the Armenians, the integrity of the Armenian nation is no longer envisioned as a problem for humanity to address. Instead, the report provides a thorough and professional analysis of transferring Armenians living as refugees in Istanbul and Greece, where their safety and ability to find work was considered problematic to the

Plain of Sardarabad, which Nansen and Quisling hoped could be irrigated sufficiently for subsistence agriculture. The report argued for assistance from the government and from wealthy Armenians in the West and indicated that the Soviet government would allow the settlers incentives to work the land. The project would never take shape in the interwar period. Instead, Armenians as individual refugees would emigrate to Western Europe or the Americas, or transform permanent refugee camps into urban ghettos in the big cities of the Levant.

In *That the World May Know,* his meditation on writing about atrocity, especially in the postgenocide, human rights theorist James Dawes confronts the assertion that "the effective dissemination of information can change the world" with his observation that "much of the work on storytelling and human rights, however, has focused on the opposite: the *impotence* of representation. Journalists and activists around the world, working from their own experiences of frustration in Rwanda, the Balkans, and elsewhere, have catalogued the many ways stories designed to shake us out of our self absorption and apathy can fail."[48] Is it right to measure the humanitarian reports of the late nineteenth and early twentieth centuries in the Eastern Mediterranean against the same standard? Clearly, the reports produced action, but they also mourned inaction and injustice—as it was happening and in retrospect. Is the moral obligation they sought to impose on their readers what journalists and activists today hope to elicit in their readers? There certainly are parallels in the way the production of knowledge of atrocity and suffering is something more than witnessing in and of itself to a range of possible actions.

The humanitarian reports of that period exist in the space between witnessing and action in that they were appended to the possible exertion of power in various forms, from American prestige to outright European occupation. But as the space for action evaporated, the meaning of humanitarian knowledge changed as well, raising the further question of whether the activist humanitarian should even write of justice in the absence of possible means to achieve it. The question of failure in the face of certain knowledge of injustice is explored in the next chapter.

CHAPTER 4

"America's Wards"

*Near East Relief and
American Humanitarian
Exceptionalism, 1919–1923*

Few passages in American writing on the First World War and its after-math in the Middle East capture the naked horror of the refugee experi-ence like Dr. Mabel Evelyn Elliott's description of her midwinter flight (February 10–13, 1920) alongside several thousand Armenians from the Anatolian city of Marash, now Kahramanmaraş, in southern Turkey. In her 1924 memoir, *Beginning Again at Ararat,* the physician recalled the long nighttime march over a snow-covered plain behind a column of French soldiers who had been ordered to abandon the city and the Armenian civilian population to a resurgent Turkish nationalist force:

> Armenian women have a way of carrying their children on their backs, hold-ing the two hands clutched against the mother's breast, and the child's weight on the bent back. . . . I do not know how many hours we had been walking, when I found the first dead child on its mother's back. I walked beside her, examining it; she trudged on, bent under the weight, doggedly lifting one foot and then the other through the snow, blind and deaf to everything. The child was certainly dead, and she did not know it. I spoke to her, touched her, and finally shook her arm violently to arouse her. When she looked up I pointed to the child and said, "Finish." The mother seemed not to under-stand at first, trudged onward for a few steps and then let go the child's hands. The body fell, and the mother went on, blind and deaf as before, all her life in that lifting of one foot after the other through the snow.[1]

Of the nearly thirty-six hundred Armenians who went with the French across the snow-covered steppe, only a third reached the relative safety of the town of Islahiye, a station on the Baghdad-Berlin railway some seventy kilometers away. All the children who had been carried by their mothers in the way described by Elliott, who herself walked along-side the refugees, died of hypothermia; the only children who did survive were the ones who walked. The following spring, Stanley E. Kerr, who had remained in the city throughout the battle and witnessed massacres, wrote his parents that travelers returning to Marash saw in the retreating snows that "a thousand bodies lay on the plain."[2]

Kerr, who had spent the World War I years working at the US Army's Walter Reed Hospital as a medicinal chemist, and Elliott, a medical doctor from Benton Harbor, Michigan, and leader in the American Women's Medical Association, were among the several hundred relief workers employed by the American Committee for Relief in the Near East (ACRNE), an organization that would eventually be known simply as Near East Relief (NER). Founded in 1915 in response to multiple humanitarian disasters in the wartime Eastern Mediterranean, most notably the 1915–1916 artificial famine in the Levant and the Armenian Genocide, the organization's earliest efforts revolved around raising funds to purchase foodstuffs in the region to be distributed by resident missionaries and by the foreign staff and faculty of the American University in Beirut. As noted in the previous chapters, over its lifetime (1915–1926), NER raised $110 million and at the high point of its operations in 1921 fed three hundred thousand people daily.

Kerr and Elliott, however, represented a distinct and new phase in the NER's mandate and operations in the Eastern Mediterranean and Caucasus. With the war's end in 1918, NER recruited Americans—veterans, Mennonites, conscientious objectors, Quakers—as relief workers, the vast majority of whom had no prior experience in or knowledge of the region, and dispatched them to the Eastern Mediterranean not just to oversee and manage food aid distribution and refugee assistance but also to serve as agents of larger societal reform and change. The desired outcome of that work is best summarized by the title of the NER's own magazine, *The New Near East*; indeed, the organization's leadership, and in particular its director, Charles Vernon Vickrey, sought nothing less than an abrupt break with what they saw as the social backwardness, and political and moral corruption, of the Ottoman and Muslim past of the region, followed by the implantation of modernity itself, albeit *à l'Américaine*. A précis of this project is seen in the elaborate "outlines of speeches" that were suggested in the NER speakers' handbook, "Coaching and Utilizing Speakers" (ca. 1921). Those giving fundraising appeals in church basements or at meetings of the local Rotary club were instructed to make their appeal:

> 1. In the name of *World Peace and Order*. . . . 2. In the name of Humanity, for women and little children who have suffered untold misery and who will die without American help. . . . 3. In the name of Civilization. . . . 4. In the name of Christianity, to which they have sealed their devotions. . . . Shall western Christianity allow the extermination of these earliest Christian peoples? . . . 5. In the name of America, who has made these people love and trust her. America cannot now, in honor, abandon the little children she has saved from death, nor pause until the work is done.[3]

Beyond addressing the immediate needs of human suffering, the entire social and political system was itself the *problem of humanity* that the NER's modern humanitarianism would fix. The way the organization understood the problem and the attendant solutions derived from the humanitarian knowledge built over the preceding generation and would be expanded by workers like Kerr and Elliott as they filed field reports, wrote letters, and eventually penned their memoirs.

The survivors of the Armenian Genocide of 1915, with the help of Americans *and* America, were supposed to play the leading role in bringing about this "new Near East." Needless to say, the decision to employ Armenians for this task—indeed, the task itself—was not universally supported within the organization, the region, or, for that matter, among Armenians themselves. The inherently ambivalent nature of the Armenian role in implementing reform corresponds with equally unsettled and unsettling questions at the very core of modern humanitarianism in the Eastern Mediterranean posed by NER's work. Many of these questions were first raised during the limited relief efforts of the war years: Which religious groups or ethnicities should be helped? What should be done with the vast populations of orphans—and the more basic issue of defining orphanhood? And how should enslaved and trafficked female genocide survivors be rehabilitated? NER's work suggests, as well, how vast the gulf can be between the intentions of Western humanitarian organizations and the realities of the work of humanitarians in the field. In the winter of 1920–1921 a tremendous distance separated those in NER's New York headquarters from the naked brutality of a place like Marash.

Nevertheless, the history of NER, from its beginnings as an ad hoc food relief organization to its interwar incarnation as a bureaucratized, multidisciplinary, nongovernmental "development" organization, parallels the larger evolution of modern humanitarianism. At the center of that transition was a movement away from a narrow focus on the *relief* of human suffering to a broader effort to address the very *root causes* of that suffering. Understanding how the organization moved from the immediate relief of a discrete humanitarian emergency to a long-term program for solving humanitarian problems brings into higher resolution issues at the core of the emergence of modern humanitarianism as both a form of practice and a manifestation of ideology. The template for what defined suffering and how to address it, in this case, had as much to do with the immediate needs of the Armenians as it did with an attempt to bring to the Eastern Mediterranean a particular American social, moral, and economic reform agenda associated primarily with the "Progressive Era"; equally, the programs resonated with elements of Wilsonian idealism and linked liberal nationalism, international intervention, and humanitarianism to development, peace, and liberal political and economic structures.

Kerr and Elliott were not amateur idealists or zealous missionaries, but rather pragmatic and results-oriented professionals who were drawing on a half-century reservoir of success, primarily in domestic humanitarianism and reform.[4] Movements against child labor, new theories in the treatment of orphans, the spread of mass education, and advances in public health justified the confidence of those who believed in the potential of liberal idealism, social and hard sciences, and medicine to address societal problems at home and abroad. The outcome of the war, which in the United States much more than in Western Europe had been portrayed as a just and humane cause that was evidence itself, in the words of the title of a chapter in Elliott's memoir, of a "A New Motive in the World," added a certitude to that belief.[5]

Disentangling—but not disengaging—the ideology of reform suffusing humanitarian organizations and institutions and the practice of the humanitarian act is critically important to a better understanding of modern humanitarianism as a phenomenon in general, and the history of NER in particular. The public and fundraising rhetoric of NER was at times imbued with appeals to Christian solidarity, dubious racist histories of the peoples of the Holy Lands, arch anti-Turkish and Muslim attitudes, and unapologetic sentimentality. At other times, those attitudes were at odds with the content of the very humanitarian reports that NER's workers in the field produced, but still influenced the organization's decision making and the implementation of its programs; that said, the social practice of the organization's humanitarian professionals on the ground often followed different paths than the fundraising appeals would suggest, and those professionals evolved a more complex relationship with the peoples, religions, and governmental structures of the Eastern Mediterranean. For yet others in the leadership of NER, its work in the field was not, nor was it ever, about Armenians, or about the implementation of a post–Progressive-era reform agenda in the Middle East, but was rather an instrument for the moral uplift of America and the exercise of "Christian citizenship."

This chapter draws on Kerr's letters home; his later monograph, *The Lions of Marash;* Elliott's memoir; and archival evidence from Near East Relief and its major philanthropic partner, the Rockefeller Foundation. It also employs the memoirs of orphans, including those of Asdghig Avakian (1907–1998), who emerged as a leader of the modern practice of nursing in Lebanon, the educator Karnig Panian (1909–1989), and the gifted Armenian poet and journalist Antranik Zaroukian (1913–1989), as a point of departure into the ideology and practice of NER's interwar humanitarianism at a moment of tremendous challenge to that very project: the Battle of Marash and the collapse of a vast refugee resettlement project in south-central Anatolia, known at the time by its French colonial designation, Cilicia.

Elliott's memoir and Kerr's letters document this first major failure in American overseas humanitarianism, and in particular a setback in the efforts of NER to adapt and successfully translate the tools of the Progressive relief and social development agenda to the vast refugee problem created by the genocide of 1915. The military debacle and diplomatic concession of the French resulted in the loss of Marash and other key cities in southern Anatolia, including Aintab, Urfa, Tarsus, and Adana, which NER considered critical centers for the repatriation of refugee genocide survivors. The new reality altered the focus of relief from restoration of refugees to their homeland to rehabilitation and resettlement outside the borders of the Republic of Turkey.

By integrating the view and voices from the theater of humanitarian action with the metropolitan archive, I can write about that humanitarian project as a dynamic and evolving process that entails encounter, engagement, and conflict, and that also opens a space to show the agency of the objects of humanitarianism. In this way I add to preexisting institutional histories of NER, which tend to ignore the way refugee communities as objects of humanitarianism experienced relief and other efforts taken ostensibly on their behalf. Indeed, these previous histories either suffer from their underlying self-congratulatory approach or take at face value the organization's propaganda and dismiss it, uncritically, as amateurish American cultural imperialism.

The events of the early 1920s put American relief workers under considerable psychological and physical strain and challenged their own preconceptions and certitudes of the mission of relief work and the role of the professional relief worker. In the face of that stress, workers in the field forged relationships—even friendships—with individuals they had come to help. Unraveling those relationships gives some sense of how concepts like compassion, mutual respect, and notions of shared humanity and empathy manifested in the interethnic spaces of encounter and exchange created by relief work. It also shows how the production of difference and ethnic superiority operated in the face of those friendships and other social exchanges. Certainly, as the Americans themselves sought to make sense of the rapidly changing and dangerous world around them on the basis of their own experiences with class and race in the United States, they tried to retain a firm hold on their own sense of cultural distance and moral superiority. The intensity of the situation in a place like Marash forced the relief workers to reassess their own judgments about moral responsibility and the causality of suffering; in an experience common to modern aid workers, preexisting moral clarity became clouded once in the field.

Underlying that change of focus were conclusions by the American and, to a lesser extent, Western relief community that Armenians and Turks could not create a viable political community, let alone cohabit the same territory; that the "Near East" as a society was incapable of embracing progress and modernity by virtue of its history and the inherent "racial traits" of its peoples; and thus that any real hope for the future meant an almost exclusive focus on the next generation through massive programs for orphan institutional care and the education of children. This assertion of the paternalistic, in the literal and figural sense, relationship between the United States and the Armenians manifested along a spectrum of ideas and policies, from calling for America to take the League of Nations mandate for Armenia to identifying the tens of thousands of Armenian orphans in its care as "America's wards."

In this last aspect, it is possible to begin to see the outlines of an exceptional American humanitarianism taking shape. This American "humanitarian exceptionalism" influenced the specific modes and characteristics of relief projects at the time, and it also influenced broader attitudes and ideas about peoples of the region and Islam in the United States, and in the region the multiple perceptions of America, Americans, and its programs for assistance and development. Understanding this exceptionalism is fundamental to conceptualizing the American presence in the Eastern Mediterranean at a time when humanitarian assistance and NER constituted the bulk of that American presence.

THE BEGINNINGS OF NER'S "NEW NEAR EAST" AND
THE POSTWAR EASTERN MEDITERRANEAN

As discussed in the previous chapters, Near East Relief (NER) had its origins in two of the most devastating humanitarian crises of the First World War in the Ottoman state: the great Syrian famine and the Armenian Genocide. In both cases the historical relationship between the victims and Americans played a major role in how the disasters were understood and addressed—how they were *problems of humanity* that became *problems for humanity*. The first case was the multiyear economic dislocation and famine in coastal regions of the Eastern Mediterranean from 1914 to 1917, which was met with the earliest expression of American humanitarian wartime efforts. Although collapsed into the "Year of the Locust" in novels, memoirs, and oral historical accounts of World War I in the Levant, the famine and debilitating economic dislocation that gripped the region lasted several years and started not just in the aftermath of a plague but also in Ottoman requisition policy, hoarding, speculation, and the interruption of transportation and communication throughout the region, which also prevented remittances being sent from abroad. The problems of the famine were exacerbated by an Allied naval blockade of the port city of Beirut, the main entry point for imported foodstuffs. The scale of misery was immense, and starvation and prostitution were common; commentators of the time blamed human avarice and natural conditions for the calamity.

The problem affected inland Syria and Iraq as well. However, the presence of American institutions, primarily the Syrian Protestant College (known after 1920 as the American University of Beirut) and the American Red Cross Society meant both that knowledge about the extent of the humanitarian disaster was communicated directly and quickly to the United States and that Lebanon and its Christians were the primary recipients of assistance. Moreover, the various communities of Syrian and Lebanese Arab Christian immigrants in the United States were instrumental in calling attention to the plight of their extended families in the affected region and advocating on their behalf.

By 1918 NER resembled the other major World War I–era relief body, Herbert Hoover's US-sponsored American Relief Administration (ARA), which brought food aid to Eastern and Central Europe and revolutionary Russia.[6] However, NER was privately funded and, in current parlance, a nongovernmental organization. Though chartered by the US Congress, and linked initially to the US Department of State via the US ambassador to Istanbul, Henry Morgenthau, NER was wholly dependent on small donors and foundations for support. Its reliance on philanthropy required NER to use modern advertising techniques, mass media, and celebrity appeals to raise needed funds; as a result, knowledge of its relief work was widespread and its efforts were generally popular. Maintaining this popularity contributed, however, to choices about which Middle Eastern populations were to continue to receive aid and what form that aid would take.

Also distinguishing the NER from the ARA was the former's social inheritance from the older Protestant missionary presence in the Middle East, which dated to the early part of the previous century: many of the organization's founders in 1915 had deep roots in the American Commission Board of Foreign Missions, and when people like Kerr and Elliott arrived, they found themselves working and socializing with American and European Protestant missionaries long resident in the region. This missionary background contributed to decisions about who received aid and why; moreover, it shaped the organization's corporate understanding of Middle Eastern society, including relations between Muslims and non-Muslims and non-Western forms of Christianity. The combined weight of the missionary origins and forms of public appeal that emphasized aid to Christians in the spirit of transnational Christian solidarity meant that, by the beginning of the interwar period, the scope and mission of NER had shifted almost entirely from general assistance, a distinctive feature of the ARA, to a more focused attempt to restore and rehabilitate (politically and socially) Armenian refugee populations in Syria and the Caucasus to their ancestral homeland in what is today Turkey.

At the armistice in 1918, approximately one hundred thousand Armenian Genocide survivors were living in and around the cities of Aleppo, Damascus, and Beirut. The southern tier of Anatolia, occupied by Great Britain and then France after the war, was chosen to serve as an area for their resettlement. Armenians had constituted much of the prewar population of the region and were found in both cities and the countryside, and thus, for many in the informal settlements, this meant a return home. By 1920, three-quarters of the displaced refugees in Syria had moved to this part of Anatolia. While NER continued to deliver direct food aid, it expanded its relief work efforts to construct a vast humanitarian infrastructure that included hospitals, orphanages, rescue homes, schools, small factories, sports facilities, and microcredit lending programs in several cities of the defeated Ottoman Empire (figure 4.1). Relief work in Marash, like similar efforts in the neighboring cities of Urfa and Aintab,

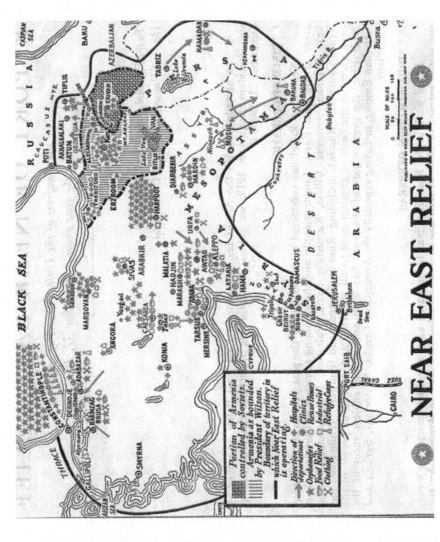

FIGURE 4.1 Map showing activities of Near East Relief, ca. 1920. Source: "Report of Near East Relief to the Congress of the United States of America for the Year Ending December 31, 1920," p. 2.

were critical to NER's dual mission of restoring Armenian refugees to their "homeland," in particular, and repairing the damage done by the war itself, more generally.[7]

However, the refugees who returned in 1920 found themselves in an unstable and uncertain political situation that had not been anticipated by NER. While the Ottoman Empire had surrendered in 1918 and subsequently agreed to the Treaty of Sèvres (1920), that peace was challenged by an insurgent Turkish nationalist movement. More critically, the security of the Armenian population in the region depended on a continued European military occupation. This aligned the Armenians with the foreign occupiers of the region. Small-scale moments of communal violence, kidnappings, rape, and targeted assassinations—alongside general lawlessness—were the norm. Nevertheless, a kind of tense standoff prevailed between the returned Armenians and the existing Turkish population. In early 1920, revolts by Turkish guerillas in the occupied cities of southern Anatolia against French colonial forces upset this status quo. Coordinated with the Turkish nationalist movement of Mustafa Kemal, later Atatürk, the situation in Marash was especially violent; Kerr and Elliott both concluded that as many as half of the city's Armenian civilian population of twenty thousand were killed in the course of the fighting. A series of diplomatic agreements between France and Turkey led to the evacuation of French forces from Cilicia; surviving Armenians—including those who had been resettled—fled back to Syria.[8]

Kerr and Elliott came to the humanitarian enterprise though divergent paths. At the time that he joined NER, Kerr had been working in the medicinal chemistry laboratory of Walter Reed Hospital in Washington, D.C., and was facing demobilization, with few job prospects and little money for his avowed goal—an advanced degree in organic chemistry. His decision to go to the Middle East was based not on any prior knowledge of the region and was instead simply a spontaneous choice made at the prompting of a superior officer at the medical center. Elliott, on the other hand, was the chief representative for the Eastern Mediterranean of the American Women's Hospitals Service (AWHS), the charitable and relief arm of the Medical Women's National Association, which had entered into an agreement with NER to provide medical expertise to a dozen hospitals scattered throughout Anatolia, Greece, and Syria. Founded after the US entrance into the war, AWHS's initial attempts to form ambulance corps for the western front were opposed by the US government, and the organization shifted its focus to the Balkans and the Ottoman Empire.[9] What Kerr and Elliott shared, however, was advanced professional training and experience in medicine and biology, and each would be required to exert exceptional managerial skill during the civil war in Marash. Neither had any background in missionary work, nor do their correspondences reveal any overt evangelical zeal beyond occasional references to their own religious practices and beliefs.

Kerr's introduction to the region occurred en route to the Eastern Mediterranean on board the S.S. *Leviathan,* a luxury liner that had been converted to a troop transport ship during the war (February 1919). Aboard ship, Kerr, alongside 250 new NER recruits, including former US Army nurses and doctors, received an abbreviated education on what had happened to the Armenians during the war itself, both from returning missionaries and what were becoming the NER's canonical texts, Toynbee's Blue Book, *Ambassador Morgenthau's Story,* and Clarence D. Ussher's 1917 *An American Physician in Turkey.*[10]

Arriving in Istanbul—then under joint Allied occupation—Kerr was assigned to Aleppo (May 1919) in the postwar Arab Syrian kingdom. That city, alongside Beirut, was the major collection point for Armenian refugees. As the initial postwar plan to restore the Armenians to south-central Anatolia took shape, Aleppo became the hub for relief work activities.

Kerr's letters home in this early period tell the story of a young man enjoying the novelty of Aleppo and southern Anatolia—from describing the sounds of Arab weddings and the thrill of boar hunting, and his collection of handicrafts, to asking his parents to send money for a planned trip floating down the Tigris on a raft at the end of his contract in the spring of 1920 (figure 4.2). In these early letters, Kerr voiced a great confidence and optimism in the NER project. That enthusiasm was shared by the NER leadership, which believed that the American relief agency would have a largely unfettered role in setting up hospitals and implementing refugee resettlement. Like Elliott, Kerr perceived his job as not just immediate relief, but also an act of what would today be called "restorative justice" for the Armenians. The key program was the repatriation of Armenians to their homelands under the auspices of a European protectorate.

However, across the summer and fall of 1919, Kerr began to encounter elements of the humanitarian crisis and larger political context that did not fit neatly into that program. Those elements forced him to begin to question the feasibility and, at times, even the justice of NER's overall strategy. The first was Kerr's introduction to the complex problem posed by the massive transfer of Armenian children from their families

FIGURE 4.2. Stanley Kerr (in glasses on left) at a picnic with other Near East Relief workers and security personnel, ca. 1920. Male NER workers wore a modified World War I–era officer's US Army uniform. Stanley Kerr Collection, photo number 42. Courtesy of the Zoryan Institute, Arlington, MA.

into Turkish and Bedouin households in Syria. As discussed in the next chapter, the Ottoman state—through formal and informal means—had taken Armenian children from their families during the deportations of 1915. In some cases, these children were placed in state orphanages, where they were converted to Islam; authorities also distributed children to Muslim families as foster children. Still others were stolen from the deportation caravans and sold or traded en route.

Kerr and NER officials in Aleppo—with the official support of the Arab kingdom—had begun to cooperate with Armenian organizations to recover these children in areas under Allied occupation. In one instance, Kerr traveled to the nearby city of Bab to recover Armenian children, primarily adolescent girls, who had been integrated into Arab households. He recalled meeting with a sheikh, who had several children in his household he claimed to have taken from the homes of their murdered parents in Aintab in the spring of 1915. The sheikh told Kerr that he had treated them as his own children, and Kerr believed the children loved the man as a father based on his brief visit. "Now are you going to take these children from me, after I have protected them during the past four years?" he remembered the sheikh asking him.[11] Kerr claims, "If I could have foreseen the future for the Armenians of Aintab [who faced similar communal violence that year] I would have decided immediately to leave these children where they were loved. But I had been commissioned to get them and allowed my sense of duty to override sentiment. 'I have no choice,' I said to the sheikh. The Emir Feisal has ordered that they should return to their own community. I must take them to Aleppo."[12]

Kerr was clearly moved by the condition of the children, who also objected to being taken to the city to rejoin their "community." For Kerr the pragmatic reality that the children appeared safe and cared for outweighed his sense, perhaps in retrospect, that the reconstitution of the Armenian community was the overriding cause. At the most basic level he was caught between the problem of the individual humanity of the children and the problem for humanity that NER had arrogated to itself to solve. The conditions that Kerr witnessed near Bab were far from unique, and among present-day Armenians, there is even a sense of gratitude to the Bedouin for taking in so many vulnerable children. However, as children were brought into rescue homes established by NER, where they were processed, including being photographed, they also were asked to explain what had happened to them in the years between the onset of the genocide and their rescue. While the records from the NER-administered Rescue Home are lost, many of the reports from the years when it was under the control of the League of Nations, as the subsequent chapter discusses, remain a useful source for understanding that the children faced conditions of slavery and, for the girls, serial rape and forced marriage.

In November 1919 Kerr wrote to his family detailing the laborious work of photographing orphaned children at the NER facility in Aintab. Similar to the work of the Rescue Home, where photographs and personal data were put to use trying to find living relatives of rescued children, the NER hoped to reunite families and raise funds: "At Aintab I photographed 960 orphans and had a record made of each child's name, its parents' names, and a story of each one's experiences during the war. These will be copied and the copies with photos, sent to America with an appeal for individuals to support or 'adopt' orphans. It was lots of fun doing this work as all the kids like to be photoed [sic]. At Marash I'm to do the same thing."[13]

By the time he had completed the work at Marash, Kerr had photographed and transcribed, with the help of a translator, the stories of nearly two thousand children. In a letter to his father in mid-December 1919, he writes, "The stories these little kids can tell about their experiences are awfully interesting . . . the way they are told." Picking one at random from his desk, he recounts the rough translation of the story of Vartanoush Seferian, a seventeen-year old orphan housed at the NER's orphanage in Marash:

> Our family was composed of eleven members, my brother . . . in America was married and his wife was with us with her two sons. My three sisters and one brother at home were married so they all started with us. First we were exiled to a place called Hasan Oglou in four months. There Turks made a massacre. They took our properties, we fled back to Kemach. At the war . . . Turk women killed with axes my father and mother and also my uncles. When we reached to Kemach Turks threw into river my nephews. An officer took one of my brother's wife so I fled to Kemach back. There the Kaimacam [mayor] of Kemach took me and I was a servant in his family as many as four years. When Russian Army came, so many Armenian widows fled to them. It was announced that none of the Turks would keep Armenians in his house so Kaimakam sent me away and I came to Marash with a Moslem. At the same time my brother's wife fled to Russian Army. After two days of my arrival to Marash I was put by the aid of Armenians to Rescue Home. There I lived nearly eight months, but now I am in [NER] orphanage.[14]

It is perhaps evidence of the increasingly difficult psychological toll that hearing those stories was having on Kerr that, despite promising to tell his family more of these stories, he never did so. Still, in his memoir of four decades later he recalled,

> The Gravflex camera was entrusted to me for this project, together with an ample supply of film, developer, and photographic paper; and I set out for Aintab on this pleasant mission. There I photographed the children in small groups and obtained information for a history sheet for each child. The stories told by the older children seemed so fantastic that at first I found them unbelievable, but one by one they corroborated each other. They had seen violence and death while small and had accepted it much as children today accept it on the television screen—it was happening to someone else.[15]

It is critical to recognize what a powerful cumulative effect those stories— testimonies—must have had on Kerr at the time.[16] The horror of the massacres and deportations that occurred during the war were no longer mediated for him through the writings of diplomats or news accounts. Now, Kerr himself was using the technology of photography and the bureaucratic tools of the report to produce humanitarian knowledge of the broader catastrophe. He was putting faces and names to trauma and its lasting impact on the bodies and minds of young people. And while he witnessed a disassociation by the orphans from their own experience ("it was happening to someone else"), he was now *associating* that traumatic experience with real children and probably having a difficult time understanding the profound emotional reaction he himself felt at the juxtaposition of the children and their experience in that moment; it was a collection of emotions, including anger and empathy, that may have only begun to make sense to him as he remembered it toward the end of his life, and only then after he had children of his own. Certainly, the time Kerr spent with the orphans was key to his later decision to remain in Marash during the worst moments of the massacres and after the abandonment of the city by French colonial forces, when he too could have left the city. While his sense of professional responsibility is enough to explain that decision, I would argue that his personal encounter with the suffering of children, in particular, made their protection a problem for Kerr's *own humanity*. His letters home from this period change abruptly in tone from that of the callow tourist to the considered and measured response of a caring professional, who understood at once the depth of need as well as the sources of suffering. Tales of hunting boars cease.

During the first few weeks of his time in Marash, Kerr sent letters home outlining the basic organizational problem facing NER's program of refugee resettlement. Funding for that project was being reduced, he observed, and the "Armenians are going to suffer terribly this winter." While money was, of course, a perennial problem, in this case, the repatriation was made more difficult because of the social and political "facts on the ground" that the genocide had created in the mixed villages and cities where the refugees were being returned. "It isn't their fault," Kerr explained,

> that they aren't ready for self-support yet. They have been held in refugee camps for so long that they haven't time now to make homes for the winter—the Turks have their businesses, homes, stores, everything—when they do get back to their homes. Even our [NER] orphanages and rescue homes are going to be terrible places to live this winter—with not enough money to buy food, *no heat at all,* and the clothing of every orphan being one summer undershirt, one [pair] Summer drawers, one dress (both boys and girls wear a sort of dress)—no shoes. For the winter they will be given woolen socks and a sweater. . . . Out in the villages thousands will die this winter. It can't be prevented. Where the [NER] is working the suffering will be much less, but even there it can't be eliminated.[17]

Kerr was among the first relief workers to understand how the transfer of wealth and property during the genocide made more complex any effort at repatriation. The magnitude of Armenian property seized by the Ottoman authorities and redistributed to the Armenians' Turkish neighbors or held by the state was little understood at the time and certainly had not fit into the broader calculus of NER, which imagined that resettlement would proceed with little opposition from the defeated Turkish side.[18] NER's calculations were also built on a misunderstanding of how damaged the very fabric of the Armenian community was as a consequence of the genocide, and how profound an impact of the death of so many adult men and the creation of an overwhelmingly female and child survivor population would have on its efforts. Not understanding how the effects of genocide cascaded throughout Armenian society was among NER's essential failures.

Before the winter rains fell on the countryside around Aleppo, making travel along its dirt roads more difficult, Kerr was transferred from the hospital in Aleppo, which was closing as the refugees were sent back into Anatolia, to Marash. He would no longer be a medicinal chemist, bur rather take on the role of NER's local chief financial officer—and join an international relief community that included not just other workers from NER, but also the YMCA, missionaries from the American Board of Overseas Missions, and Armenian communal organizations and political parties. Kerr arrived in Marash just as the British occupation forces turned the city over to the French military—made up primarily of soldiers from France's overseas colonies, but led by European officers—a low-grade insurgency arose, targeting both the army of occupation and the civilian Armenian returnees.

Dr. Mabel Evelyn Elliott (1881–ca. 1944) was significantly older than Stanley Kerr and a seasoned professional at the time of her deployment to the postwar Eastern Mediterranean. Photographs of her from the time show a small woman with white hair and a stern visage behind wire-rimmed glasses. Elliott arrived in Marash before Kerr, within weeks of the initial British occupation of the city. She took charge of the Hilfsbund hospital from the elderly German nurse who had directed it for two decades; German nationals had been ordered to leave Ottoman territory after the state's surrender.

Prior to her arrival in Marash, Elliott had spent time in Istanbul providing medical services at the NER's Rescue Home in Üsküdar, a suburb on the Asian shore of the Bosphorus. This Rescue Home was a parallel institution to those established in other Allied-occupied parts of the Ottoman Empire, including Marash and Aleppo; again, its function was to receive and rehabilitate Armenian women who had been kidnapped, traded, or sold into Turkish and Kurdish households during the genocide. This particular Rescue Home was somewhat unique, however, in that the young women gathered in it were the products of Western-style missionary schools like Robert College and generally had origins in the upper middle class of the Ottoman state's vibrant Armenian community. They spoke foreign languages like German, English, and French and had been raised to be respectable and respected wives and mothers in their community.[19]

Similar to what had happened in the cities and villages of Anatolia, the young women and their families had been deported; and like them, these women and girls had faced trafficking, enslavement, forced marriage, and rape—often leading to unwanted pregnancy. At the Rescue Home, Mabel Elliott met with some women who had been liberated from the households into which they had been placed. In certain cases this rescue had occurred after house-to-house searches in Istanbul by British military police; still other women reached the safety of the Armenian patriarchate or similar institutions on their own. The stories of trauma and survival retold by Elliott in her memoir are as haunting as the ones told by the child orphans to Kerr. When reading Elliott's memoir, however, one sees glimpses in her matter-of-fact prose that these women had faced—and were facing—a different horror that she, despite her training, had been unprepared for. As each girl came in for her medical examination, which included checks for pregnancy and venereal disease, they began to tell their stories. In most cases they had been at the home for a relatively short period of time, and Elliott claims that this was their first opportunity to explain what had happened to them. Beyond the immediate context of gathering data for the checkup, Elliott's status as a female professional (or just the fact that she was foreign) quite possibly made the telling safer. The women told of being forced to convert to Islam, of being mutilated to prevent their running away, and of bearing children that they had to or chose to abandon to enter the Rescue Home. One in particular, who was found to have been impregnated by the head of the household in which she lived, told Elliott that upon giving birth she would return the child to its father.[20]

Elliott took away from her conversations at the Rescue Home the conclusion that the girls were not particularly confident that Americans like her could repair their lives and restore them to the path they were on before the genocide. Where the Americans planned to rehabilitate them and make them whole, they themselves recognized that, although they had been rescued from a terrible situation and had rejoined the Armenian community, having been raped, impregnated, and sometimes mutilated by their captors, that return could not be seamless and it was difficult to imagine that they could be the kinds of wives and mothers they had been raised to be. They were caught in what Lerna Ekmekci-oglu describes as the double bind of patriarchy in the postgenocide.

Similar to Kerr's experience with the registration and photography project of the orphans in Aintab and later Marash, in Üsküdar, too, the eyewitness testimony of, in this case, educated young women influenced the way Elliott understood the problem of humanity and her role in addressing suffering. "The things that I heard were unbelievable," she explained, remarking:

> A doctor sees more deeply into the abysses of human society than any other person . . . but I knew only America. This was Asia, strange, bestial, incomprehensible. It was my first personal encounter with such things—the things that human beings can do, carelessly, without rancor, laughing, to other human beings. It was incredible, too, that these girls could have seen and endured them, and survived to sit there telling of them. The stories did not vary greatly.[21]

The recurrent horror of these stories, told not by waifish orphans but rather by educated young women to whom Elliott would have felt some degree of class, gender, and social affinity, connected her to the humanitarian project in a profound way. Her growing awareness of the depth of her own connection to these women was evidence of the unfolding of a larger attachment, built on the principles of shared humanity between Armenians and Americans, and uniquely so: "No two peoples of the same family of human races could be more different than the American and the Armenian. The bond between them is unique in history—the purely humanitarian interest of one nation in another."[22] For Elliott, the advent of modern humanitarianism as practiced by Americans in the Eastern Mediterranean was itself a historical departure from the dominance of war and self-interest in international affairs. "But today," she argues, "the rule has exceptions. One of them is the relations of America to the Armenians. We see America, with nothing to gain, with no intention of annexing land, of finding cheap labor or seizing concessions, act as though Armenians were not an alien people, but members of her own family."[23] And while there are significant differences between Armenians and Americans by virtue of history, religion, and geography, "they are united by a new reality between peoples, the idea of human solidarity."[24] That new force, which Elliott calls a "young motive in the world," is "a weakling."[25]

Elliott's vision was not unique and reflects the sense of historical mission that underlay the work of NER—namely, that the efforts on behalf of Armenians were a manifestation of American Progressive leadership away from the Old World's affinity for war and colonialism and toward a peaceful world built around new humanitarian principles. It is evidence that Elliott, among others, was experimenting with the idea that modern humanitarianism went beyond professional and neutral caring and was potentially a form of ideology itself, enfeebled though it might be in the face of what she would have seen as stronger, older, and, to her mind, morally corrupt prevailing ideologies of colonialism and nationalism, and perhaps even ideologies on the Left. But beneath Elliott's rhetoric of American humanitarian exceptionalism, her memoir is acutely sensitive to the depths of human suffering that preceded her arrival as well as the atrocities that would take place in Marash, and again what she witnessed as she spent the next several years in the region, culminating with her work in Soviet Armenia. Especially moving is Elliott's account of the suffering of mothers, as seen in her description of the flight to Islahiye. Equally, it was important to her to portray the humanity of the Armenians she worked with. "I wish that the people at home who had sent us to the Near East to help the Armenians could know them as we know them—more as neighbors, and less as symbols."[26]

Clearly, however, the cumulative effect of being exposed to the deeply traumatized population was taking a toll on Elliott. As she confided in a letter from Marash to Dr. Mary Crawford, "This work is quite a strain. No matter how one tries, the stories of these people can't help but affect one. I never seek their stories and often they will be about for weeks without your realizing what a terrible burden they are carrying."[27] Her memoir provides evidence as well of the potential of friendship across the humanitarian object–subject divide. Clearly the inherent and intense paternalism that suffuses humanitarianism colors anything resembling friendship with dynamics of power. Nonetheless, Elliott built friendships with local Armenians. True, these relationships were contingent on class and education and were primarily made among the Western-educated medical staff of the Marash hospital. Kerr recalled Elliott's "sensitivity of spirit and the warm relationship she developed with the Armenian doctors and nurses."[28] The most significant of these friendships was with Dr. Haroutioune Der Ghazarian, a medical doctor educated at the

Syrian Protestant College who had returned to Marash to work in the former German hospital. Known as "Dr. Artine," he was remembered by Elliott as "a surgeon whose skill touched genius; he was also a cultured and gentle man, intelligent, widely read, humorous."[29] He became Elliott's window onto Armenian culture and politics and emblematic to her of the resurrection of the Armenian community in Cilicia.

The possibility of friendship across the social and cultural gulfs between Der Ghazarian and Elliott is a distinctive characteristic of modern humanitarianism that distinguishes it from missionary paternalism. These kinds of friendships were also evident in the relationship between some of the Western educators in Beirut, whose personal connections with the local Beiruti middle class informed choices about relief work and collaboration. It is clear from her memoirs that Elliott did not see in Der Ghazarian, during the time they spent together in Marash, a potential convert or a client of missionary patronage; it is even possible to imagine that his acceptance of her as a fellow professional and the respect he showed her was refreshing for a female doctor who may have experienced little of that respect from her American male colleagues. Nevertheless, the concept of friendship and linked ideas of mutual respect and collegiality remains an unstudied and underexamined element of the interface of the Western humanitarian presence in the post-Ottoman Eastern Mediterranean. Humanitarianism at its root acknowledges shared humanity *in the abstract;* what the relationship between Elliott and Der Ghazarian shows is a more intimate and less intangible manifestation of that core principle as it unfolded in the field. For Elliott, as well, Der Ghazarian was evidence of the success of the American approach to Progressive development; he was the consummate modern man.

That friendship, and experiences with stories of trauma experienced by both Kerr and Elliott—in particular Kerr's photographing of orphans and Elliott's encounter with the middle-class trafficked rape survivors at Üsküdar—formed their sense of professional commitment to the refugees and survivors among whom they were working. It was not missionary zeal, but rather a commitment to *fix* the problem of humanity facing the Armenians in their care. Their memoirs and letters are replete with references to their sense of professional responsibility, both to individuals and to the larger community of Armenians. That sense of responsibility would be sorely tested as Marash became the scene of the bloodiest intercommunal violence of the interwar period. Both Kerr and Elliott remained in the city throughout the worst of the conflict, and if they contemplated abandoning the Armenians, those sentiments are not present in their letters home or later recollections. As Kerr wrote to his parents on the night of the flight to Islahiye: "There is no doubt about our duty. No one even suggested another course. Perhaps by the time this reaches you a cablegram will have told you that all is well here and that we are safe. But until you know certainly, don't give up hope. We are in great danger, but not without hope. Out thoughts are with the orphans in our care rather than ourselves at present."[30] Kerr and Elliott were both painfully aware that their status as Americans was no guarantee of safety. Early in that conflict two Americans from the YMCA were murdered en route to Marash, and each recalls being shot at and having to take shelter from indiscriminate shelling.

The Battle of Marash has attracted a great deal of attention in Armenian and Turkish historiography because of its central role in the so-called Turkish War for Independence.[31] It is not the purpose of this chapter to rewrite that episode. However, the battle—which took place over the winter of 1919 to 1920—culminated with the French withdrawal in February 1920. The ultimate outcome was the expulsion of Armenian returnees and inhabitants from not just Marash, but also the other cities and villages of the areas under French occupation. Alongside that loss was the loss of the immense infrastructure that NER had built to assist in the rehabilitation of the Armenian community, and in many cases the loss of Armenian professionals and leadership that was to have been instrumental in building a self-sufficient community and creating a new Near East.

Kerr remained in the city after the French withdrawal, hoping to shelter as many of the Armenian orphans and elderly as he could. He could do little to protect them except assert that they were under the care of a US organization and were "neutral" in the conflict. It is quite possible that he chose to remain in the city as Turkish nationalist forces and irregulars mounted a massacre to bear witness to the atrocity as a final professional act, and as an act of conscience. The morning after the French retreat, Kerr, in concert with NER officials, was able to broker a ceasefire that spared many of the remaining civilians. He spent the rest of the winter feeding orphans and helping organize a committee of ecclesiastical leaders to manage food distribution. Planning to take up a fellowship at the University of Pennsylvania, he left that summer. But within a few months, he was back in Marash, this time as director of operations and accompanied by his sister, Marion Kerr, and another relief worker, Elsa Reckman. Kerr discovered that despite assurances by the new Kemalist government that it would respect Armenian rights and property, the new Marash had become utterly inhospitable to the handful of remaining Armenians, and indeed the institutional integrity of NER operations had collapsed as well.[32] After organizing the sale and transfer of NER assets and the movement of orphans to Lebanon and Syria, Kerr left Marash for the last time on July 29, 1922, with what was left of the NER staff in the city.

Elliott had fled Marash with a mass of refugees alongside the retreating French military column in February 1920. She arrived utterly exhausted and suffering from exposure at the Islahiye train station; most of the nurses from the hospital had survived. The flight alongside the refugees stripped away from her much of her sense of distance from them. As she searched for her friend Dr. Der Ghazarian, she noticed how like the refugees she herself had become:

> I kept asking for Dr. [Der Ghazarian]. No one had heard of him. This, I thought, is the way Armenian families are broken up. This is the way they tramp the roads of Turkey, asking for news of each other. I am a refugee. This is what it means. If I had been born in Marash instead of in America, all that I know, all that I am, would not keep me from this; hunger and cold and heartache, refugee camps and lines of refugees, bread lines, dirt, disease. Why should I wish and pray that [Der Ghazarian] escaped alive? It would be easier for him to be killed by the Turks.[33]

But she did find him. He had also left the city leading a group of refugees. Elliott was able to find an interpreter position for him with NER and he eventually rose to administer the organization's hospital in Adana. Thinking about her friend, Elliott wrote what could also serve as the epitaph for the NER project in Cilicia: "Wherever he is, he will always be a gallant, gentle intelligent man. But his personal life, his career, and his hopes were killed in Marash."[34]

For American relief workers and many of the Armenian professionals who had worked with them, Marash was the pivotal moment in the broader historical experience of humanitarianism—not only did it renew flows of refugees and create new populations of refugees from communities that had survived genocide, but with failures on the diplomatic front, it forestalled the creation of a *modern* Armenian nation under American tutelage. What was left was a population of refugees and no longer potential citizens of a new Armenia or, in the argot of NER, the building blocks of a new Near East. The refugees were citizens of no state, bereft of rights and disconnected from place; they were so much human flotsam flooding down from the mountains of Anatolia and washing up in waves as new *khleakner*, wrecks, into massive refugee camps taking shape on the arid plain north of Aleppo and in a malaria swamp at the mouth of the Beirut River.

ORPHAN AND REFUGEE CHILDREN

Writing a field report to NER's New York office in 1923, Enoch R. Applegate, the Aleppo director of the organization, explained that the "general evacuation of Cilicia by the Armenians in 1921 realized the great necessity for founding a refugee school for the hundreds of Armenian children deprived from education and roaming the streets underfed and sparingly clothed."[35] Applegate's report documents the creation of a network of "refugee schools" in Aleppo that were part day school and part orphanage. These schools—how they were organized and staffed, what subjects were taught—became the focus of much of the NER's work in the region and provide evidence of the institutional shift away from the project of returning Armenians to their homeland to a more limited goal of what was termed, in the post–Cilician disaster policy framework of NER, a "restoration to normalcy." Normalcy, in this sense, was some combination of a return to home life—deinstitutionalization—or self-support as a laborer, but certainly not a return to citizenship or to place of origin. The project in Aleppo was matched on a similar scale in Beirut and at other centers of refugee settlement, including Jerusalem and Nazareth. "By the word 'school'," Applegate, himself a World War I veteran who had been wounded while evacuating Armenian children under fire from the city of Kharpert, continued, "the impression should not be conceived to signify schools as known in America and Europe with their sanitary class rooms, and modern school equipment etc. A refugee school is usually composed of three to four grades consisted of 150 to 200 pupils in a large wooden hut . . . sitting on the bare ground and the various grades having different lessons at the same period."[36]

Orphan care had been part of NER's mandate from the earliest period of its involvement in the region and was primarily focused on the health care and feeding of children. The creation of refugee schools expanded that mandate and shifted the focus of the organization to educating and preparing young people to enter the non-Armenian societies where they were in refuge—French mandate Syria and Lebanon, British mandate Palestine and Greece.

At the same time, that process had the intended effect of preventing the full assimilation of the Armenians into those societies, helping them retain a distinct identity and forms of communal belonging. Exemplary

TABLE 4.1   NER-AFFILIATED ARMENIAN REFUGEE SCHOOLS IN ALEPPO, CA. 1923

Name of refugee school (origin of students)	Total enrolled	Male	Female	Half orphan[1]	Full orphan	Teachers employed
Cilician Benevolent Union (Aintab), Marash, Killis, Sivas, Adana, etc.)	1,316	712	606	345	150	33
Armenian National (Aintab, Killis, Marash, 'Urfa, Ankara, etc.)	451	259	222	292	52	27
Armenian Protestant (Aintab, Marash, Gürün, Erzerum, Zeitun, etc.)	361	239	122	56	18	16
Kharpert Compatriotic Union (Kharpert Province, Killis, Istanbul, etc.)	308	135	173	233	45	6
Camp-Based Protestant School (Marash, Aintab, Killis, Erzerum, etc.)	220	134	66	60	2	2
Camp-Based Orthodox School (Marash, Aintab, Kharpert, 'Urfa, etc.)	158	108	50	35	1	5
Malatia Compatriotic Union (Malatia Province)	150	75	75	41	64	5
Usumsirets Union (Zeitun, Marash, Aintab, Killis, etc.)	107	60	47	16	2	2
Çarsanjak Compatriotic Union (Dersim Province)	90	45	45	46	16	3
Total	3,161	1,767	1,406	1,124	350	99

SOURCE: "The Armenian Refugee Schools in Aleppo," E.R. Applegate (Aleppo) to Chairman (New York), October 25, 1923, RAC-NER.

[1] "Half-orphan" generally meant a child without a living father.

of this retention of communal identity is seen most particularly in the way that many of the schools in Aleppo were organized with the support of what were called "compatriotic unions"—societies of survivors from Anatolia who organized themselves on the basis of their cities and towns of origin. For example, in addition to schools run in cooperation with the Armenian Orthodox and Armenian Protestant churches, and philanthropies like the Usumnasirats (lit. "lovers of education") Society, refugee schools were affiliated with the compatriotic unions of the cities of Kharpert, Çarsanjak, and Malatia (table 4.1).

In addition, the curriculum at the schools supported this measured process of assimilation. The subjects taught were English, French, Arme-

FIGURE 4.3. Female orphans in a Near East Relief facility in Aleppo learning to tat,
ca. 1922. Courtesy of the Nubarian Library, Paris.

nian, arithmetic, geography, history, religion, grammar, and gymnastics;
for girls, sometimes also needlework and aspects of home economics (figure 4.3). Missing from the curriculum were both Turkish and Arabic. A
large portion of the Armenians who arrived in 1921—certainly those
from Marash and Aintab—would have spoken an Anatolian dialect of
Turkish as their native language; far fewer were Armenian speakers, and
certainly even fewer were literate in the written Armenian of Istanbul,
which had become standard modern Western Armenian. Their parents—
had they been literate at all—would have been so in Turkish. More to the
point, they were living in what was nominally Arabic-speaking Syria.
Critically, the emphasis on Armenian-language instruction to young
Armenians who may not have spoken Armenian at home was a crucial
element in building an Armenian community in diaspora, and one that
could successfully oppose complete assimilation.[37] Alongside the refugee
schools, NER took control in 1921 of a series of workshops-cum-indus-
trial-arts-schools that had been established during the war to provide
employment to orphans and displaced young people. Master craftspeople
taught young men and women carpentry, shoemaking, baking, black-
smithing, tailoring, tatting, and needlework. These tended to be self-sufficient enterprises and, indeed, the NER tailor shop secured government
contracts to produce uniforms for the Syrian military and gendarmerie.[38]

Beyond the significant curricular lacunae, what is striking about the makeup of the student body of these schools is the relative parity between male and female students at a time when girls' education in larger Syrian society beyond the most rudimentary levels was quite rare outside of the urban middle class. This attention to female education, as well as to orphan education, is among the most significant residues of the Progressive agenda of NER. It is also a testament to the degree to which an emerging Armenian diaspora community was responding to the impact of the mass killings of men and older boys by recognizing the increased value of girls to the survivor community.

What Applegate's 1923 letter shows, however, and the basis for his writing it, was the chronic underfunding of education by NER. The schools in Aleppo and elsewhere operated on a combination of tuition, gifts from organizations, including the YMCA, and subsidies from NER. And while 1923 saw over five hundred thousand dollars distributed, most of that money was spent on feeding programs in the Caucasus and Greece. By 1924 the organization's overall disbursements fell to less half that total amount.[39] This decrease in funding was a consequence both of the passing of the most acute phase of refugee need, but also of donor fatigue in the United States itself. NER had tried to stem this tide of fundraising decline with a renewed focus on the organization's efforts on behalf of children, reinvigorating the older idea that the children of Armenia and its "orphans" were America's wards, and that Americans were uniquely positioned to help them.

Exemplary of this conceptual framework is a fundraising pamphlet from 1924, produced at a time when NER was coming under increasing criticism from the Rockefeller Foundation and other organizations for its focus on orphan care to the exclusion of family reunification. The competency of the organization's New York–based leadership was also being questioned. As early as June 1922, the RF had been alerted to administrative and ideological problems in the implementation of NER's work, in particular how its publicity and seeming lack of neutrality had drawn the ire of Turkish nationalists, as well as its apparent instrumentalization of orphans in service of a Protestant American agenda.[40]

Still, money for NER was necessary, the advertising copy read, because Armenian children were being "reared by Americans," thus "instilling American ideas and methods into the conservatism of the East."[41] The copy continued, "Children reared by Americans are inspired by certain American qualities—optimism, desire to cooperate, initiative.

The black days of the past distress are lost sight of in the steady light of present security. . . . A generation of leaders, self-confident because of their training and aggressive because self-confident, is growing up to fill the vacancies made by war."[42] There was little evidence in the field of this *Americanization*, as the care and education of Armenian young peoples was dominated almost exclusively by Armenian professional teachers and administrators. Applegate's staff was entirely Armenian and included Haig Boyadjian, Haroutiune Nalbandian, Louis Hekimian, and Adour Levonian. Nonetheless, the NER schools had an impact on the refugee communities, and indeed they were capable of producing young people who did transition into positions of cultural and social leadership in the Armenian diaspora. Despite what at times seems an ostentatious Americanism streaming through the public relations and promotional materials produced by NER, the preeminent role of the organization in a multifaceted process of an authentic Armenian survival in diaspora is a fact.

ORPHAN LIVES

NER had gone to the Eastern Mediterranean to make Armenians the vanguard of a new, modern, and moral community. With the collapse of the humanitarian project in Cilicia, where the organization had sought social transformation within the context of French colonial nation building, it faced in the refugee camps in the cities of the region instead the problem of survival. Nevertheless, as the organization rebuilt its infrastructure in the Levant, elements of that transformative project were reintegrated and adapted into orphan care. Evidence of the organization's clear break with its missionary past is seen, likewise, in its 1921 decision to cooperate with the Armenian Orthodox Church hierarchy, a decision that would have been anathema a generation earlier among the American Protestant missionaries in the region. The information from the field, like Applegate's report telling of increasing cooperation with diaspora civil society institutions created by Armenians themselves, indicate the formation of partnerships that were not foreseen by the more paternalistic leadership of the organization in New York and anticipate more contemporary collaborative practices between the objects and subjects of humanitarianism. These partnerships provided NER with personnel, funds, and local knowledge that made what work the organization was able to do somewhat more effective through the mid-1920s.

That final transition is visible in three of the few surviving memoirs of orphans who passed through NER institutions: Karnig Panian's unpublished addendum to *Husher antourayi vosbanotse* (Orphanhood and childhood) (Beirut, 1992); Asdghig Avakian and her *Stranger among Friends* (Beirut, 1960); and Antranik Zaroukian's *Mankut'iwn ch'unets'ogh mardik* (Men without childhoods) (Beirut, 1985). On the one hand, all the memoirs illustrate the potential social mobility offered by the education and socialization provided in the orphanages; they also tell of terrible cruelty at the hands of administrators and teachers and the generally precarious nature of refugee orphanhood. The life stories of Panian, Avakian, and Zaroukian are somewhat out of the ordinary, in that they document the lives of young people who became quite successful in adulthood, but they are far from unique. Of the three, Avakian had the most contact with Americans and American institutions throughout her life and, indeed, she is an example of the *real* impact of the exceptionalism of NER's project: instead of making new Near Easterners, NER had helped make new Americans in the Middle East, or at least Armenians who were both modern but still "out of place" in the societies where they found refuge. Though Avakian did not emigrate, thousands of others in situations similar to hers found assimilation in Arab Syria and Lebanon untenable, and their transition to Western society was smoothed by their education and training at the hands of NER.[43] Zaroukian and Panian remained in Beirut, too, wrote exclusively in Armenian, and became part of the cultural revival of what was an autonomous, or, perhaps more correctly, ghettoized, Armenian community in the logic of the consociational regime of independent Lebanon.[44]

Avakian was from the village of Körpe in south-central Anatolia. Upon her father's death in the years before the outbreak of World War I she was sent, as a "half orphan," to live at the German missionary orphanage in Kharpert, where she remained until her mother remarried. She was briefly reunited with her mother and abusive stepfather. Her mother returned her to the orphanage as war began and in all likelihood perished along with most of the Armenians of the Kharpert district. Young Asdghig survived the genocide in the orphanage, but was witness to terrible atrocities between 1915 and 1919, including the mass execution of male deportees. With the end of the war, NER took control of her orphanage from the German nuns who had run it for a quarter century. In 1922 Avakian was evacuated to the new NER orphanage in the seaside Beirut suburb of Antelias. She had little contact with NER

American relief workers, whom she invariably and inaccurately called "NER missionaries" (Armenian writers had no word for relief worker) until she was selected to participate in a pilot nurse education program that was run by the American faculty at the hospital of the American University in Beirut:

> In 1923, several months after my arrival at the orphanage in Antelias . . . two missionaries from [American University Hospital] arrived to select some girls to be taken to Beirut and trained as nurses. Several of us were called to Superintendent's office and lined up for inspections. I was wearing a long, dark shabby dress, and my hair was done in pigtails tied with a red ribbon. The kind smiling eyes of Mrs. Graham and Miss Ella Osborn, the two missionaries, studied us carefully, [the administrator] . . . spoke in my favor and was over generous in her praise of my conscientiousness, willingness and helpfulness. She spoke highly of my intelligence and a few other virtues which she had seen in me. With her help I was chosen as one of the four who were to be taken for training. We blushed modestly and went to pack our belongings. We did not possess a great deal, so this operation took but little time. . . . I remember packing my 12 brightly dressed dolls [which she had made herself] and my Bible. These were my only possessions.[45]

Fifteen years old at the time, Avakian spoke little English but quickly adapted. In 1926, Bayard Dodge, who had become the university's president, handed her a nursing diploma. Experiencing feelings that must have been common among successful orphans, a profound sense of survivor's guilt engulfed her in that moment: "Why had mother pushed me into this position? Why hadn't I been allowed to perish with the rest of my family? And now alone having to face the unknown, was her sacrifice worthwhile?"[46] Within two years she was made head nurse of one of the hospital's floors. Her nursing and nurse educator career would last well into the 1970s.

Panian's memoirs tell of a comfortable childhood in Gürün, a small town near Sivas in central Anatolia, where his extended family owned orchards and his father and grandfather worked in home building and construction. His father was drafted into the Ottoman Army and never seen again, and the family was deported by foot in 1915 to a concentration camp near Hama in central Syria. There, most the family perished, and young Panian was put in the care of a German orphanage. He was transferred by the Ottoman military authorities to a state-administered orphanage near Beirut at Aintoura in 1917. As discussed in the next chapter, that orphanage was the site of an experiment by a member of the Young Turk elite, Halidé Edip Adıvar, to "Turkify" young Armenians and Kurds through abusive practices and the erasure of social identity. Panian survived that orphanage and after the war was transferred to the care of NER.

Panian was among the first group of orphans dispatched from the Levant to Aintab as part of NER's resettlement project in Cilicia. He recalls of that moment the restorative nature of their "return," not necessarily home but a new Armenian enclave under American humanitarian protection:

> Obviously, in Aintab, our education and our nutrition were equally important to the orphanage's administration. We ate three meals a day, every day, and the food was always plenty to satisfy us, as was the bread. We now also had the chance to take a bath with hot water once a week, and we very much appreciated this new privilege. In Aintoura, the orphans had bathed perhaps four times in four years. Some of the boys had even forgotten how to wash themselves. Our Turkish caretakers had completely neglected to teach us basic hygiene. . . . Soon, we began making real progress. We could read, we could write, and our vocabulary was becoming prolific. Even out in the courtyard, during recess, we often read aloud to each other, though we were not allowed to sing aloud. We were in a Turkish neighborhood, after all, and hearing Armenian children singing happily just may irritate the locals.[47]

NER's ultimate plan was to continue to train and educate the young people as the basis of a revitalized community that was now largely without the white-collar professionals and artisans who had been exterminated during the genocide. The education Panian received empowered him to see himself in that kind of social role. "I could read fluently," he remembered after a year at the Aintab facility,

> and I had read my textbook cover-to-cover. I had learned some of the stories within it by heart and often entertained my friends by reciting them. They were amazed at my ability to absorb and retain information, and I remember, one day, one of them looked at me and prophetically stated, "Just you wait, you'll be a teacher someday!" . . . This was a fresh, new idea, and I mulled it over for quite some time. I let my imagination run free, and I wondered whether I really could, one day, become a teacher. These reflections kept me busy for many days.[48]

Nonetheless, the fighting, which had convulsed Marash in 1920, soon reached Aintab as well. The young people were brought into the old Armenian quarter, which the Americans believed could be more easily defended during communal violence. The NER efforts in Aintab were led by Ray Travis (1906–1965), whom Panian remembered fondly as a great giant of man who enjoyed eating and playing with the orphans. In a departure from the nonviolent actions Kerr took in the face of the rising communal violence, when the Armenian district of Aintab was attacked by armed Turkish irregulars, according to Panian, Travis took up arms himself, firing on the attackers and securing weapons and ammunition from the French colonial forces for the Armenian fighters. The fighting took the life of one of the orphans, Manuk, who died from a bullet wound.

With the French total withdrawal from Cilicia, Panian, Ray Travis, and the others were evacuated back to Lebanon, and Panian was placed with three hundred others in an NER facility in the town of Jubayl. Reflecting on the failure of the "return" to Aintab, Panian recalled: "I remember standing in the twilight near those ruins and thinking—nor was I the only one to have these thoughts—that we had come to a new country and we would have to start from scratch again. But, at least, here we knew that we would have everything necessary to survive. We also knew we would receive the best possible education. We would now have to work as hard as possible to rebuild our shattered lives."[49] Panian would continue his education and go on to be a beloved teacher at Beirut's Jemaran (gymnasium), the premier Armenian-language high school in the Levant. In Panian's story, with its recurring emphasis on the role NER played in Armenian education, the organization's contribution to preserving Armenians as a people comes through. Education was more than just a pragmatic effort, but was seen as a central element to the restoration of the humanity of the survivors by reattaching them to their community's language, culture, and history. That emphasis is one of the most unique elements of the entire NER project in the region and definitive of its place in the formation of the Armenian diaspora.

Zaroukian was also from Gürün, and only two years old when he was deported with his mother, Yeranouhi. His father, Toros, had joined a resistance movement, but had been captured and executed in Marash. The mother and son survived a period in the Syrian desert and were interned at a camp near Aleppo. With war's end, Zaroukian's mother, whose job as a cleaning woman at the city's famous Baron Hotel left her in a precarious existence, could not care for him and placed him, as a "half orphan," in the Armenian Protestant Orphanage, which at the time was a converted enormous courtyard home in one of the city's walled neighborhoods. Zaroukian was later transferred to the NER facility at Jubayl.[50] Returning to Aleppo in 1920, he was eventually reunited with his mother and then sent to Beirut's Jemaran on scholarship.

Zaroukian's memoir, which he wrote later in life after a career as an author, poet, and journalist, describes Dickensian conditions at the orphanages—perpetual hunger, lack of blankets and clothes, corrupt caretakers, abusive treatment, and occasional moments of laughter and humor. Zaroukian had a deep sense of how orphan life had damaged him and those around him; it is a profound reminder of how the dehumanizing and debasing elements of genocide continue to be visited on survivors, no matter how effective programs of relief could be. "We weren't just orphans" he recalled,

> We never wore the orphan's mask of sorrow and desolation because we never felt the absence of goodness or affection. Ours was one collective face, rude, bitter, mischievous. We hated everyone, we hated each other. Every manner of lie was our defense. It was natural law to beat up the weak, to be beaten by the strong. For a piece of bread the size of a fist we battled, bit, bled. Love was an incomprehensible word, friendship an unknown feeling. Bread was comrade, friend, and love.[51]

Unlike Avakian and Panian, both of whom became almost ideal products of NER's efforts, Zaroukian had only a brief and sporadic experience with American modern humanitarianism. Most of his education was at the hands of Armenian Protestants; indeed, it is hard to imagine, with his description of the poor education they were receiving in the orphanage, that he would have had the literary career he did had he not been returned to the care of his mother and enrolled elsewhere.

Zaroukian did have one very significant encounter with NER, a Christmas gathering in honor of an Armenian intellectual, the Istanbul-based satirist Yervant Odian. Odian, whose own encounter with humanitarian disaster and rescue is discussed in the next chapter, was inspecting Aleppo's orphanages and distributing presents after a visit to the killing fields near Dayr al-Zur, where he himself had once been exiled. His arrival was greatly anticipated by the boys in the orphanage, who had learned of his reputation as a humorist and expected that he was coming to entertain them.

Zaroukian was ushered into an assembly at the orphanage, where Odian, two unknown female representatives from NER, and the administrators of the facility were arrayed on stage. The director introduced Odian with great flourish, which Zaroukian and his friends, around seven years old at the time, little understood. After the introductions, the director asked Odian to say a few words. "We waited for him to speak," Zaroukian recalls,

> to laugh, to make us laugh. One word would have been enough to set us roaring. . . . After a long, awkward interval, he opened his mouth: . . . "Children, orphans . . . " He went silent again . . . and tried to return to his seat;

but the [director] stopped him. . . . The guest tried once more to speak, this time a little louder. . . . "Orphans, I love you very much . . . " He didn't say another word. He returned to his seat, dabbing his eyes with his handkerchief.[52]

As important as the refugee children and orphans were to the American project in the Middle East, the *vorper,* as orphans were called in Armenian, meant much more to what was left of the Istanbul-based Armenian elite, like Odian. And seeing them there in an American orphanage—safe, or at least safer, in French-occupied Syria—was a relief. But it also must have been a reminder of the loss of humanity that had produced this army of parentless boys, boys Odian knew were so deeply scarred that they would have no childhood and then only the slimmest chance at a normal life as adults. The intense sorrow and anguish of being an adult powerless in the face of the pain and trauma of children he had been unable to protect during the war and now to whom he could only provide the most modest of assistance must have placed an almost unbearable burden on Odian—a burden that would have been familiar to Kerr and Elliott. With that burden in mind, it is hard to imagine that NER's Americans in the field, those who knew in detail the suffering these children had endured during the genocide, and then witnessed those same children facing renewed ethnic violence and displacement, would have found themselves imagining them as mere instruments of a quasi-colonial American political project in the "New Near East."

Odian stared at the floor of the stage and never looked up. The director quickly summoned a beautiful older teen, known to the boys as "Miss Zabel." The boys believed that she would soon travel to America as a mail-order bride. Without accompaniment, and in the mournful tones of the tetrachordal scale, she sang "Barzir Aghpyur" (Run Pure O Spring!):

> Run pure o spring! so I can take water to the Kurd's son.
> Run pure o spring! so I can give water to the bey's son.
> Spring do you know what the Kurd does to us?
> He robs us, he hunts us down, he murders us.
> . . .
> There was a time when we lived free.
> We roamed mountains and plains free and without fear.
> Spring: our world is now cloaked in black
> Oppression, oppression, massacre, terror and darkness . . .[53]

The children looked on in stunned silence. Then, as the adults, even the American women, wept, they too began to cry.

CHAPTER 5

The League of Nations Rescue of Trafficked Women and Children and the Paradox of Modern Humanitarianism, 1920–1936

Satılık çocuklar var mı? (Are there any children for sale?)

—A cry heard by Yervant Odian in the Armenian concentration camp at Sabil, Aleppo, ca. 1916

Few Armenian intellectuals of the Ottoman state survived the extrajudicial murder, deportations, and exile of the 1915 genocide. Among those who did was Yervant Odian (1865–1926). Odian, a journalist and satirist, published a serialized memoir of his ordeal shortly after the end of the war in the Armenian-language Istanbul newspaper *Zhamanag*. Entitled *Anidzyal Dariner, 1914–1919* (Accursed years), this remarkable first-person account of surviving genocide is comparable to the canonical human rights literature of Primo Levi or Elie Wiesel in its scope and reflective nature. Unique to Odian's chronicle, however, was the particular attention he paid to the fate of the Armenian children and young women whom he encountered during internal exile in the Ottoman state's Levantine provinces. He described at length Ottoman policies that placed these young people in Muslim households, and the widespread practice, as discussed in previous chapters, of Ottoman military officers and other officials of seizing girls, in particular, to serve as domestic and sexual slaves in their entourages. Indeed, Odian was among the first Ottoman Armenian intellectuals to identify the large-scale transfer of children and trafficking of young women as not the by-product of genocide, but an element central to it. It was one of the crimes that constituted what is to Armenians the Medz Yeghern, the Great Crime.

Odian had been caught up in a state-organized liquidation of intellectuals and was deported from Istanbul to Aleppo in what in now Syria in the early summer of 1915. Though his personal financial resources enabled him to spend the first days of his exile in the city in the relative comfort of the Baron Hotel, the local military police ordered him to remove himself to a concentration camp in a nearby field known as Sabil. The Sabil camp was temporary and the bulk of its inhabitants faced transfer to the desert in the region of Dayr al-Zur, where most would later perish. A few with skills were sent to work as slave laborers in Ottoman state workshops being established in the Syrian cities of Homs and Hama.

It was in Aleppo that Odian first encountered a form of child transfer unprecedented in its horror: the sale of children by their own desperate parents. Amid accounts of disease, starvation, and unremitting hardship in the camp, Odian described the daily visits of "Arab, Turkish and Jewish women [who] would come from Aleppo in carriages and start going from one tent to another asking, 'Are there any children for sale? ('Satılık çocuk var mı?')." Odian writes that, while wealthy families rejected these inquiries outright, poorer families under duress did sell their children for tiny sums, sometimes after the purchaser promised to return the child if the internally displaced family survived. Other times, the purchaser persuaded the families that they were going to die as it was, so why not let at least one survive?[1]

> The women would put one or two [silver] *mecidiyes* in the husband's hand and, putting the child in a carriage, mother would cry, regret what they did, and wish to run after the carriage, but it would already have left. . . . I saw a woman go mad a few hours after selling her two children. Others fell into a sort of lethargic, stupid state, silent, their gaze distant, sitting for hours on the ground. You'd think that their feelings and consciousness were dead; they'd become animal-like. . . . Thousands of boys and girls were sold in Sabil in this way to Arabs, Turks and Jews from Aleppo. The small children of about 7–10 years old were usually considered to be valuable, especially the girls.

For Odian, "the sale of children" constituted a complete moral collapse in the face of genocide itself; it was "the most terrifying side of the dreadful crime of deportation. It is impossible to imagine that humanity could sink any lower." The sale of children was not unique to the camp in Aleppo and happened elsewhere during the deportations, including episodes where children were auctioned.[2]

Elsewhere in his memoir Odian acknowledges that, "to be honest, these children [those taken by non-Armenian families] for the most part, were better cared [for] and received better food and were happier than those who were with their poor parents [in exile]." As an example, he writes of an Ottoman official he met in Hama somewhat later, one Selim Effendi, "who, being childless, had adopted a little [Armenian] girl. Both husband and wife idolized the little one. Once when the little girl became ill, they brought a doctor . . . from Aleppo and, according to his own statement, spent over 100 liras to provide for her recovery."[3] Indeed, Armenian oral histories and memoirs from the time are replete with accounts of moments of generosity toward child survivors, though generally these accounts are by Armenians who rejoined the Armenian community after the war and following large-scale efforts at humanitarian rescue. Despite an emerging literature in Turkey by the grandchildren of transferred Armenians, little is known of those who were integrated into Muslim households. Odian's horror at the sight of Armenian children being sold led to his clearly painful admission—an admission Stanley Kerr had also made—that for the children themselves, sale under duress or extralegal adoption could mean survival bereft of their Armenian identity. That admission is among the complex dilemmas at the center of the history of the forced transfer of children, an element of the crime of genocide, and humanitarian rescue, a central concern of modern humanitarianism.

For Odian and others, like the Armenian feminist intellectual Zabel Yesayan, this dilemma was understood as the preeminent *problem of humanity,* and consequently a *problem for humanity,* wrought by genocide. The Armenians were a community in extremis, for whom the loss of the transferred children was an act victimizing both children and parents, as well as an element in the Ottoman state's conscious destruction of what they considered the Armenian nation.[4] It is difficult to overestimate the importance that the history of transfer, transformation through loss of identity, and recovery of Armenian children has had on the formation of modern Armenian identity, especially in its diaspora. The Armenian community itself is now, to a significant extent, a community of descendants of children who faced their own forced transfer or loss of their immediate family, known collectively as the *vorper,* the "orphans" (figure 5.1). How is that story understood and explained within families and the community, what did it mean for the rebuilding of social structures and social networks, and, in particular, what did it mean to be an Armenian woman or child after the genocide? These are profound, far-reaching, and multigenerational questions that arise from this aspect of genocide. Of equal importance, how does this history

FIGURE 5.1. Young Armenian refugees in Aleppo, ca. 1915. Source: George Grantham Bain Collection, LC-USZ62–88621 (b&w film copy neg.), Library of Congress Prints and Photographs Division, Washington, DC.

shape modern conceptions of Turkish identity as more and more contemporary Turks, who call themselves the *torunlar*—the grandchildren—confront the reality that their grandmothers were transferred Armenian girls, taken during the genocide that lay the foundations of their modern state—a state that emphasizes the homogeneity of Turkish identity and denies that the Armenian Genocide even occurred?

After the war, Odian sought to answer these questions as he led efforts to recover children, support the work of orphanages to rebuild the Armenian community—which is why he visited the orphanage where Antranik Zaroukian (discussed in the previous chapter) lived for a time—and reclaim his own humanity. And in a preemptive rejection of Adorno's maxim about poetry after Auschwitz, Odian describes in his memoir how on the first day after he returned from exile to Istanbul, he sat at his desk and resumed his satirical writing.

Collectively, the efforts to reclaim and liberate survivors, like the ones encountered by Odian, were known as the rescue movement. This chapter explores the movement as it unfolded in the early 1920s, especially as the responsibility for rescue moved away from Armenian organizations and Near East Relief (NER) to the League of Nations. Employing the records of various committees and subcommittees of the League; correspondences and supporting materials submitted by its relief workers in the field; communications with the Ottoman state and

Armenian diaspora organizations; and memoirs and local histories of the movement in Arabic, Armenian, and Turkish, the following discussion illustrates the complicated and often paradoxical historical experience of the humanitarian rescue as it was conceived and implemented in the early interwar Eastern Mediterranean. It presents a case in which the rescuing of trafficked genocide survivors—a seemingly unambiguous good—was at once a constitutive act in drawing the boundaries of the international community, a critical moment in the definition of modern humanitarianism, *and* a site of resistance to the colonial presence in the post-Ottoman Eastern Mediterranean—a presence that was often defended in the language of humanity, progress, and civilization. Rescue would also play a role in binding the international community to Armenian communal survival, serve as an ex post facto warrant for the world war, and threaten, nonetheless, late Ottoman ethnic, religious, and gendered hierarchies, as well as the unalloyed dominance of post-Ottoman society by Turkish- and Arabic-speaking Sunni Muslims.

In addition, this chapter uses the history of the rescue movement to explore the ideological and bureaucratic changes associated with interwar modern humanitarianism as it became increasingly managed by the League of Nations. Critical to this new humanitarianism was its explicit connection with peacemaking, as both a causative and preventative measure, and its alignment with another emerging concept, that of "collective security," in the League of Nations' raison d'être.[5]

This chapter also traces how the rescue movement's very idea of suffering, and thereby what constitutes its root causes, had changed from earlier conceptions. It shows that in the first decades of the twentieth century, while the definition of suffering broadened, it was also influenced by liberal nationalism's emphasis on the extension of categories of rights to nations and, in the modern sense, ethnicities. This extension would have profound implications for the international reach of humanitarianism, particularly in formulating the elements of the crime of genocide. Child transfer, involuntary marriage, servile concubinage, and compulsory conversion to Islam, in addition to mass extrajudicial killing, fell into an expanded category of "cultural" or "national" suffering, in which the victim was not just the individual but also the nation; in other words, the rights, in this case, of the Armenian nation entered the orbit of humanitarian discourse alongside the rights of individual Armenian survivors and refugees. For dominant Ottoman society, this had the not wholly unanticipated effect of transforming quasi-legal or at least widely accepted forms of customary domestic and intercommunal practice into elements of human suffering. A final element of this new humanitarianism was the anticipation that the international community—itself a concept of recent origin—could and would take *action* in response to humanitarian concerns.

This connection between intention and action was predicated in the unique case of the Eastern Mediterranean by the outcome of the war and the occupation of the region by European forces. The fact of foreign occupation meant the possibility that certain kinds and categories of Western-originated humanitarian intervention were feasible, certainly more so than in the antebellum Eastern Mediterranean because of the parallel reduction in Ottoman sovereignty. This had been anticipated by NER and its projects in Anatolia. Even more so, the establishment of the interwar mandate system in the Arab provinces of the empire extended and institutionalized that subordinate status and reduced sovereignty accordingly, again allowing for humanitarian intervention and management throughout a broad range of state–society interactions. While questions about the nature of state sovereignty remained unresolved in the theoretical understanding of the League's role in the interwar world, conceptually—and ironically to some—the most internationalist dimension of the League's larger efforts took place only in the shadow of interwar colonialism; the liberalizing and tutelary agenda of the mandate system created an unprecedented opportunity for League initiatives to be implemented unrestrained by questions of national sovereignty because sovereignty itself was held in trust, as it were, by a colonial power and member state. In this sense, the boundaries between humanitarianism as an emerging Western imperative and humanitarianism as an element of colonialism become blurred. However, this does not mean that this form of humanitarianism should be dismissed merely as another facet of imperialism, cultural or otherwise. Rather, it speaks to the need to investigate the relationship between colonialism and humanitarianism, and the tensions that arise at their intersection, more thoroughly.

From the perspective of the historiography of the Eastern Mediterranean, the rescue movement was a collision between emerging Western expectations of how women and children should be treated and not enslaved and late-nineteenth and early twentieth-century Ottoman Islamic conceptions of domestic patriarchy, property, and the inferior legal and social position of non-Muslims in Muslim society. Understood in this fashion, the reaction to rescue in Aleppo, Istanbul, and elsewhere sheds light on whether Ottoman reform efforts of the previous century, during the Tanzimat and First Ottoman Constitutional period (1839–1878) and the more recent Second Constitutional Period (1908–1918), had successfully extended civil rights of equality and emancipation to non-Muslims as part of larger social modernization. The evidence suggests that such a process had not taken root within Ottoman society and could not withstand multiple and existential crises and widespread social and economic dislocation.

Finally, the rescue movement—situated at the nexus of Ottoman and European diplomacy, the work of relief workers, and the experience of the rescued and those who had held them—provides a unique opportunity to understand how ideas about individuality, equality, race, and emancipation, and perhaps even limited discussions of rights, were in circulation at the start of the interwar period in the interface between the West and the Eastern Mediterranean. Possessing multiple points of bureaucratic, ideological, and ethical intersection, the history of the rescue movement is a powerful tool to theorize what happens when a problem for humanity is understood to be a disciplining tool of Western institutions and colonialist agendas.

THE VOICES OF RESCUE AND THE WORK OF THE LEAGUE

The archives of the League of Nations include the Aleppo Rescue Home's roughly two thousand intake surveys of Armenian girls, boys, and young women who had been rescued—or, as was more often the case, rescued themselves—from Arab, Kurdish, and Turkish households into which they had been trafficked during the Armenian Genocide of 1915. As detailed in the previous chapter's discussion of Stanley Kerr's project to photograph orphans in Urfa and Aintab, this practice of connecting life histories and images was part of standard humanitarian practice.

The story of Zabel, whose arrival in the mid-1920s is documented in figure 5.2, is typical of the rescue histories in the home's records and highlights the myriad challenges facing individual survivors.[6] Zabel, the daughter of Bedros, arrived at the home in Aleppo on May 18, 1926, at the age of eighteen. Deported along with her family when she was seven or eight years old, she recalled that she was from Arapkır, a town in southeastern Anatolia known for its wine grapes and woven textiles. She told the Danish director of the home, Karen Jeppe, enough that Jeppe was able to reconstruct the following biography:

FIGURE 5.2. Photograph of Zabel attached to the intake survey that was conducted upon her admission to the Rescue Home. She is still dressed in the traditional garments of rural Mesopotamia. Records of the Nansen International Refugee Office, 1920–1947, Registers of Inmates of the Armenian Orphanage in Aleppo, 1922–1930, 4 vols., ALON-UNOG. Courtesy of the United Nations.

In the beginning of the deportation, Zabel's father was separated from her family and was sent in an unknown direction. Zabel was exiled with her mother, 5 sisters and a younger brother. The caravan which consisted of men, women, boys, girls and infants, was formed to go on foot 3 months, wandering upon the mountains, passing through the villages, crossing the rivers and marching across the deserts. . . . The gendarmes had received the order to kill the unfortunate people by every means in their power. Near Veranshehir, they collected all the beautiful girls, and distributed them among the Turks and the Kurds. The rest of the caravan had to go further on in the deserts to die. Zabel had been the share of a Kurd, who married her. She lived there 11 years, unwillingly, til an Armenian chauffeur informed her that many of her relatives still were living in Aleppo. Having made her escape in safety, she reached Ras al-Ain, from where by our agent she was sent to us.[7]

A notation made on the next page explains that Zabel eventually left the orphanage and was placed with relatives. Hers is similar to the story Lütfiyye Bilemdjian told a League relief worker: At the onset of the genocide, she and her family had been forcibly displaced to Upper Mesopotamia, where they were set upon by Ottoman irregular soldiers. She witnessed the killing of her mother, father, and one of her brothers. A soldier took her as booty and sold her to someone, who then resold her to a wealthy man named Mahmud Pasha. He sent her to his house, where she remained for eleven years. In 1926, Lütfiyye escaped across what had become the international border between Syria and Turkey and reached Aleppo, where she found one of her surviving brothers. And Zabel's and Lütfiyye's stories are not unlike that of Khachadour Beroian, from the city of Kharpert (now Elazığ in Turkey), whose picture shows him wearing a *kaffiyya* and a wool-lined *'aba'* coat—clothes he wore as an unpaid agricultural laborer in eastern Syria before he ran away from the farm he had been forced to work at for nine years. He was around twelve years old when his father, Avedis, was killed at the beginning of the genocide. Like other orphaned children in his city, Khachadour had been rounded up and sent to Syria in a deportation caravan.

Other narratives of the Aleppo Rescue Home's intake forms describe the intensely precarious living conditions women and children survivors faced in the city and countryside of Upper Mesopotamia and southern Anatolia. Fehmi, the son of Terthagian, was taken by a bedouin from a passing deportation caravan at Mardin and sold to a Christian Arab named Habib, who taught him the tailoring trade. Habib fell on hard times and gave Fehmi to a local Turkish family, which treated him poorly, causing him to flee to Aleppo. Dikranouhi, daughter of Panos, who entered the home at sixteen in 1925, making her six years old at the beginning of the genocide, explained that her father died serving in the Ottoman Army, and she was deported with her mother. On the road, a Kurd took them both and forced her mother into servile concubinage. After some time, the mother fell ill and died, and Dikranouhi became a servant in the Kurd's household. When Dikranouhi reached sexual maturity at fourteen years of age, the Kurd attempted to take her as a concubine, but she fled and was abducted by an Arab in a neighboring village where she became an abused maidservant.[8]

Most surveys echo those of Zabel, Khachadour, Dikranouhi, Fehmi, and Lütfiyye with unremitting consistency: those arriving in Aleppo told of deportation, separation, mass extrajudicial killing, and rape—though only in euphemistic and elliptical terms—followed by years of unpaid servitude as agricultural workers or domestic servants, servile concubines, and involuntary wives and mothers.[9]

The Rescue Home and the Neutral House, its cognate in Istanbul, were situated in the institutional and ideological framework of the League of Nations' efforts on behalf of deported and vulnerable populations of Armenian and, to a lesser extent, Greek women and children (1920–1927). These efforts, called in Armenian *vorpahavak,* "the gathering of orphans," provide further evidence of the critical turn in humanitarianism during and after World War I.[10]

At the seventeenth plenary meeting of the League of Nations, on September 21, 1921, Hélène Vacaresco, the Romanian delegate, delivered the final report of the "5th Commission on the Deportation of Women and Children in Turkey, Asia Minor, and the Neighbouring Countries."[11] The work of the committee, established a year earlier, had become a central concern of the League during its first months of existence and was seen as a preliminary step in implementing the 1920 Treaty of Sèvres between the victors of the world war and the Ottoman Empire. Of particular significance was article 142 of the treaty, which vacated all conversions to Islam between 1914 and 1918 and required the Ottoman Empire to cooperate with the League of Nations in the recovery of displaced and trafficked people and generally to "repair so far as possible the wrongs inflicted on individuals in the course of the massacres perpetrated in Turkey during the war."[12] The League's formation of the commission was also in response to calls to aid women and children from both Western Protestant denominations and transnational nongovernmental organizations, most notably the Women's International League for Peace and Freedom, which equated the cause of displaced women and children with that of the repatriation of male prisoners of war. Writing to the League in May 1920, suffragist Helena Swanwick (1864–1939) suggested, "This question [of] the enslavement and dishonoring of women and children all over the East as a result of the war is one which might well be taken up by a special Commission of the League of Nations upon which women of standing in the East would be found to take an active part." Addressing the League a few years later, Emily Robinson, secretary of the Armenian Red Cross and Refugee Fund of Great Britain, argued:

> Will you also kindly represent the intense bitterness of feeling that has been fostered on many sides owing to the fact that many scores of thousands of Armenian women and children are still detained in Moslem houses, where they have been captive since 1915. The Armistice with Turkey provided for the release of 'all prisoners of war.' *Only the men* were released and the terms of the Armistice as regards women have not been carried out. Some of us who have this matter much at heart earnestly trust that the League [will intervene]. . . . The present state of things is hazardous in the extreme to the cause of peace in the East besides being a scandal and a disgrace to the civilization of the 20ᵗʰ century.[13]

The General Assembly charged the commission with both collating reports by League relief workers Karen Jeppe in Aleppo and Dr. W. A. Kennedy and Emma Cushman in Istanbul and recommending remedial actions to the body. Indeed, the commission's report and supporting materials stand as one of the first and most comprehensive reckonings of the postwar situation facing survivors of the early phase of the Armenian Genocide (1915–1920) and in particular of the conditions under which young people like Zabel were living. Critically, the commission had come to understand, as Zabel explained, that ranking members of the military, or Kurdish and Arab pastoralists and rural people, had taken children and young women by force or following a bribe to their escorts. Members also learned that the bulk of the young people had been delivered to brothels and orphanages or were integrated into Muslim households.

This style of integration was a common Ottoman social practice for elite and rural peoples, though the sheer volume of trafficked children and women was not. Among pastoralists, rural smallholders, and the landed elite of Anatolia and Mesopotamia, households often included an array of members, with some related by marriage or filiation to the patriarchal figure, alongside a collection of unrelated servants and retainers who belonged, as it were, to the household. The relationship of the latter group to the household was one of dependence and a set place in a gendered hierarchy, and displaced persons without the support or protection of a natal group found themselves situated at the very bottom.[14] They had little recourse in cases of mistreatment. In times of economic stress or the death of the patriarchal figure, they could be sold or transferred without their consent. Unrelated girls and boys in the household—regardless of religious or ethnic origin—were sexually available to senior males. Often the girls were considered attractive as wives, especially second wives, because they had no viable family of their own to protect their interest or demand a bride price, and any children born of these unions would belong to the father and his family. This was the kind of situation Zabel had left. Boys were more difficult to integrate and usually worked as shepherds or in other roles on the margin of the households.

Those women, girls, and boys taken by Ottoman officers were brought into their own households or placed in elite and middle-class homes in the major cities of the empire by state officials. In part, this was consistent with Ottoman policy on displaced girls and boys dating from the mid-1800s. As waves of Caucasian Muslims took refuge in Anatolia as a consequence of Russian expansion into the southern Caucasus (ca. 1864), the Ottoman state had placed "unattached" Muslim girls—in order to forestall their being sold by their refugee parents—with elite and middle-class Ottoman families as *evlatlıklar*, which roughly translates as "foster children," to be educated in proper gender roles and prepared for life. In both a legally and socially inferior position, the *evlatlık* children, like the Armenian children during and after the genocide, belonged to the household, were generally employed as domestic help, and could be used as sexual objects. As this practice continued through the nineteenth century, this source of inexpensive labor and wives came to be viewed as a natural privilege of the Ottoman middle and upper classes.[15]

However, any strictly materialist explanation can only go so far to explain the motives for large-scale child transfer. Indeed, transfer of children from the victim's group to the perpetrator community is a recognized element of genocide, but why it takes place is less understood.[16] In this instance, the fact that large-scale transfer had happened to the children of those the Ottoman state had come to consider an internal enemy certainly adds a triumphalist dimension to the effacement of an entire generation of Armenians into a larger Muslim and Turkish-speaking society; perhaps, for some, the women and children were even considered legitimate war booty, a sentiment captured by the Turkish phrase *kılıç artığı*, "leftovers of the sword," which was used to describe Armenian women who had been integrated into Turkish society.[17] Nevertheless, in both rural and urban settings, the women and children were caught in a legal gray area that afforded them little measure of protection beyond the good will of those holding them. Ironically, prevailing Islamic doctrine on slavery, which had been made illegal in the empire in 1908, had given slaves some very limited avenues of recourse in the case of ill treatment.[18] However, beyond escaping and reaching a rescue home or similar institution, women and children integrated into households in such a fashion had little hope of altering their status.

Humanitarians considered the Armenian women and children sequestered in Muslim homes in this fashion slaves, consistently describing their condition as slavery and citing not just lack of wages but also child marriage, forced conversion, and subjection to trafficking as constitutive of their enslavement. League relief workers frequently contributed stories and photographs of rescued Armenian girls to the London-based periodical the *Slave Market News,* and Karen Jeppe, in particular, made analogies to the experience of American slavery described in Harriet Beecher Stowe's *Uncle Tom's Cabin,* not only to illustrate the conditions in which the Armenian captives were living but also to locate her efforts on behalf of Armenians within a tradition of nineteenth-century movements for emancipation; she and her counterparts in the Eastern Mediterranean and their interlocutors in the West imagined themselves as the inheritors of the abolitionist tradition. As Jeppe explained in 1922, "We have to do with many, who have lived in slavery similar to that of the one in 'The Uncle Tom's Cabin' [*sic*]. They have been purchased and sold more than once, have drudged to obtain only unsufficient [*sic*] food and endured much ill treatment."[19] For the League relief workers, this generally accepted form of domestic practice was the most pernicious *root cause* of the trafficked women and children's suffering and confirmed both relief workers' corporate sense of how out of step Ottoman society was with modern legal and moral norms and why the League needed to aggressively intervene on behalf of vulnerable populations. Equally objectionable to League workers were the forced conversions and marriages that accompanied the transfer of women and children and the way in which such marriages presented a situation of "racial chaos" akin to miscegenation. This last objection perhaps explains why there is no evidence that League workers at the time extended any concern to Muslim women and children in the same or similar conditions.

For the human rights theorist Barbara Metzger, the work of Jeppe at the Aleppo Rescue Home in particular constitutes evidence that human rights was being implemented in practice prior to its formal elaboration in theory.[20] This observation is drawn from an anachronistic conclusion about how Jeppe saw her work. In imagining Jeppe as a prototypal human rights activist, Metzger's discussion obscures the fact that Jeppe was not anticipating a future human rights regime; rather, her work was a manifestation of the basic terms of modern humanitarianism itself. While Jeppe might have agreed, in a general sense, that her duty to humanity was universal, her own description of why she assisted Armenians but not other groups signals a profound particularity. For Jeppe, and more broadly for modern humanitarians, the purpose of humanitarianism was ending suffering; but equally important to them, practically and by choice, was the conviction that some people or groups were simply more eligible for and deserving of assistance than others. The object of humanitarianism in this case was not the universal, but the particular.

The Aleppo Rescue Home

The Fifth Commission focused first on the Aleppo Rescue Home.[21] Earlier efforts of the NER and various Armenian organizations to locate child and female survivors had enjoyed relative success with the backing of the British Army of occupation in the early days after the armistice.[22] In general, these survivors were placed with living relatives or housed in ad hoc institutions. At the time of the report, however, Jeppe estimated that perhaps thirty thousand Armenian boys, girls, and women were still being held in various conditions in the countryside of Upper Mesopotamia, and she had grown increasingly concerned about managing the rehabilitation of the growing number coming in off the desert or out of brothels with no easily found remaining relatives.

Jeppe's career in the Middle East began in the late Ottoman period (1903), spanned the Young Turk Revolution (1908) and the genocide, and ended with her death in Aleppo in Syria under the French mandate (1935). In her early twenties Jeppe had been attracted to a Danish liberal Lutheran movement, Grundtvigianism, which stressed the value of one's personal relationship with God and Jesus over membership in any particular denomination and emphasized the importance of a sense of national belonging to human freedom and development. Dispatched to Eastern Anatolia before the war on behalf of the Danish Friends of Armenia (DA), Jeppe worked initially with Johannes Lepsius, the noted German missionary and author of a critical humanitarian report on the Hamidian massacres, in 'Urfa.[23] Her work at this time focused primarily on collaborative education and health programs and not on conversion from the Armenian Apostolic church to Protestantism, which in

Grundtvigian terms would have robbed the Armenians of their natural or essential culture and prevented their further national development.

Suffering a mental breakdown during the war, Jeppe recovered sufficiently and resumed her association with the DA, taking up a post in Aleppo. Lobbying by Scandinavian delegates to the League—in particular Henni Forchhammer, at the time the vice president of the International Council of Women—led to Jeppe's appointment in 1921 as a League of Nations' commissioner.[24] As her biographer, Matthias Bjørnlund, concludes, "She saw herself as an aid worker and rescue worker, and, increasingly, as an activist working for national self-determination for the oppressed . . . Armenians who had been . . . almost completely eradicated by the Ottoman Empire."[25] What Jeppe's career also suggests is how the institutions of missionary work could provide additional avenues for modern humanitarian efforts, as well as the ease by which some categories of missionaries could make the transition to working for secular institutions.[26]

Jeppe's understanding of why these particular women and children should be found and rehabilitated reflected her strong conviction that, as a result of the war, the unchallenged dominance of Ottoman society by Sunni Muslim political and legal structures was no longer, and modern social reform and the liberal political and economic agenda emerging in the West would be exported to the Middle East. She *expected* that the new humanitarianism embodied by the League would give it power as a moral agent of change and would reverse the calamitous impact of the war on the Armenians *as a people* and not just work to provide immediate aid; this reversal was a reaffirmation of both the dignity and the humanity of Armenians, and of her sense of the potential inhumanity of Islam and Muslims. Jeppe's optimism aside, she suspected that Armenians could never resettle among Muslims, even with international assistance, and that they should be found a separate home in the Caucasus or Brazil.[27] Critically, for Jeppe, the process of rehabilitation, as she explained in her report and later supporting documentation, was not just an educational and training process, but also a cultural act, in which the rescued would be turned back into, in her words, "human beings."[28] For her, the restoration of the Armenians transcended a traditional humanitarian project and rather was an act of restoring the rescued and by extension society to a proper moral ordering:

> The standard of civilization of the Armenians . . . is on a higher level than that of those beings with whom the young people are forced to associate. Their race is far more developed, which will be most evident from the fact,

that the Armenian nation never could sink to Islam but sticked [*sic*] to the Christianity even [when] subjected to the most incredible sufferings. . . . There are two things which attract these young people [religion and ethnic identification], even if it is not quite clear to their consciousness. The purer and stronger the character is, the more powerful the attraction. Weak or degenerated individuals yield more easily and become Mahometens [*sic*].[29]

Jeppe's negative attitude toward Islam, which changed over time, was not especially unique among her missionary contemporaries. However, her commitment to the national survival of Armenians was, and it is evidence of a departure in how she conceptualized not just Armenians but also her role in their relief. Indeed, her origins, career, training, and prewar fieldwork anticipate elemental features of the shift in postwar humanitarianism and formulation of professional relief work as a form of practice. Jeppe's discussions of the moral superiority of the Armenians and the labeling of their status as illicit slavery were for consumption outside of the region only, and she anticipated that it would remain that way. Within Syria, she encouraged survivors to be as discreet as possible to avoid any conflict.

Nevertheless, the rescue movement—both the method and how it was changing the nature of the relationship between Muslims and non-Muslims in the shadow of humanitarianism—elicited a strong response among the region's Muslim elite. Exemplary is Kamil al-Ghazzi's series of complaints about Armenian refugees in Aleppo in his three-volume history, *Kitab nahr al-dhahab fi tarikh Halab* (River of gold in the history of Aleppo), first published in 1923.[30] Al-Ghazzi was a leading intellectual and reform-minded Muslim cleric and jurist, and he was representative of the region's emerging Sunni Arab middle class of white-collar bureaucrats, educators, and professionals. After commenting on the financial impact and criminality of some of the approximately fifty thousand refugees living in and around his city, he notes, "There were a large number of Armenian girls and their children living with Aleppines. The Aleppines had given them shelter from the very first moment they took refuge in Aleppo. They had gathered them from the desert and saw to their upkeep and cared for their children. Some took from the legally mature girls, legal wives and adopted their children."[31]

For al-Ghazzi, the origin of these women—whether they had been purchased during the deportations or trafficked thereafter, or had entered into relationships with Muslim men as a consequence of their vulnerable status as refugees—was irrelevant, though he did acknowledge that "we do not rebuke the Armenian sect for wanting to return their children to their bosom, because this is what their racial traits directed them to do, yet we condemn them for the way that this prejudice aided violence and assaulted friendship."[32] To illustrate that "assault," al-Ghazzi relates two stories. In the first, an unnamed Armenian refugee woman married to a Muslim man is located by her brother, who demands that she return to her husband, once thought dead but in fact alive. The Muslim man refused to release her, "as was his right under Islamic law." The police arrested the Muslim husband and sent the woman to the Rescue Home. Locked away in a rooftop room, she refused all food and drink. Meanwhile, her daughter by the Muslim husband was taken from her. In a daring escape she leaped from her room to the street below and returned to her Muslim husband, who had since been released. The police arrested him again and returned her to the Rescue Home. Interrogated by an Armenian priest, she stated that were she not allowed to return to her Muslim husband she would kill herself. Seeing her resolve, her Armenian husband gave up and allowed her to return. "So she returned to their house, and she has stayed with him [her Muslim husband] until today, having given him many more children."[33]

More troubling still for al-Ghazzi, the legitimate children of local Muslims, in addition to the Armenian children adopted by them, risked "rescue." One six-year-old boy was taken from his family and, despite the testimony of the family's Muslim and Christian neighbors to the contrary, an Armenian man took him to his home. While this particular boy was eventually returned to his "true father," many others remained with Armenians.[34] Striking in al-Ghazzi's discussions is that, unlike much of the rest of his book, the passages on Armenian refugees in Aleppo and the rescue movement lack specific places, names, and dates, and the descriptions resemble rumors more than historical events and court cases. It is worth noting that al-Ghazzi, a jurist, does not reflect on the fact that the reappearance of the Armenian husband in the first case would have rendered the second marriage invalid, as polyandry is equally illegal under Islamic and Armenian canon law; the Armenian refugee woman's marriage was never legally dissolved. Instead, he asserts in both instances the patriarchal rights of the Muslim man as an absolute, superior to any other legal or ethical consideration. Regardless, the underlying sentiment is clear: while the multiplicity of agencies or institutions involved in the rescue efforts seemed quite opaque, al-Ghazzi did recognize the movement as a serious intervention into established norms of social interaction and hierarchy. To him, the effort at rescue was an unjustified and outright illegal intervention in the domestic sphere, but it was also unnatural in that it upset the moral order on behalf of heretofore subordinate elements of society—non-Muslim women and children. For al-Ghazzi, these acts of rescue were an unwarranted interference in a Muslim man's home, his *harim*, something that was unprecedented, illegal, and a violation of his patriarchal and property rights. Al-Ghazzi's writing about postwar society emphasized similar problems of moral decline, alterations to the domestic sphere, and tumultuous relations between Muslims and non-Muslims. Certainly, however, his conception of "family" and "household," in which clear categories of slave, free, children, and property were blurred, was at odds with the notions of emancipation and bourgeois domesticity championed by Western humanitarians.

The Neutral House

The Fifth Commission's investigations focused as well on the work of Istanbul's Neutral House, an institution established first in Şişli and later reestablished by Near East Relief in Bebek, a suburb of Istanbul and the location of Robert College, the premier American educational institution in the city. As indicated by the report, the situation in Istanbul presented similar challenges to those in Aleppo and Mesopotamia. After the armistice of 1918, French and British forces occupied Istanbul and a rump imperial government continued to rule. With general lawlessness throughout the countryside, culminating in the post–World War I war between Greece and Turkey for Anatolia (1922), variably known as the "Anatolia disaster" or the Turkish War for Independence, waves of refugees, including displaced orphans, flowed into the Ottoman capital.

In the course of their work, the League commissioners—Emma Cushman, an American nurse, and Dr. W. A. Kennedy, an Anglo-Irish medical doctor and representative of the London-based Lord Mayor's Fund for Armenia—had gained access to registries of Ottoman state orphanages. They noted that the names of Christian children had been overwritten with Muslim names and concluded that about 50 percent of all orphans in the city (five thousand) were Armenian in origin, with another six thousand orphans in other parts of Allied-occupied Anatolia. Moreover, the commissioners accepted the Armenian patriarchate's estimate that sixty thousand Armenian children were still held in Ottoman orphanages and Muslim homes. The report also noted that "innumerable women, mostly young, rudely torn from their hearths and homes, compelled to perform the most degrading tasks, are shut up in harems, into which it is almost impossible to penetrate."[35] The committee had been especially frustrated in its efforts to gain access to the orphanages and women, complaining that "it is almost impossible to get at them, as an entire people is an accomplice to this crime. . . . Rape, violence, fraud, the force of inertia, bad faith—all are employed by men who manifest a particularly odious form of fanaticism in carrying off women and children to captivity and degradation."[36]

Of the two commissioners, Cushman had the most extensive background in the region and is exemplary of the kind of middle-class female relief worker that developed during the humanitarian turn of the interwar period. Originally from New York, Cushman was trained as both a schoolteacher and a nurse. Leaving a job as the superintendent of a Kansas City hospital, she took up a leadership position at the American Hospital in the central Anatolian city of Konya. During World War I, she refused to evacuate and consequently became the acting consul in Anatolia for several countries. With the onset of the Greco-Turkish War (1919), she oversaw the evacuation of some twenty-two thousand Armenian and Greek orphans to Greece and Bulgaria. Ill, she retired first to Greece and then to Egypt, where she died in 1930. Unlike Jeppe, Cushman seemed motivated less by any clear ideology and more by a general altruism and professional ambition. More important, engaging in relief work abroad placed her beyond the glass ceiling imposed on American professional women, like Mabel Elliott in the early twentieth century, and she could thereby assume levels of responsibility that would have been unavailable to her had she remained in the United States.[37]

In the original plan for the Neutral House negotiated during the first months of the British occupation of Istanbul, "disputed" children and young women were to be observed by a team of representatives from the Armenian and Greek communities—either secular political officials or delegates of the respective patriarchates—in addition to a representative from the Ottoman Red Crescent Society) and advisors from the British government. The Armenian delegation included Zarouhi Bahri (1880–1958), a prominent writer and socialite and a founder of the Istanbul Armenian Red Cross. Indeed, Bahri's account in her memoir stands as one of the only contemporary Armenian discussions of the Neutral House's operations.[38] After their status had been determined, these children were returned to their "community." Decisions about the fate of the children were made on the basis of observations by these community representatives, who voted on each child. The children arrived often without documentation, and the observers encouraged them to recall nursery rhymes and folk songs from their past to determine their origin.[39] Very few, if any, of the disputed children were ever determined to be Muslim. Claiming bias in the Neutral House's operations, the Ottoman Red Crescent Society's first representative, Naziye Hanım, resigned after several months, as did her successor, Nakiye Hanım.[40]

In a variation on the intake surveys conducted at the Aleppo Rescue Home, relief workers documented the lives of those processed at the Neutral House. The cases confirm many of Zabel's observations about rape, separation, and enslavement, but unlike the stories collected at Aleppo, the relief workers in Istanbul also described how reluctant the children often were to admit their Armenian background. Cushman attributed that reticence to a combination of abuse and incentives at the hands of their foster families, noting, "with the girls, experience has taught me that this attitude of mind is usually brought about by gifts of clothing, personal adornments, such as beads, cheap jewelry, etc. with the boys, it seems to be largely produced by fear, threats, blows, etc. until the child really believes that he is being protected by the Turks from a much worse fate."[41]

The registries at the Neutral House first list the child's Muslim name and then, in the text, the child's original name. The story of Ceman, a.k.a Verjine, is illustrative of the process used by the Neutral House to make the determination:

> 10–11 years old. Brought from Eub Soultan, Dergahe Emuele [a neighborhood in Istanbul] Sinan Hodja Sheih Nourollah's [Sinan hoca sheyh Nurullah] house. A very beautiful and charming girl, they have kept her in "Muduriet" [police detention] three days in a subterraneous den explaining to her that if she tells, she is "Giavour" (Christian) the Armenians and the British will kill her. She kept silent under this terror for two days and confirmed that she knew nothing. By and by her terror passed she got used to us and began to relate that she was from Angora [Ankara], her name Virgin [Verjine], father's Vitchen [Vigen], mother's Foulik [?], sister's Josephine. During exile she has gone as far as Aleppo with her family; there, they have separated her from them and brought [her] to Constantinople. She knows the Armenian letters, but cannot speak.[42]

Other entries describe more difficult cases: For example, in the case of eight-year-old Nadiye, a.k.a Shevester, who was purchased by one Acı Badem Essad Pasha, Naziye Hanım produced a woman claiming to be the child's mother, who then failed to recognize her. The child was transferred to an Armenian orphanage. It was this case in particular that triggered the resignation of the Red Crescent representative.[43]

Like the Rescue Home's efforts in Aleppo, the Neutral House's program again elicited strong resentment among Istanbul's elite, including Halidé Edip Adıvar, the leading Turkish feminist of her day, who was herself deeply involved in wartime relief efforts through her professional association with the Red Crescent and her personal associations with members of the Committee of Union and Progress military junta, known in the West as the Young Turks.[44]

During the war, Halidé Edip briefly administered an orphanage in Aintoura, north of Beirut in Lebanon. In her own postwar memoirs she noted that at the time she had expressed some reservations to Cemal Pasha, the military governor of Greater Syria, about the forced mass conversion of Armenian orphans to Islam. A standard element of late Ottoman social policy was to convert orphans in its care to Sunni Islam, the religion of the empire—similar to practices in Europe or North America. During the genocide the scope of these orphanages expanded so much that it is important to distinguish them from prewar state orphanages or those run by Christian missionaries, which were limited in use.[45] To draw a close analogy, wartime Ottoman orphanages resembled American Indian boarding schools, where children of Armenians, other Christian minorities, and non-Turkish Muslims (primarily Kurds) were acculturated into the dominant group; and indeed there was a great deal of support for them from members of the upper echelons of Ottoman society, who perceived these schools to be merciful, charitable, and modernizing. In her memoirs, Halidé Edip described her role at the orphanage as a manifestation of a "civilizing mission," with religious conversion to Islam as a secondary consideration. The children in that orphanage were to emerge as modern citizens whose Armenian and Kurdish identities were no longer an impediment to complete membership in the new national community. This transformation was to be accomplished through forms of coercion and unremitting physical abuse: children were given Muslim names and falsified birth records, the speaking and reading of Armenian were grounds for beating, and no attempts were made to reunify children with living relatives, especially Armenian relatives. The loss of identity even followed the orphans after their death: in his orphan memoir, Karnig Panian, who was six years old when he entered the facility, wrote: "The dead orphans, who were buried in a hole and covered with dirt, were attacked, the same night, by the hungry jackals, ripping off the little bodies and scattering their bones all over the place. . . . The only thought on the orphans' minds was food. In desperation, they would often collect the bones of their dead friends, grind them and use them in soups as food to survive."[46]

Critically, the history of the orphanage at Aintoura was reproduced at orphanages throughout the empire. Indeed, what was happening in the Ottoman state parallels historically contemporaneous programs for enculturation of indigenous children in North America and Australasia—justified also by appeals to civilization and the best interest of the child and accompanied by regimes of abuse, emotional torture, and coercive language policies. And with the take-over of many of these orphanages, including Aintoura in 1918, by the NER, the reentry of Armenian orphans into Armenian survivor society was also at risk. Indeed, the American agenda was less in line with Armenian expectations of restoration than with an American desire, as discussed in the previous chapter, to use Armenian children as a vanguard for, as the title of the NER's journal suggests, a "new Near East," constituting thereby a possible double loss to the Armenian community as these children became wards of the Americans. However, unlike during the war, American humanitarian workers cooperated with Armenian community leaders in teaching the children Armenian, identifying living relatives, and organizing the orphans into clubs and groups that eased their transition into adulthood.

The turning over of the orphanage to the care of American relief officials as Ottoman authority melted away in the Levant provides a window onto children's resistance to transfer, perhaps the least-understood part of this element of the crime of genocide. Writing in a 1918 report, Bayard Dodge, the president of the American University in Beirut, explained that immediately after the management of the institution was placed in the hands of the American Red Cross, "the Armenian children *asserted their rights.* They refused to use their Turkish names and they brought out Armenian books, which they had hidden away in secret places during the Turkish régime."[47]

Halidé Edip's concerns about the situation in Istanbul paralleled Kamil al-Ghazzi's objections to the apparent illicit transformation of Muslim children into Armenians. Indeed, it is in Edip's writings about the situation of children in the postwar empire that her hatred and distrust of Armenians is most pronounced; her writing has a texture similar to contemporary anti-Semitic writing in the way it casts Armenians as a mythical and existential enemy of the Ottomans, even to the point of borrowing tropes from blood libel and child cannibalism in describing a conspiracy to turn Turkish children into Armenians, thus also turning the accusations leveled against the Turks back toward the Armenians themselves. Hence, she complains, "When the children were brought in large numbers from orphanages of Anatolia they were sent to the Armenian church in Koum Kapou [Kumkapı], a hot-pot which boiled the Turkish children and dished them out as Armenians," and she concludes that "the children who were brought to the [Neutral House] were left in the care of the Armenian women, and these Armenian women either through persuasion or threats or *hypnotism,* forced the Turkish children to learn by heart the name of an Armenian woman for their mother and the name of an Armenian man for their father."[48] As a motive for this treatment, Halidé Edip provides no reason beyond fanaticism ("so far even the Christian missionaries could not go in their zeal") and dismisses the assertions of the "Armenians"—and implicitly those of the League's representatives—to the contrary, because "the Moslem Turks do not have the missionary instincts of the Christians of the West."[49]

As her discussion of the Neutral House's pernicious role in Istanbul concludes, Halidé Edip linked the house's operations to a question of national survival. Relating the story of young Kâzim, Edip explained how, as he had no papers, he was determined to be an Armenian, despite the fact that he was able to remember his father as a Muslim. In protest, the boy had told the commission—as recalled by Nakiye Hanım, the last Red Crescent representative to the Neutral House—"Kiazim is small, Kiazim is weak, his fists cannot protect him, but time will come when Kiazim will be strong: then he will show the world that he is a Turk." For Halidé Edip, Kâzim's case was "a symbol of the helpless Turkish nation at the moment."[50] Again, this rhetorical strategy of inversion—depicting the dominant groups as the real victim—underscores Edip's sense of how potential threatening this humanitarian intervention had been to the established social order.[51]

This inversion takes on additional meaning in the face of a conclusion drawn in the report of Cushman and Kennedy that Halidé Edip, alongside other leading Young Turks in conjunction with the Red Crescent Society, had been involved in a program to place Armenian children from southeastern Anatolia and the province of Aleppo with elite and middle-class Ottoman Muslim families in Istanbul. Edip had played some role in the history of the children being reclaimed by the Neutral House.[52] Nevertheless, she certainly viewed her actions as within the universe of humanitarianism, and quite possibly as a form of charity, in the manner that boarding schools for American Indian children were once perceived in the West. Indeed, during the Balkan Wars, the Ottoman Red Crescent Society bore some responsibility for administering *evlatlık* placements of Muslim refugees and orphans from southeastern Europe.[53] From the perspective of a committed nationalist, seizing and placing Armenian children in Muslim homes could be read as an attempt to erase national difference in a moment of extreme threat; the fact that the program pivoted on conversion to Islam as an elemental feature of becoming a Turk confirms the relative importance of religion in the broader conceptualization of that identity. Left unacknowledged in Edip's text, but on display in the reports on the reclaimed orphans, was the fact that many were being held in the homes of Istanbul's military, political, and religious elite. These were people within her own social class and circle of acquaintance. The customary practice of that class to possess and exploit human beings from subordinate groups had come into plain view, casting doubt on the civility and modernity of Turkey and Turks. Her assertion that modernity was a major theme of her work and of her reluctance to protect or even voice empathy for Armenians as victims of genocide shows how class and the persistence of Muslim privilege trumped relevant forms of cross-confessional feminist solidarity or basic human compassion. For Halidé Edip—as was the case with the Western relief workers—questions of social distinction and religion placed limits on the asserted universal nature of humanitarianism and its subjects, but it must be recalled that Western relief workers, unlike Edip, were not accessories to genocide.

Combined, the work of the Neutral House and the Rescue Home and the reports collated in the field—not just at the established centers in Aleppo and Istanbul but also throughout Anatolia and Mesopotamia—led League observers to conclude that sexual and domestic enslavement or forced sequestration of women, girls, and boys was a widespread consequence of the war that the current Ottoman state was incapable of addressing and that Ottoman society either ignored or explicitly sanctioned. The committee asked the Assembly to resolve to (1) appoint a commissioner to serve as the League's representative to the Allied occupiers of Istanbul, the Turkish government, and the religious leaders of the Armenian and Greek communities; (2) instruct Great Britain, Italy, and France (who were occupying portions of the Ottoman Empire at large) to coordinate with the League's representative; (3) create a "mixed board"—meaning Turkish (i.e., Muslim), Armenian, and Greek—to oversee the "reclamation" of women and children; and (4) open additional Neutral

Houses in other parts of the empire.[54] It was clear from the resolutions that the League anticipated a much more vigorous and intrusive inspection process—backed by force of arms if necessary—that would allow unrestrained access to Muslim homes and Ottoman state institutions.

Remaining at the rostrum after completing her report, Vacaresco, the Romanian delegate, delivered a lengthy speech, punctuated three times by applause, that amplified to the commission the sense that their work had been interfered with, but more importantly excoriated the Ottoman Empire in general for its treatment of Armenian and Greek orphans, girls, and women. Hélène Vacaresco (Romanian: Elena Vacarescu) (1864–1947) was an author and folklorist who is remembered primarily for her poems and connection with the Romanian royal family.[55] While many women served in the national delegations at the League, she was the only one ever designated with the rank of ambassador. Like most other women, primarily in the delegations from the Scandinavian countries and Great Britain, Vacaresco had been involved in early twentieth-century movements for international peace and women's rights, including the Paris-based Ligue du Droit des Femmes; at the League of Nations, women were channeled into working on issues of human trafficking, public health, and children—the so-called "social questions." More important, by 1920, most League efforts on behalf of women and children in the Ottoman Empire and then Turkey and the Levant were led by European and American women, not only at the level of relief work in the field, but also in administrative and executive positions in Geneva.[56] Unlike other women in the League's delegations, however, Vacaresco had been born an Ottoman subject in the principality of Wallachia, and her father had fought against the Ottomans in the Russian-Ottoman War of 1877–1878. Ultimately, the speech she gave blends the emancipatory language of suffrage and women's rights with the religious and racist lexicon of Balkan nationalism and perhaps even a degree of revanche. Moreover, as discussed below, Turkish responses to Vacaresco's speech highlighted her profession and gender as a tactic to undermine her as an expert and authority—and to undermine by extension the entire edifice of relief work in the former Ottoman Empire; more generally, the fact that much of the criticism of the actions of Turkish, Muslim men was being made by Western, Christian women seemed to arouse explicit resentment from the Ottoman representatives.

"You all know the story: women withering in their youth in the degrading languor of the harem," Vacaresco began, coloring the matter-of-fact prose of the committee's report with Orientalist, classical, and other literary references, "children torn from the bosom of their family and cast violently from one race into another, trained to serve those who are bent on the extermination of their own race, and perhaps some day doomed to fight in the ranks of their enemies, each one a new Oedipus trained to kill his parents with his own hands. (*loud applause*)'[57] In Vacaresco's estimation, the treatment of the orphans was an act of cultural erasure:

> Attempts are being made, before all things to teach these little Armenian children to forget; attempts are made to deprive them of their innocent memory—that first bond of man with the infinite, memory which, moreover, a mother trains and nurtures with such tender care. They must know neither their parents' name nor the place of their birth, and, destined to sleep later under an apocryphal epitaph, they are to drag out their mournful existence unmindful of the spot which was the cradle of their childhood. (*Renewed applause*)[58]

For those women enslaved in Muslim Turkish households, forgetting their "true nature" was also at stake, "as it would be vain to expect that these women and these outraged maidens will forget merely because they are asked to do so, their resistance is gradually worn down; persuasion, presents, threats are all employed in their turn for this end." Vacaresco's conclusion was a call to action that encapsulates key elements of the new humanitarianism: "I should trespass too long on your attention were I to enumerate all the means of putting an end to these horrors. In this case we are not confronted by one of those human disasters . . . [in which the international community] is impotent. . . . These iniquities may be countered by barriers and sanctions. Nothing should stop the will of a collective body when its high and noble will is also the will of the whole civilised world."[59]

Following a reiteration of the resolutions proposed by the commission, Vacaresco concluded that "the Assembly and the Council of the League of Nations, . . . will, I feel sure, prove once again that, thanks to them, the reign of brute force is over and the era of justice is at hand. *(Loud applause.)*" No members of the Assembly rose to respond to Vacaresco and, following a quick voice vote, the recommendations of the commission were adopted unanimously.[60]

The commission's report, Vacaresco's speech, and the enthusiastic response both to it and to the resolutions authorizing an increased League presence in relief activities in the Ottoman capital and provinces highlight the degree to which fixing the problems caused by the war and genocide was a moral imperative consistent with the League's larger purpose. It was telling evidence, as well, as far as the international community was concerned, that the "Turks"—here both an ethnic designation and code for Muslims—were implicated in an ongoing crime against humanity and that their collective responsibility had placed them beyond the pale of civilization.

THE FACES OF REJECTION

The Ottoman government responded quickly to Vacaresco's speech and the League's proposals in a pamphlet published in 1921 by the Ministry of Interior's General Directorate of Emigration, entitled *Cemiyet-i Akvam ve Türkiyede Ermeni ve Rumlar (The League of Nations and the Armenians and Greeks of Turkey)*. English and French translations were produced simultaneously. In substance the pamphlet resembles other texts produced in the period of what historical sociologist F. Müge Göçek calls, in her periodization of Turkish Armenian Genocide denial, the moment of the "Ottoman Investigative Narrative," most especially the Turkish National Congress's *The Turco-Armenian Question: The Turkish Point of View.*[61]

Cemiyet-i Akvam ve Türkiyede Ermeni ve Rumlar is typical of this period in its rebuttal of Vacaresco, noting that Armenians and Greeks had lived together with Turks for centuries in peace and harmony. Yet the former had fallen under the influence of revolutionary committees and had taken up arms against the state, and what had happened, while unfortunate, was a national necessity. In the English version, the pamphlet's author expressed his frustration that this was not being acknowledged by noting: "and after centuries thus spent together—[why is it] that the Turk should one day wish to deport them? IT IS MAINLY THIS POINT WHICH HAS NOT BEEN DULY INVESTIGATED."[62] Still, in a nod to the 1919 war crimes trials of several Young Turks, those responsible had been prosecuted: "The perpetrators of these incidents [excessive brutality toward deportees] have been searched out both during the world war as well as after the armistice and have been executed."[63] This transference of blame to the victims is reproduced in the pamphlet's second objection to Vacaresco's speech and the League's decision, namely that they are the outcome of a misinformation campaign launched by the Armenians, Greeks, and their supporters.

The final objection engages directly the question of the treatment of women and children in the postgenocide era. Previous Ottoman publications of the period, as described by Göçek, do not address the issue of trafficked and enslaved women and children. The rhetorical shallowness suggests that no strategy had been developed to address this area of concern; in other words, whereas various lines of counterargument had evolved to respond to other elements of culpability and Western criticism of the Ottoman state, the introduction of this particular line of argument was both new and unprecedented—it caught the Ottoman bureaucracy off guard. More to the point, as discussed above, addressing the postconflict rescue and rehabilitation of women and children was relatively new for the international community, as was the way such concern derived from the notion that ethnic groups were entitled to protection and categories of rights. The Ottoman reaction indicates that those rights were not recognized as rights per se within late Ottoman society, despite reform efforts to the contrary and some evidence that legal protections did exist on paper. As this final argument unfolded, the pamphlet's unnamed author asked: how can the League of Nations appoint an inspector of harems when the organization has no evidence that anyone is being held? The passages deny that slavery persisted or that trafficking had occurred and conclude, "We claim very openly and positively that other than the Greek and Armenian servants who in return of definite salaries customarily stay in the houses in CONSTANTINOPLE, there is not a single Greek or Armenian woman or child kept forcibly in the Turkish families. . . . [It is] obvious, that the incidents published about Turkey with mean intentions are nothing other than mere imagination and dirty calumny."[64] Taken as a whole, the rejoinder suggests that the Ottoman elite believed it was being held accountable for what in practice was the lawful treatment of not just women and children, but the women and children of what they saw as ungrateful, and seditious, ethnic and religious communities.

That sense of anger and resentment was amplified in Ottoman diplomatic responses at the League. A letter from Cevat, the Ottoman ambassador to Switzerland and the de facto head of the Ottoman legation, to the Assembly (March 31, 1922) encapsulates again the self-righteous and selective outrage:

The whole Assembly of the League of Nations, that League of universal brotherhood, moved by Mademoiselle Vacaresco's lyrical talent applauded her expressions of hatred; and though it was far from accurately informed and far from possessing any knowledge of *the East and its customs*, it responded to this isolated challenge, and, without hearing the accused party or giving him an opportunity to defend himself, without weighing the significance of its action or measure its consequences, it endorsed the judgment of the poetess, which slandered and cruelly attacked an honest and honourable people, which has been persecuted for centuries and always been vilified as the persecutor. Can such a procedure be called justice—a procedure the disastrous consequences of which affect *not merely individuals but a whole peaceful and peace-loving nation?*[65]

Again, like *Cemiyet-i Akvam ve Türkiyede Ermeni ve Rumlar,* Cevat's response did not engage the issues of trafficking and rescue and instead focused on Vacaresco's clearly anti-Muslim sentiment, introducing a species of cultural relativism into the discussion. Taken as a whole, his claim was less that Ottoman society writ large was consciously covering up a crime and more that it could not or would not acknowledge that what was termed a crime by the international community was in fact so. While Ottoman leaders did recognize that certain categories of war crimes had taken place—in particular massacres of civilians—and claimed that those responsible had already been condemned, they were unwilling to admit collective responsibility for what they considered not criminal, but rather an established and customary social practice.

In the end, the entirety of the Ottoman response struck the League's officials as improbable and unpersuasive, so much so that further discussions and attempts to clarify the residual empire's position were met with derision on the part of the body's secretariat, an attitude summed up best in a handwritten note attached to a dossier that included Cevat's letter: "A long intolerable whine from the Turkish Minister, the burden of which is that no Turk ever hurt a living creature, but that everyone bullies Turks and the Assembly was monstrously unfair."[66]

The final paragraph of *Cemiyet-i Akvam ve Türkiyede Ermeni ve Rumlar* is a striking departure in the way it argues that the League's actions are unjust not just to Turkey, but to Islam as a whole: "The Moslem World would have, alas, rightly expected that the Honourable Society of the League of Nations would at least have expressed a word of sympathy in the name of civilization, if not send an inspector or commission of investigation for the hundreds of thousands of Moslems of Turkey now moaning as a living emblem of poverty and misery in the interior of ASIA MINOR and in CONSTANTINOPLE."[67]

This sentiment echoes the responses to the efforts of the Rescue Home and Neutral House by al-Ghazzi and Halidé Edip—although in Edip's case, in her role as a protagonist of Turkish nationalist secularism, the insult was to the Turkish nation. Regardless, it points to how the motives of the humanitarian regime were interpreted and received in elite Ottoman and post-Ottoman Turkish and Arab Muslim circles in the Eastern Mediterranean. For them, the attempts to reclaim women and children were understood not as a humanitarian act repairing the damage of the war, but as a punishment and affront to Islam. In public, the Ottoman delegates were declaiming the violation of their national sovereignty, defending the social practices of their society in a rhetoric of cultural and religious superiority, and denying a preponderance of evidence of human trafficking and enslavement. But in private, these same men faced the prospect of being forced to open the doors of their own homes, their individual domestic spaces, to foreign inspection. If the League had its way, they risked having what was, at least in their collective consciousness, property—foster children or additional wives—seized. They were unable to participate in the universalist and cosmopolitan impulses of the rescue movement's proponents in the international community and dismissed this key facet of the new humanitarian regime as an anti-Muslim, anti-Turkish cudgel.[68]

Following the political and military successes of Mustafa Kemal and his nationalist allies (1920–1922), the conditions under which the Neutral House was constituted and the inspection of Muslim homes had been conceivable no longer existed. The Treaty of Lausanne affirmed Turkey's unmitigated national sovereignty, and while it included gestures toward the rights of minorities, these were unenforceable. This outcome had been anticipated by professional diplomats at the League at the time of Fifth Commission's report—a moment when much of Anatolia was already in the hands of nationalist forces. One of these professionals, Thanassis Aghnides, had even labeled the entire enterprise from the beginning "a pious wish devoid of all practicability."[69]

Conversely, in Aleppo, which had become the most populous city of French mandate Syria, conditions allowed the Rescue Home to continue to function—reinforcing the link between the success of interwar modern humanitarianism and the prevailing forms of late colonialism. Indeed, by 1927, Karen Jeppe concluded that "practically all the deported women and children, detained since the war against their will among the Moslems, will have been offered an opportunity to return."[70] The following year's report notes that the only women and children survivors entering the Rescue Home that year had been smuggled across the Syrian-Turkish border, meaning that no additional survivors had been located in Syria itself. While about 75 percent of those entering the home eventually found living relatives, others remained, and Jeppe turned her focus toward using the home as a center for training and rehabilitation, providing education and instituting a micro-credit lending program to help adult women earn a living by producing lace and other arts and crafts for export to Europe and the Americas. Jeppe's efforts mirrored those by the international community, which began the process of creating the international institutional framework for resettling existing refugee populations and sponsoring institutions for orphans, rather than seeking to restore and return refugees to their ancestral homelands.

As a residue of the early interwar conception that Armenians had suffered as a community and communal entity, as discussed in the following chapter, efforts were taken to assist Armenians in maintaining their cultural distinction, institutions, and language in the face of the pressure to assimilate. These efforts dovetailed neatly with French colonial strategies in Syria and Lebanon to foster the political development of non-Muslim, non-Arab communities as a countervailing force to incipient Arab nationalism and calls for independence. More to the point, the effort at rescue signaled that the definition of human suffering—as the prompt for humanitarian action—had expanded in a way that included the legal status of women and children and was inflected with Wilsonian ideas about community and nation.

Despite, or rather in spite of, the attention to the rights of women and children, a common thread running throughout the discussion within the humanitarian community—and indeed in the local elite reaction to the implementation of the rescue movement—was the degree to which women and children were abstracted into nationalist, conservative, and humanitarian discourse as empty vessels into which anxieties and beliefs about change, national honor, and civilization could be poured. Halidé Edip's memoir and Vacaresco's speech are perhaps the best examples of how this emblematizing took shape. For the latter, the treatment of Armenian women and children achieved an elaborate symbolic value as an example of alleged Muslim depravity, the inherent guilt and backwardness of Turks, and the general moral disorder and chaos of the war; for the former, it was a brutal reminder of how low Turkey's fortunes had fallen—and in part at the hands of a disloyal internal "other." The virtuous Armenian woman, victimized by the rapacious, terrible Turk and requiring rescue by the West, was a leitmotif in the forms of publicity and fundraising campaigns initiated by missionary and nongovernmental relief organizations like Near East Relief during the war. This image no doubt contributed to the way the humanitarian community situated itself in relation to both groups, and has had a lasting impact on Turkish-Armenian relations. For the community of relief workers, also at stake in the restoration of order was the prevention of any further mixing between "white" Armenians and "Asiatic" Turks; the creation of the "unnatural" unions of Armenian women and girls was an act of miscegenation they found both offensive and contrary to the moral discipline of modernity.[71]

Certainly, the Armenian women and children involved in rescue had been stripped of their individual histories within official discourse—though thankfully not in the records of the Rescue Home and the Neutral House—and reduced to a synecdoche for broader formulations through which modern humanitarianism itself was being constituted. Beyond the implications this has for recovering female and children survivors as discrete historical actors, in a very profound way, the act of infusing their rescue with this constitutive meaning impeded rescue or at least the extension of direct humanitarian assistance to the vast majority of those survivors held in various capacities in the residues of the Ottoman state. The ideological and cultural meaning of rescue and the immense symbolic value of the women and children was predicated on grander assumptions by all sides about non-Muslims in late Ottoman society, paternalism, emancipation, and equality, which at that moment may have helped define humanitarianism and the League's role in the Eastern Mediterranean, but also underscored a loss of Turkish national prestige and Muslim social control and preeminence. The Ottoman reaction to the Fifth Commission's recommendations, which rejected not just the proposals but also the underlying facts, left no ideological or ethical space in which humanitarian concerns and compassion would be the overriding principles, and consequently very few rescues were effected in post-Lausanne Turkey, leaving the vast majority of trafficked survivors in place.

As the process of recovery in Anatolia was forestalled permanently with the establishment of the Turkish Republic, the vast majority of Armenian children and female survivors integrated into Muslim households remained there for the rest of their lives. Assimilated into families and communities as Muslims and Turkish speakers, these "former" Armenians, for lack of a better description, started their own families and left descendants. It is estimated that as many as two million contemporary Turks have at least one Armenian grandparent, though the possible costs of revealing Armenian ancestry in public are so high as to preclude arriving at an accurate number. Excised from official Turkish history, this demographic reality has garnered increasing attention nonetheless, and discussions of Armenian heritage have become interwoven

with efforts at Armenian-Turkish reconciliation and official acknowledgment of the Armenian Genocide.[72]

Turkish human rights lawyer Fethiye Çetin's memoir, *Anneannem:
Anlatı (My Grandmother: A Memoir)*, provides an example of how the
recognition of the fact that many Turks have Armenian ancestors has
implications for reconciliation—at least on the level of the family. In it
she tells of her discovery that her grandmother, whom she had known
growing up as Şeher, had been born Heranush and was a child survivor
of the genocide. Çetin's retelling of Şeher/Heranush's story is haunt-
ingly reminiscent of Zabel's story: after the men and older boys of her
village of Havva were executed, the women and children were sent on a
march toward Mesopotamia. Among the horrors Şeher/Heranush witnessed en route was her grandmother drowning two of her infant
grandchildren, only to then fling herself into the water after them. Eventually, she and the other girls in the caravan were separated and
"adopted" by various officers, she by one Colonel Hüseyin. Later she
learned that her brother, Khoren, now named Ahmet, had been sold to
a local farmer and was working as a shepherd. Their father, who emigrated to America before the war, returned to Aleppo, where he located
her mother. He sent word to both his children via smugglers for them to
join him. Khoren did, but Şeher/Heranush, now married to a local
Turkish man, was unable to do so. Nevertheless, Şeher/Heranush maintained some contact with her family until the 1950s. A respected and
beloved grandmother, she engaged in traditional Armenian rituals,
including the baking of a sweet bread, *çorek*, at Easter, which she shared
with other *kılıç artığı* women in the village; she and other former Armenians never quite fully assimilated and maintained in forms of practice
a memory of their origins. Çetin has renewed contacts with her Ameri-
can-Armenian cousins, the children of her uncle Khoren.

CHAPTER 6

Between Refugee and Citizen

The Practical Failures of Modern
Humanitarianism, 1923–1939

Once they had left their homeland they remained homeless,
once they had left their state they became stateless; once they
had been deprived of their human rights they were rightless,
the scum of the earth.

—Hannah Arendt, *The Origins of Totalitarianism*

In Aleppo, Syria, home to the largest community of descendants of survivors of the Armenian Genocide in the Middle East, a map once greeted
visitors at the entrance of the Karen Jeppe Jemaran, a preparatory high
school on the site of the League of Nations Rescue Home named in
honor of the Danish relief worker who administered it. The map shows
the boundaries of the medieval kingdom of Armenia overlaid with the
borders of "Wilsonian Armenia," a geographical construction drawn
by the American president as the victors of the Great War divided the
Ottoman Empire among themselves (figure 6.1). The map, which Wilson presented to the Paris Peace Conference in 1920, has become the
basis for an image of a lost homeland affixed to the walls of Armenian
schools, cultural centers, and churches throughout the world. For
diasporic Armenians, it is a reminder of a nation-state once promised
them in the wake of an attempt to destroy them as a people, then
briefly established, and finally lost as the principle of national self-
determination was sacrificed by the League of Nations and the United
States, Britain, and France in the face of the military and political
ascendancy of the Republic of Turkey and its integration into the international order.[1] The failed project embodied by the map is also a stark
reminder of the real limits facing America as it sought to extend its

FIGURE 6.1. "Boundary between Turkey and Armenia: As Determined by Woodrow Wilson, President of the United States of America." Map by Lawrence Martin, ca. 1920. Source: G7431.F2 1920 .M3, Library of Congress Geography and Map Division, Washington, DC.

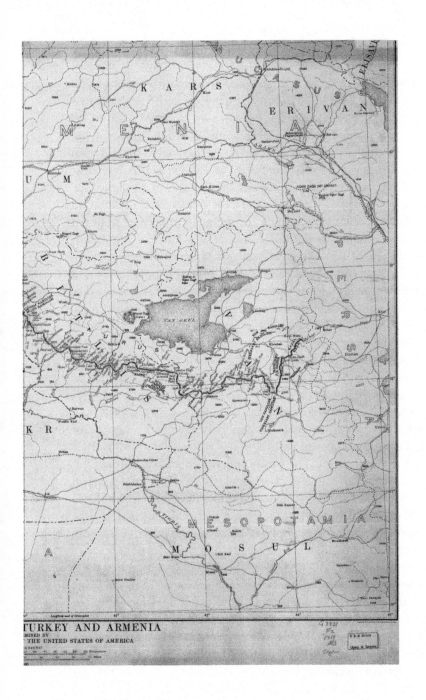

TURKEY AND ARMENIA
...MINED BY
...' THE UNITED STATES OF AMERICA

will in the interwar period, even at the very apex of its power in the early 1920s.[2]

The relationship between Armenians and Armenia (the nation-state that was not) and the League of Nations, especially in the League's first decade, bears out a history in which Armenian national aspirations were abandoned. Nonetheless, member states' shifting and evolving attitudes and League policies still affected the status, position, and even survival of Armenian refugee communities and individual Armenians. In the face of the failure of the victors of the Great War to secure the establishment of Armenia—that is, a state for Armenians, understood at the time as the preeminent vehicle for the achievement of national aspirations—the League of Nations formulated a *particular* humanitarianism on behalf of Armenians. The *problem of humanity* posed by the existence of a denationalized and stateless refugee population would still be a *problem for humanity,* not at the level of the state, but rather at the nexus of international institutions, philanthropic organizations, and diasporic political parties and civil society groups. The relegation of the problem of the postgenocide Ottoman Armenians to that level after decades of international advocacy on their behalf demonstrates how swiftly a humanitarian emergency can fade from view or become an inconvenient and forgettable problem for humanity.

This substate and residual humanitarian enterprise (a) asserted the national rights of the Armenians; (b) explicitly linked the League of Nations to the communal survival of that Armenian nation; and (c) sought to achieve that survival by promoting the collective and individual welfare of Armenian refugees. The emphasis on communal survival rather than just assimilation distinguished this project from the policies the League developed during the same period on behalf of Russian refugees, who were expected, for example, because of their putative Europeanness, to acculturate and assimilate. Still, despite the exceptional nature of the League's Armenian policy, elements of it intersect with other questions that drew the attention of interwar humanitarians. Their concerns included the treatment of Jews facing de facto denationalization by the states of Eastern and Central Europe and the extension of citizenship to refugees or migrants in colonial and settler states, which ultimately laid the groundwork for the elaboration of relationships between international humanitarian organizations—such as the League, the International Committee of the Red Cross, and then the United Nations—and the theory and practice of protecting civilians during and after conflicts, but not necessarily in the context of international war.

The convergence of colonialism, nationalism, and communal survival in the League's work also marks the interwar period as somewhat distinct in the genealogy of humanitarianism itself, and certainly distinguishes it from the humanitarian practices elaborated in the decades following the Second World War, when concepts like national self-determination were absent altogether and a regime of individual human rights had *some* influence on the ambit of humanitarianism.[3] More broadly, what the history of humanitarian policy toward the "refugee" in the 1920s and 1930s confirms is that modern humanitarianism as an ideology and a collection of practices could not escape the prevailing cultural norms, moral economies, and politics encircling it. The inherent weakness of humanitarianism has been a constant in this book, all the more so in this case: humanitarian policy was shaped by the forces that acted on it, and consequently it could exert minor force, perhaps only in the form of resistance by its practitioners or its subjects, the other way. In the end, while the interwar international humanitarian response was marked by unique departures from previous forms of relief and assistance and is at odds with elements of the form of contemporary practices, what happened to the Armenians, as well as later to the Assyrians of Iraq and Palestinian refugees in the immediate post–World War II period, is an early example of what today's relief or development workers would call the substitution of humanitarianism for politics. This was a truly ersatz substitution, in which the actual root cause of human suffering was generally understood as the clearly illegal or unjust actions of a state (or colonial power)—denationalization, mass extrajudicial murder, land expropriation, foreign occupation—but was met with purposeful silence and a formal indifference.

The multifaceted relationship between the League and the Armenians constituted a proving ground on which prevailing ideas about minorities, refugees, and concepts of cultural and national survival played out in the wake of World War I and the colonial division of the Middle East into mandates. At the same time, as the League elaborated a series of novel projects to address Armenian suffering, the ideological content of interwar modern humanitarianism became clearer. Critical to an understanding of humanitarianism's evolving role in interwar politics and society is showing where the humanitarianism of that moment intersected with prevailing and evolving conceptions of human dignity and shared humanity, as well as how it was ultimately subordinated to the demands of twentieth-century nationalism and the persistence of late colonialism.

Based on archival materials from the League of Nations, reports by League officials, archives of the French mandate for Syria, and contemporary legal writing, this chapter follows the relationship between the League and the postgenocide Armenian communities of the former Ottoman state. Beginning with the construction of Armenians as the objects of humanitarianism sine qua non, it continues by examining critical episodes in that relationship: the rescue movement of the previous chapter, the grant of the Nansen passport to Armenian refugees (both communally and individually), and the "final settlement" of Armenian refugee communities in French mandate Syria and Lebanon. The last episode is framed by the League's diverse plans to solve social conflict by removing and resettling peoples, a policy that later shaped the exchange of populations between Greece and Turkey at the end of the Greco-Turkish War and the transfer of other groups of Armenian refugees to southeastern Europe and Soviet Armenia in the late 1920s.[4] While the focus here is primarily on the League's engagement with the Armenian survivor communities of the Middle East, rather than the engagement of Armenians worldwide with the League, it is critical to note that Armenians as individuals and through international organizations like the Armenian General Benevolent Union shaped and reshaped their relationship with the League and asserted a degree of agency that is often missing from the accounts found in the League's own archives.[5]

THE ARMENIAN AS UNIVERSAL HUMANITARIAN OBJECT

In concluding his discussion of the relationship between the Armenians and the Great Powers of Europe in his 1926 *La Société des nations et les puissances devant le problème arménien* (The League of Nations and the powers confront the Armenian problem), André Mandelstam, an émigré Russian jurist and former diplomat who had become the leading European critic of the League's abandonment of Armenian national aspirations, argued that the Armenians had "earned" the right to a national home following years of oppression by the absolutist Ottoman state and through the support of the international community:

> The humanitarian interventions undertaken by the Powers in Turkey in the course of the nineteenth century created, without any contradiction, a customary *right* in favor of the oppressed nations of the Ottoman Empire, a right, so to speak, that persists. In the case of this particular oppressed [Armenian] nation, this right, which at first was to protect the primordial

interests of man *[les intérêts primordiaux de l'homme]* (life, liberty, and equality) was with time, because of the incorrigible tyranny of Turkey, transformed into a guaranteed right to autonomy and the right to secession.[6]

Mandelstam was representative of a large group of European and North American politicians, writers, and diplomats who were profoundly disappointed with the collapse of the prospects for an Armenian national home in the decade following World War I. The *cause* of the Armenians, which had been relatively popular in the West starting in the late nineteenth century, continued through the war years and into the immediate postwar period. As discussed in previous chapters, during the Great War, European and American civil society had mobilized on behalf of the Armenians, raising money for relief and exerting pressure on governments to provide assistance. In the period after the war, the Armenians loomed large in an emerging Western modern humanitarian consciousness, so much so that even in the increasingly isolationist United States, proposals for an American mandate for Armenia had enjoyed more support than the League of Nations itself. As a consequence, the Armenian cause became emblematic of the larger goal of establishing a just world order, and Armenians themselves the prototypical object of humanitarianism. Concern for Armenians translated into how the League and its bureaucracy would conceptualize Armenian suffering, and also how much effort would be exerted on behalf of Armenian issues. Simply put, the Armenians were not the only people who entered the interwar period without a sovereign and viable state, but they were unique in the degree to which their cause mattered at Geneva and Washington, and in the capitals of League members.

For Mandelstam, the Armenians had been the object of humanitarianism for quite some time, and his observations on both their national rights and the failures of the international community to act on their behalf were shaped by his experiences as first dragoman at the Russian Embassy in Istanbul in the waning days of the Ottoman state. In that capacity, he had tried to negotiate the last in a series of autonomy plans for the six predominantly Armenian eastern provinces of the Ottoman Empire and the separate noncontiguous province of Adana (Cilicia). Known as the *Mandelstam Draft* (1913), the plan for autonomy included sectarian-based forms of representation like those implemented following the Western "humanitarian intervention" in Mount Lebanon (1860) and the establishment of a unique administrative form, the *mutasarrifiyya*. The *Draft* echoed, as well, the political and administrative reforms imposed by European states on the Ottoman Empire's Balkan provinces over the course of the late nineteenth century. It included many features that became commonplace elements in various "minority treaties" in the interwar period—for example, the emphasis on access to legal services and education in minority languages. Beyond political reorganization in favor of greater Armenian political participation and administrative control; the elimination of the irregular tribal cavalry (the Hamidiye corps), which had been implicated in the Hamidian massacres of the 1890s; the creation of a gendarmerie made up of Turks and Armenians led by European officers; and the expulsion of newly settled Muslim migrants from the Balkans and Caucasus to other parts of the Ottoman state, the *Draft* also included cultural elements. Thus the proposed agreement added Armenian and Kurdish to Turkish as the official languages for administration; and it gave each community (here meaning Armenians, Kurds, and Turks) the right to create their own schools, publicly financed through taxes. The European powers would enforce compliance.[7]

While the Sublime Porte did agree to the plan, the onset of the war several months later made it a dead letter. Altering the demographic makeup of the provinces at the heart of the *Mandelstam Draft* was among the motives for the Armenian Genocide as it unfolded in the Ottoman state from 1915 to 1922. The reasoning behind this was that, if Armenians were no longer concentrated in significant numbers—or if they were eliminated altogether—in those particular provinces, Western and Armenian calls for autonomy would be a nonissue after the war.[8] The process outlined in the 1913 *Draft* seemed to have achieved implementation in the division of the Ottoman Empire as outlined by the Treaty of Sèvres (1920). That treaty acknowledged the establishment of the Republic of Armenia in the South Caucasus and the creation of Cilicia as a predominately Armenian French client state.

As discussed in chapter 4, elements of the Ottoman state and military resisted the occupation and division of the empire, a movement that culminated in what is remembered in modern Turkey as the Kurtuluş Savaşı, or "War for National Salvation" (1919–1922). Best characterized as a combined anticolonial and civil war for Anatolia, it pitted nationalist Turkish forces against Armenian, French colonial, and Greek armies. The conclusive Turkish victory prevented the division of Anatolia: France withdrew from Cilicia, evacuating the hundreds of thousands of displaced Ottoman Armenians who had been resettled there to camps in and around Aleppo and Beirut; the Republic of Armenia ceased to exist, and its residue was absorbed into the Soviet Union.

The political reality created by the Turkish military victories was recognized first by the Treaty of Ankara (1921), sometimes called the Franklin-Bouillon Agreement, and then by the Treaty of Lausanne (1923). The latter included several provisions protecting non-Muslim religious minorities (it eschewed any ethnonyms, most notably "Armenian" and "Greek")—in particular their property, religious, and communal education rights—but these protections fell far short of providing anything resembling political autonomy, let alone a national home. Moreover, Turkey had become in practice a religiously, though not ethnically, homogeneous state as a combined result of the war, the genocide, and then the League-administered exchange of populations with Greece. Later, official Turkish policy prevented Ottoman Armenians from returning home, making them stateless. Those Armenians who remained in the new republic lived in small pockets in major cities or isolated in tiny provincial towns, and they faced terrible forms of informal and formal discrimination.[9]

Mandelstam viewed these developments as the triumph of politics over law; he also considered them contrary to the spirit of the League of Nations: "Indeed, the attitude of the Powers toward Armenia appears to be an accidental and momentary deviation from the great principles of the Treaty [of the League of Nations]."[10] For him, the various humanitarian projects of the League on behalf of the Armenians through the early 1920s were evidence that, "while at the League's beginning it did not respond to the ardent hopes of Armenia, . . . since then, on the strength of the continual increase of its prestige and influence in the world, it has not ceased to raise its voice high in favor of this needlessly sacrificed nation, in other words, in favor of the triumph of rights [or law] over misguided politics."[11]

The humanitarian activities on behalf of the Armenians took on a certain urgency after the absorption of the Republic of Armenia in 1920 by the nascent Soviet Union, precisely because of this sense that the moral authority of the League, in its commitment to both international law and idealism, had been compromised by what had happened to the Armenians at Lausanne, and that its future success and credibility in other fields hinged on rescuing, repairing, or perhaps just preserving what remained of the Armenian nation. As the previous chapter's discussions on race and cultural assimilation also show, the sense of mission implicated in the League's discourse emphasized the success of Christian civilization over putative Muslim barbarism. That sense of mission enveloped emerging interwar racist ideologies that viewed the Armenians as white "Europeans" who needed protection from the masses of Semitic and Turkic Muslims among whom they were now living.

This sense of mission likewise stemmed from the League's understanding of the plight of the Armenians in the interwar period. It viewed them not merely as civilian victims of war or survivors of massacres, but rather collectively, as a nation that had faced (and continued to face) extermination. A consistent narrative in the form of *humanitarian knowledge* of what the Armenians had endured emerged early in the League's history, based primarily on accounts by two diplomats as discussed in chapter 3: *Armenian Atrocities, the Murder of a Nation* (1916), by Arnold J. Toynbee (1889–1975); and *Ambassador Morgenthau's Story* (1918), by Henry Morgenthau, Sr. (1856–1946). The scientific nature of their reporting met the standards of proof and "factfinding" on which the League—and the Secretariat in particular, constituted as a deliberative body—rested. That narrative was reinforced throughout the period by "minority petitions" to the League, but also by accounts provided by Armenian ecclesiastical leaders and organizations, including the Armenian National Delegation and the Armenian General Benevolent Union, as part of their ongoing advocacy efforts.[12]

In sum, the League, and in particular its Secretariat, understood the cause of the Armenians in the most paternalistic terms possible. The Armenians were a stateless but "deserving" people, made up primarily of widows, orphans, and young women. The rescue of the Armenians was entwined with the success of the League itself on a number of levels. For some, these goals even defined the broader humanitarian purpose of the League, whose moral authority was at stake and depended on redressing the wrongs inflicted on the Armenians during the genocide *and* as a consequence of postwar diplomacy.

LEAGUE HUMANITARIANISM AND ARMENIAN COMMUNAL SURVIVAL

The fact of Armenian statelessness in the interwar period meant that any relationship between Armenians, the Armenian "nation," and the League perforce fell outside of its usual sphere of activity at the intersection of states, and came instead under the rubric of humanitarianism.[13] As noted above, critical to this particular form of humanitarianism was the underlying principle that it was not just intended to ease the suffering of individual Armenians, but would also endeavor to prevent the further erosion of the Armenian nation by forestalling the effacement of that nation through dispersal and cultural assimilation. As these plans and programs unfolded during the League's existence, they registered changing attitudes about intervention—especially in the shadow of the British and French occupation of the Middle East—refugees, and the persistence of colonialism.

The rescue movement, the broad-based effort to locate child and trafficked female survivors of the genocide and return them to the control of the residual Armenian community, as detailed in the last chapter, was the earliest manifestation of this plan. Among the very first acts of the League of Nations was the establishment of the Fifth Committee. Its final report, *Deportation of Women and Children in Turkey, Asia Minor and the Neighbouring Territories* (1921), stands as one of the most comprehensive reckonings of the situation facing postgenocide Armenians.[14] The rescue movement is unique in that it began when there was a real possibility of establishing an independent Armenian national home in the Caucasus and an Armenian-dominated French client state in Cilicia and endured when those two projects collapsed altogether. The specific meaning of humanitarian rescue had evolved across the period of its implementation, just as the responsibility for it moved from Armenian families and organizations into the hands of Near East Relief (NER) and later the League. When the prospect of an Armenian national home was still present, the rescue of these young people fit into the project of nation building and the making of citizens writ large. With the failure of that project, the recovery of Armenians to their community, which meant that they would swell the ranks of refugees primarily in Syria, has a different texture. In reading the reports of relief workers from the time, it is clear that rescue had become more about the basic humanity of the individual survivor and, to some extent, that survivor's intimate right to dignity outside of enslavement and, in the best possible world, reunification with family.

The Nansen Passport

That sense of individual dignity in the face of the inhumanity of war's impact on civilians resonates with the League's primary tool to address Armenian statelessness, the Nansen passport. In 1922, as the international community was assessing the implications of the Kemalist movement's success in Turkey, the League's high commissioner for refugees, Fridtjof Nansen (1861–1930), received the Nobel Peace Prize. Nansen's laureate lecture, entitled "The Suffering People of Europe," encapsulated the polar-explorer-turned-humanitarian's distress over the unprecedented levels of suffering in the wake of the Great War. In the course of the speech, he issued a humanitarian challenge that was also a précis of the programs in which he was involved: "This is not the struggle for power, but a single and terrible accusation against those who still do not want to see, a single great prayer for a drop of mercy to give men a chance to live."[15]

At war's end, the League of Nations had charged Nansen with over-seeing the repatriation of prisoners of war, primarily in Eastern Europe. He was among the first Western humanitarians to grasp the full extent of the unfolding Russian refugee crisis. War, revolution, and food shortages had displaced 1.5 million subjects of the former Russian Empire—Russians, Poles, Latvians, Ukrainians, Turkic Muslims, Jews, and Caucasian Armenians—as well as so-called "white émigrés." With the redrawing of boundaries, the Soviet government passed legislation denaturalizing large portions of that displaced population, producing thereby a large and heterogeneous mass in various forms of statelessness. In particular, it was Nansen's encounter with 120,000 Russian refugees in Istanbul that first indicated to him the gravity of the situation.

With the collapse of the repatriation provisions of the Treaty of Sèvres and the rise of extreme Turkish nationalist policies denying Armenians the right of return to their homeland and denaturalizing those living outside the borders of the newly constituted state, the survivors of the Armenian Genocide living in southeastern Europe and the Middle East became in effect stateless as well (1920–1922). Not counting those Armenians who had emigrated to the United States or who were living in the Soviet Republic of Armenia, the League estimated the number of Armenians in this precarious situation to be approximately 340,000, with roughly half living in refuges camps, orphanages, or shantytowns near the major cities of the Levant.

Nascent international aid organizations—sometimes, but not always, in concert with the League—were undertaking monumental relief work for these displaced populations. The American Relief Administration delivered food aid to Russia and the post-Ottoman Eastern Mediterranean, as did NER. However, neither organization had the authority to address the legal status of displaced peoples. Food, shelter, and sanitation were certainly critical to their welfare, but with the passage of time, the sense that these refugees were never going home grew, given that these populations faced legal or extralegal denationalization. The next most pressing challenge was the lack of an internationally recognizable legal framework to deal with their statelessness in the war's immediate aftermath. These stateless persons lacked identity papers (or if they did possess them, the papers had been issued by states that no longer existed), and they were perceived as an economic burden, a health risk, and a security threat to their host societies. Equally, they were vulnerable to expulsion, exploitation, or trafficking.

This precarious status prompted what has since become a question lying at the heart of modern humanitarianism: who is responsible for displaced and stateless peoples? For Nansen and others at the League, the answer suggested itself: there was an international responsibility to "do something" about refugees.[16] But the form this responsibility ought to take was a complex and vexing issue. It also prompted the reverse question—namely, whether this meant that, as a refugee, one had an individual right to protection by the international community. Clearly, however, notions of rights at that moment adhered more closely to national citizenship than individual human rights, and it is hard to identify with any certainty a recognizable legal body of rights outside of that framework. In other words, as the underlying theory of the Nansen passport regime showed, an individual's access to protection was predicated on that individual's membership in a specific national group—despite the very clear rhetorical commitment to individual dignity.

The international management of the refugee crisis prompted the establishment of the Office of the High Commissioner for Refugees, which eventually became the Nansen International Office for Refugees. Among the office's earliest acts was the creation of a League-administered travel document called the Nansen passport—first for displaced subjects of the erstwhile Russian Empire in July 1922, and then for formerly Ottoman Armenians in May 1924. Fifty-four states agreed to recognize travel documents issued to Russians, and thirty-eight later also acknowledged those held by Armenians.[17] By May 1926, the League had further defined what constituted a refugee in accordance with Nansen's proposals, formalizing the eligibility requirements for the travel documents:

> The Conference adopts the following definitions of the term "refugee":
> Russian: Any person of Russian origin who does not enjoy or who no longer enjoys the protection of the Government of the Union of Socialist Soviet Republics and who has not acquired another nationality.
> Armenian: Any person of Armenian origin formerly a subject of the Ottoman Empire who does not enjoy or who no longer enjoys the protection of the Government of the Turkish Republic and who has not acquired another nationality.[18]

During the same interval, the United States Congress passed legislation extending refugee status to Ottoman Armenians.

The ideological and theoretical dimensions of the interwar refugee regime were further elaborated in the *Convention of 28 October 1933 Relating to the International Status of the Refugee*. The language of the document, like that used by the rescue movement and Nansen's Nobel speech, is redolent with what appears to be the shibboleths of shared humanity and universality, seen as well in Nansen's Nobel acceptance speech. Its preamble notes several aspirations:

> Desirous of supplementing and consolidating the work done by the League of Nations on behalf of the refugees;
>
> Anxious to establish conditions which shall enable the decisions already taken by the various States with this object to be fully effective, and desirous that refugees shall be ensured the enjoyment of civil rights, free and ready access to the courts, security and stability as regards establishment and work, facilities in the exercise of the professions, of industry and of commerce, and in regard to the movement of persons, admission to schools and universities . . .[19]

But then the document shifts from the universal to the particular: "The present Convention is applicable to Russian, Armenian and assimilated refugees, as defined by the Arrangements of May 12th, 1926, and June 30th, 1928."[20] These measures taken by the League confirm what the term refugee meant at that moment in the evolving framework of international humanitarian law—that is, "a refugee is a member of a group that has no freedom of international movement because its members have been effectively deprived of the formal protection of their government."[21] And the only states to which this definition applied were the ex-Ottoman state (functionally the Republic of Turkey) and the Soviet Union. What is also important is that the definition turned exclusively on state protection and its denial and not on the kinds of conditions that tend to inform contemporary definitions of the refugee, and certainly not on any acknowledgment of the human rights of the refugee.[22] With these distinctions in mind, it is critical to avoid conflating our understanding of the limited nature of the measures taken to care for and manage vast populations of refugees in the post-Ottoman Middle East and postimperial Eastern Europe with the kinds of refugee policies that took shape after the *1951 Convention Relating to the Status of Refugees*.

It was precisely the inherent and intentional limitation of the Nansen passport that rendered it appealing to League members. The Nansen passport promised to free host countries of the social and economic burden of sheltering refugees by allowing the free flow of refugee labor, as well as by allowing the mechanism of the market and liberal economics to ameliorate or improve their condition. The passport was issued by member states and was basically a travel document; it included minimal anthropometric data, a photograph of the subject, and information about place of origin, date, and place of issuance. Visas, entry stamps, and the like could be affixed to it. According to the international agreements worked out between the League and member states, holders of the document had the ability, *not the right,* to (1) travel from their place of refuge to a second country, generally in search of work, without fear that they would be unable to return to their country of refuge, and without *refoulement* (involuntary return to the refugee's country of origin); and (2) possibly move on to a third country.[23] For the countries through which the refugees circulated, the documents constituted a de facto temporary residence permit—far less than citizenship—which meant, among other things, that refugees could be easily deported in times of economic stress or in the face of political upheaval. Nevertheless, the extension of the ability to travel established for Armenian refugees a modicum of legal status at the intersection of states and at the behest of an international organization. This meant, however, that in a narrow window of activity the League had become a virtual state for refugee Armenians. In retrospect, that act provided dignity in the sense suggested by Nansen in his Nobel lecture, but it also provided a way for Armenians to participate in economic (though not political) structures with relative ease. It allowed them to regain some control over their own lives, letting them connect to the "market" with recourse to some social and legal guarantees.

Onnig Isbenjian's Nansen passport and its visa stamps (figure 6.2) tell his story as a refugee. It confirms that Armenians from the Ottoman Empire could make a successful transition to Western Europe and beyond, where they often, but not always, managed to become naturalized citizens. Born in Izmir in 1907, Isbenjian had a passport issued by Britain and he used it to travel to Belgium and Germany, which faced severe labor shortages after the war. He used a second document to travel to Great Britain and then eventually to Manhattan, where he attended Columbia University. He died in 1988. Nevertheless, as Michael Barnett concludes of the inherent weakness of this Nansen passport and the work of the High Commission, "It was wholly dependent on states to carry out its recommendations; when states did not want to cooperate, little happened."[24]

Authority issuing certificate... Home Office.
Indication de l'autorité qui délivre le certificat.

Place of issue of certificate... London.
Lieu où l'on délivre le certificat

CERTIFICATE OF IDENTITY.
CERTIFICAT D'IDENTITE.

Valid until 7ᵗʰ February 1928.
Valable jusqu'

The present certificate is not valid for return to the country which issued it without special provision to that effect contained in it. It will cease to be valid if the Bearer enters Turkish territory.

Le présent certificat n'est pas valable pour le retour dans le pays qui l'a délivré sans une mention spéciale inscrite sur le présent document. Il cessera d'être valable si le porteur pénètre, à un moment quelconque, en Turquie.

Surname... ISBENDJIAN.
Nom de famille.

Christian Names... Onnig
Prénoms.

Date of Birth... 15ᵗʰ September 1907.
Date de naissance.

Place of birth... Smyrna
Lieu de naissance.

Surname of Father... Isbendjian
Nom de famille du père.

Surname of Mother... Maronian
Nom de famille de la mère.

Person of Armenian origin not having acquired another nationality.
D'origine arménienne n'ayant acquis aucune autre nationalité.

Occupation... Nil
Profession.

Former residence in Turkey... Smyrna
Ancien domicile en Turquie.

Present residence... 27 Priory Road London
Résidence actuelle. N.W.

The undersigned certifies that the photograph and signature hereon are those of the bearer of the present document.

Le soussigné certifie que la photographie et la signature apposées ci-contre sont bien celles du porteur du présent document.

Signature of the issuing authority,
Signature de l'autorité,

H.M. CHIEF INSPECTOR,
ALIENS BRANCH,
HOME OFFICE,
LONDON, S.W.1.

This Certificate is issued in conformity with the plan submitted by Dr. Nansen, High Commissioner for Refugees, on May 31st, 1924, for the approval of interested Governments.

Ce certificat est délivré conformément au projet soumis le 31 Mai, 1924, par le Dr. Nansen, Haut-Commissaire pour les Réfugiés, à la Société des Nations, à l'approbation des gouvernements intéressés.

Signature of Holder,
Signature du titulaire,

DESCRIPTION.
SIGNALEMENT.

Age... 18.
Age

Hair... Black
Cheveux

Eyes... Brown
Yeux

Face... Oval
Visage

Nose... Small
Nez

Special peculiarities...
Signes particuliers.

Remarks
Observations

This Certificate is available for holder's return to the United Kingdom during its validity. Subject to visa —

9764

FIGURE 6.2. Interior of Onnig Isbendjian's Nansen passport, issued in London in 1928 and used for travel to Belgium and Germany. Note the description of the travel document as "in conformity with the plan submitted by Dr. Nansen, High Commissioner for Refugees" in the lower right quadrant of the first image. Courtesy of the Zohrab Information Center Digital Collection, New York.

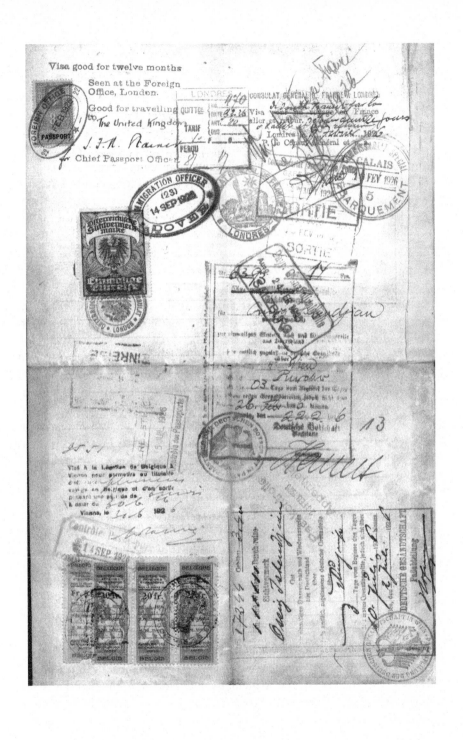

The humanitarian practice of the Nansen passport, and the level of the League's commitment to Armenians in particular, brings into stark relief the limited reach of the interwar refugee regime. Efforts to expand its coverage to other stateless refugees, including Jewish refugees in Romania and Roma and Hungarians scattered throughout Europe, were generally opposed and failed. Before 1938 the only group to receive recognition similar to the Armenians and Russians were Assyrian and Chaldean refugees in Syria and Iraq. Other European states with groups considered for this kind of protection made the argument that those groups had not been legally denationalized, despite their inability to benefit equally from citizenship in the states in which they resided. This was, of course, also a result of the ethnicity and location of the European refugees.

From the perspective of colonial mandate authorities in Syria and Lebanon, it was easier, in this regard, to make room for non-Muslim, non-Arab refugees as a way to alter demographic realities in favor of their style of rule. In the Levant, the Nansen passport became less relevant as Syrian and Lebanese citizenship was extended to Armenian residents in 1928, whereupon Armenian men voted in that year's constituent elections. Since the Nansen passport was generally not extended to new groups of refugees, the Nansen Office for Refugees turned its attention to refugee development schemes, microcredit, and educational programs. Nansen passports continued to be used in Europe through the Second World War.

As much as Nansen had hoped to restore dignity to refugees through the League's policies, the passports themselves bear witness to the moral and ethical vacuity (even uselessness) of the interwar refugee regime. This was not an intervention on behalf of political grievance or on the basis of justice claims. The Nansen passport made no provision for the refugees to have any ability to act politically in any arena. It provided states with a reservoir of controllable workers deprived of any ability to claim political agency or civil rights; thus the refugees could expect no legal protection from their host countries, and the host countries had no binding obligations to them of any kind.

Moreover, the use of this humanitarian-bureaucratic tool relieved countries like Turkey of their responsibility to their own citizens-made-refugees. In the case of the Armenians, like Isbenjian, the Nansen passports they received were valid for much of the world with the exception of their own homeland. As his passport explains: "The present certificate is not valid for return to the country which issued it without special provision to that effect contained in it. It will cease to be valid if the

Bearer enters Turkish territory." Thus the Nansen passport constituted an early international juridical notice of the permanence of the refugee's exile. In this sense the interwar humanitarian regime assisted the Republic of Turkey in its desire to complete the process of genocide begun by its Ottoman state predecessor.

"FINAL SETTLEMENT"

The largest portion of Armenian Genocide refugees was concentrated in and near the major cities of the Arab Eastern Mediterranean, Aleppo and Beirut in particular. As the discussion of the Nansen passports indicates, by the mid-1920s it had become clear that returning home to Anatolia was no longer an option for most Armenian refugees. Immigration to Soviet Armenia had some appeal and was implemented on a limited scale; the League's Nansen Office explored developing, in cooperation with the Soviet government, even larger-scale programs aimed at transforming it into the Armenian national home. However, the bulk of survivors in the Middle East preferred to either stay or emigrate in search of better economic opportunities in Western Europe and North and South America.

As if to emphasize the fact that the problem of humanity represented by former Ottoman-citizen Armenians was no longer a problem of states, in late 1927 Nansen formed a committee of nongovernmental organization representatives to ameliorate the refugee problem in French mandate Syria and Lebanon. This committee included delegates of French, Belgian, Italian, and British "Phil-Armenian" organizations, as well as representatives of Near East Relief and the Red Cross. Two Armenians were appointed to the commission: M. Leon Pachalian of the "Armenian Organizations" and M. A. Hacobian of the "British Armenian Organizations."[25] Pachalian was a protégé of Boghos Nubar Pasha, of the Armenian General Benevolent Organization, which had emerged as the primary Armenian diasporic voice at the League. He would continue to represent Armenian interests through the early 1930s and the negotiation of the 1933 international refugee treaty.[26]

The French mandate was an invention of the League of Nations. However, the establishment of the French mandate did not anticipate the massive flow of Armenian refugees to the states of the Levant. As the relationship between the League of Nations and the French mandate evolved, the treatment of Armenians became increasingly important. This is apparent in the fact that the League closely monitored the way mandate authorities implemented its Armenian policies, and in the fact that France used the treatment of the Armenians to demonstrate to the League and its own public its commitment to colonial-humanitarian responsibilities. In internal discussions preserved in the French archives, however, it is evident that French colonial officials increasingly came to view the Armenian refugee population in Syria and Lebanon as a community that was vulnerable to political exploitation, due to its dependent and precarious status, and thus that it could be instrumentalized as a useful adjunct to colonial rule. The basic organizing principle of French politics in Syria was the identification of a cross-confessional constituency within urban society—Muslim, Christian, and Jewish—that was unwilling, for various and distinct reasons, to support Arab nationalist claims made by country's traditional Sunni elite.[27] The Armenians fit neatly into that construct, and in the electoral politics of the 1920s and early 1930s they were reliably antinationalist in their voting behavior.[28]

This process of alignment was shaped also by the League and its concerns that the Armenians be settled in a way that prevented their full assimilation with the Arab population.[29] In many ways, this international sanction of cultural heterogeneity was among the few remaining residues of the League's original project for the repair and preservation of the Armenian nation. In part, "separateness" was accomplished through the establishment of agricultural installations along the Turkish border and in the province of Alexandretta.[30] But by far the most ambitious scheme was the transformation of entire refugee camps on the outskirts of Beirut and Aleppo into modern neighborhoods and the making of Armenian refugees into a respectable urban middle class. As French high commissioner Henri Ponsot (1877–1963) explained in 1936,

> One must lend support to the real distress, which this situation [the status of refugees] creates. This is what has been done in Syria and Lebanon. This has been brought under control in material terms through loans of money, and in moral terms by a human welcome which has allowed them [the refugees] to acquire citizenship in the country which has opened its doors to them. It is necessary to help the refugees primarily to establish them permanently. This is what the goal is. *With the Armenians, what one fears is that as soon as they have a little savings, they will wish to go elsewhere.* This must be avoided, and to avoid it we must make of them small-property owners, of a house, of land or of a field. This task is underway: what has been done in the Levant towards this goal *does honor to the League of Nations.*[31]

As described in the Nansen Commission reports from the era, the plan's implementation included purchasing land; constructing homes, the ownership of which was transferred to the refugees; employing refugees in government jobs and professional apprenticeships; and providing small-business and agricultural loans. Armenian organizations, Near East Relief, and other aid organizations also participated through League coordination. The settlement project, like other aspects of Nansen's work, depended on settled refugees paying back initial capital outlays to expand the projects.

The first major project took place in the northern suburbs of Beirut, where a refugee camp had taken shape along the Beirut River. The plan was to house 2,500 urban refugees and to purchase additional land for an additional 3,500 agricultural refugees. As these suburbs took shape, the 1936 Nansen Office report to the League acknowledged that these new neighborhoods had transformed "Aleppo and Beyrouth from Oriental into modern cities."[32] By the end of the first stage in the process of settlement (1936) in Aleppo, 2,061 new homes had been built, housing some 3,000 families, or over 15,000 people. The homes were semidetached or attached, and they had plumbing and electricity when this was still relatively rare in the rest of the city.[33] In addition, new churches and schools were built or older structures remodeled for new purposes, including the building that would become the Karen Jeppe Jemaran mentioned at the beginning of this chapter. The Nansen Office opened welfare bureaus throughout the neighborhoods. The visitor to contemporary Aleppo is still struck by the form of suburban Armenian neighborhoods like Midan, which the Armenians call Nor Giwgh, "New Town." The district's wide avenues and straight streets, the ubiquitous use of Armenian signs, and the sounds of Turkish and Armenian instead of Arabic mark it as a unique space and furnish evidence of the communal survival of a distinct Armenian community in Syria.

Nonetheless, the protection and promotion of a distinct Armenian community during the French mandate had the intended effect of creating a section of the population that, as noted above, would support French rule and oppose Arab nationalist aspirations; of course, this policy had the added consequence of creating the Armenians as a subject population who were seen by the majority—and saw themselves—as not-quite-Syrians.

THE "IMPOSSIBILITY OF A RADICAL SOLUTION"

The popular antipathy toward Armenian refugees and their integration into post-Ottoman Lebanon and Syria was tremendous. At the time of the 1928 elections, for example, handbills were posted on the walls of Aleppo decrying the French mandate authorities; for, "not satisfied with these acts of oppression, they [the French] have recently introduced unto our land 100,000 Armenian refugees, of whom many have been raised to a high rank. . . . All our commerce and finance have gone to these usurpers."³⁴ Massive Armenian settlements of the kind implemented by the League had been possible only because of French control of Syria. Had the Syrian and Lebanese nationalist elite that eventually replaced the French been ruling the country, it is unlikely that such a blanket extension of citizenship to Armenians and their cultural encapsulation would have taken place—certainly not under the terms negotiated by the League and France. The way Palestinian refugees were (and were not) integrated into the political structures of Syria and Lebanon after 1948—when citizenship was accorded to some, but denied to most—gives some sense of what the postgenocide Armenian refugees might have faced.³⁵

Where the League's unique humanitarian approach to the problem of Armenian communal survival existed in the political space made available by interwar colonialism, the larger question of what to do about refugees in sovereign states and states emerging from colonial mandates began to push the entire concept of the refugee into unknown territory. The Armenian refugee experience with "final installation" had been suggestive of what the High Commission for Refugees called the "radical solution" of the naturalization of refugees in the states where they were resident. Nevertheless, by 1929, the commission

> recognized that it would be impossible for the various countries in which the refugees are located to proceed to a mass naturalization of those refugees. It would be even less possible, as a means of resolving the problem, to consider the possibility of refugees being faced with the alternative of either obtaining the naturalization in the country in which they are located or of returning to their country of origin. On the one hand, naturalization is a privilege which cannot be granted without distinction to every person who requests it and, on the other hand, respect for individual liberty excludes the exertion of pressure on foreigners, even those without nationality, in order to oblige them to apply for naturalization.³⁶

The commission's conclusions are noteworthy inasmuch as they appear to juxtapose an individual right to refuse to seek naturalization with an option that was not, in fact, afforded to the Armenians in Syria and Lebanon. It also confirmed the centrality of the state to the process. Later in the same document, the commission recognized those states that had regularized naturalization mechanisms for refugees, indicating the beginnings of some kind of international norm.

This rejection of the "radical solution" was taking shape against the growing economic anxieties of the late 1920s, the rise of anti-Semitic politics in European successor states, and forms of nationalism that forced the League to view refugees as a problem of international security and not just as the beneficiaries of its humanitarianism. In the face of reduced options for refugees, the 1929 report insisted on the desirability of moving refugees en masse to South America.[37] The limited success of the "final settlement" of the Armenians was not reproduced in the analogous efforts made by the League to address the suffering of the Assyrian refugees of independent Iraq. Recognizing the differences in context, the Assyrians of Iraq were still a postgenocide refugee community that had been instrumentalized by European colonialism and faced terrible violence and discrimination by a nationalist postcolonial state.

The creation of an independent Armenian state had been a significant cause for governments and the general public that created the League of Nations, and Armenians had been constructed in the humanitarian imagination of many Western Europeans as perhaps the definitive "deserving" oppressed people in the early history of the League. However, the facts on the ground in the Middle East forestalled the creation of an Armenian nation-state in the homeland of the Armenians. Genocide, denationalization, and expulsion changed the demographic reality in Anatolia to the point that in the interwar period such a home was only aspirational, and while it may have made some sense legally or even morally, it had no real chance of success. This reality challenged the League's self-appointed role of setting the world aright in the wake of the war. It also created a situation in which the implementation of a system of international laws and global norms were dependent on the League achieving a kind of absolute moral credibility.

The absence of a state through which to act on behalf of the Armenians led the League to vest its efforts for Armenian communal survival in modern humanitarianism. In the process it expanded the scope and reach of humanitarianism itself. The new practices employed to care for the Armenians, including programs for rehabilitation, travel documentation, and resettlement, defined the very nature of humanitarianism in this era. Equally emblematic of this moment was the manner in which the humanitarian imagination incorporated dominant beliefs about nation and ethnicity—often couched in racist terms—into the characterization of suffering. Recognizing the extent to which nationalism, ethnocentrism, and race thinking shaped the definition of suffering and the humanitarian response indicates the difficulty of reconciling interwar humanitarianism's emphasis on notions of shared humanity and universalism with the reality of its implementation. As aspects of this form of humanitarian practice have persisted into the postwar era, understanding these links and how they have and have not been challenged sits at the center of any attempt to write the history of modern humanitarianism. A fundamental question to pose of this history is when, or even whether, modern humanitarianism emerged from the paradigmatic shadows of nation and race.

By the same token, interwar humanitarianism failed to challenged the dominance of states' rights and their sovereignty, as exemplified by the Nansen passport regime; the basic forms of oppression and unequal power relations inherent to late colonialism, as in the case of the rescue movement and the settling of refugees in French mandate Syria and Lebanon; or even the more obviously settler-colonial act of planting entire communities in South America. The connection between humanitarianism and the rhetoric of colonial justification—indeed, the entire edifice of the League of Nations mandate system—suggests that interwar humanitarianism breathed some new life into that increasingly moribund institution. Still, echoes of the relationship among humanitarianism, colonialism, and nationalism clearly persist in the cruel logic inherent to the other Eastern Mediterranean refugee crisis of the first half of the twentieth century. The preservation of post-Holocaust European Jewish identity (among other goals) achieved its success through a colonial project that in turn created the Palestinian diaspora, which has faced multigenerational statelessness. It is no coincidence that the international response to Palestinian dispossession—perhaps only until the 1990s—resembled the interwar humanitarian practices employed on behalf of the Armenians: ad hoc travel identification documents that stopped short of citizenship; the maintenance of separateness through vast urban refugee camps; the political and social vilification of refugees by host societies; and the use of limited emigration to the West of those Palestinians with access to education and capital, while those without often exist at the very margins of the states where they live, and usually without the benefit of full citizenship.

With these observations in mind, how can we explain why the League's humanitarian discourse on the treatment of refugees, women, and minorities seems to come so close at times to asserting the role of individual human rights in the practice of humanitarian assistance?

Especially since, in retrospect, these projects appear to some observers to have laid the groundwork for contemporary elements of modern human rights law and action, particularly for refugees.[38]

The interwar understanding (operative for most of the twentieth century) of why certain categories of people should or should not receive humanitarian assistance often had very little, if anything, to do with the protection or promotion of their human rights per se, and instead usually had more to do with their ethnicity, religion, citizenship, and utility to states and ideologies. In this sense, a too-early integration of questions of human rights into the history of humanitarianism deforms rather than informs our understanding of both concepts. It can also obscure what is most interesting and provocative about modern humanitarianism, in particular what its history—when examined without being instrumentalized for the history of human rights—can reveal about the early twentieth-century understanding of concepts like shared humanity (and inhumanity); the construction of difference across the colonial divide; and the problem of empathy in a world in which media, emigration, colonialism, and commerce had transformed the very roots of those concepts.

Still, by the late 1930s, ideas about universal human rights and humanitarianism were being floated by League-affiliated organizations, including André Mandelstam's own Institut de Droit International, where he served as rapporteur for the protection of the rights of man and citizen and of minorities. Historian Daniel Whelan, for example, argues that Mandelstam's work at the Institut contributed to the conceptual framework for the American contribution to the Universal Declaration of Human Rights. Moreover, Mandelstam clearly identified a series of minimum rights—life, liberty, and, later, conscience—to which a citizen of a state is entitled from that state, or perhaps more accurately that the state cannot interfere with. In the years before the outbreak of the Second World War, Mandelstam even suggested that if states failed to protect these rights they risked military "humanitarian intervention."[39]

All this calls into question how the "rights talk" that emerged at the edges of League discourse around humanitarianism subsequently moved to the center of the formulation of human rights instruments and treaties at the United Nations. Perhaps the element of interwar humanitarianism most relevant to this question is the evolving definition of the "refugee." But what the discussion of the Nansen passport confirms is that interwar refugee assistance, in theory and practice, exhibits a substantial difference from the contemporary refugee regime. In my thinking, the critical turn in this discussion is found in the move away from identifying collective denationalized populations as refugees eligible for assistance, and toward conceptualizing the refugee as an individual victim of intolerance, tyranny, or oppression, whose circumstance are made more miserable because of war, revolution, or conflict. A poignant example of this shift is seen in Hannah Arendt's brief 1943 essay "We Refugees," in which she laments the status of the individual refugee as a *human being* in the face of systems and ideologies that can no longer (or were never intended to) protect them. As this line of argument expanded in Arendt's work, it would form the basis of her concept of the "right to have rights." Tellingly, in her case—though she was stripped of her German citizenship in 1937—she would not have qualified as a refugee under any established refugee convention at the time of her humanitarian rescue from France to America by the US diplomat Hiram Bingham and the journalist Varian Fry, a rescue that took place outside of any international legal framework.

Clearly, it is possible to find individuals and groups within the working environment of the field of humanitarianism who were engaged in forms of struggle, political and otherwise, on behalf of universalizing individual rights and limiting the sovereignty of states. It is precisely this struggle on the part of individuals within and around the League of Nations that sheds light on the evolving frustration many had with the scope of interwar humanitarianism, the multifaceted failures of the limited refugee regime, and the collapse of the haphazard system of group rights that emphasized membership in national communities. Human rights as they emerged at the time of the writing of the Universal Declaration in the 1940s were in part a response to those failures. These basic questions about the origins of human rights discourse and policy during the Second World War—and even before, in the late 1930s—should be seen as a starting point for the contemporary study of human rights history.

Finally, the humanitarian work of the League of Nations did play an ambiguous and ambivalent, though critical, role in the interwar survival of Armenians and an Armenian community. Those programs transformed the lives of hundreds of thousands of individual Armenians, enabling some to exert limited agency over their own futures. Like the memory of betrayal evoked by the map of Wilsonian Armenia, for many Armenians the relics of the League's work on their behalf—rescue homes, Nansen passports, and the refugee neighborhoods—are important milestones in their own and their families' stories of survival.

CHAPTER 7

Modern Humanitarianism's Troubled Legacies, 1927–1948

ISTANBUL: MAY 16, 1927

Barclay Acheson, the patrician executive secretary of Near East Relief (NER) and later of its institutional successor, the Near East Foundation (NEF), traveled to the Eastern Mediterranean and convened a conference on the campus of the American Robert College (now Boğaziçi Üniversitesi) that would inexorably alter the American humanitarian presence in the Middle East. A typed transcription of Acheson's diary from that summer remains in the archives of NER. In it he details visits and meetings, as well as games of golf and souvenir buying in Istanbul's grand bazaar. He had traveled to the region at a moment when the philanthropic coalition that had first come together during the "Year of the Locust" (1914) to support relief work in the Middle East was crumbling rapidly. Nonetheless, his presence in the region marked a critical juncture in the broader history of modern humanitarianism, when a substantive transformation of the work and meaning of relief—the movement to professional development and technical assistance in particular—and the relationship of humanitarianism to Middle Eastern states and societies was set in motion. This period also marks perhaps not quite an end, but a resounding caesura, in the possible inclusion of rights-based—or social justice—elements in the practice of humanitarianism.

The coalition's collapse had its origins in the international political realities detailed in the previous chapter: the Armenian state imagined in the postwar treaties vanished; the Greco-Turkish and Anatolian civil wars led to the expulsion from their homelands of the refugee communities that the organization was serving; the newly established Soviet Union grew hostile to the presence of Western aid workers in the Caucasus; the Arab Eastern Mediterranean fell under British and French colonialism; and the United States absented itself from humanitarian opportunities embodied by participation with the League of Nations. And there were also more mundane reasons for this collapse, including donor fatigue, poor leadership, and the transformation of the very *problem of humanity* that had so engaged the American humanitarian imagination. This transformation occurred as the annihilation of the non-Muslim communities of Anatolia brought an end to the religious conflict that had formed a foundational appeal to Christian solidarity, if not an end to intra-Muslim violence itself; likewise, orphans aged into adults—with different but far less sentiment-evoking problems—and refugees settled and integrated into their new communities, thus disappearing as a discrete and needy mass. The acute phase of need—the humanitarian emergency—had passed, and with it the opportunity to impose the preferred solution of something akin to an American humanitarian empire, the desideratum that had been attractive to many of the early proponents of relief in the "Near East."

By the mid-1920s, NER's primary institutional sponsor, the Rockefeller Foundation (RF), had grown increasingly wary of supporting the organization, especially as NER's leadership under Barclay Acheson's predecessor, Charles Vickrey (1876–1966), seemed more concerned about preserving NER as an institution, regardless of actual and demonstrable need in the field and in the face of a marked decline in popular support for the organization. At the center of the effort to preserve NER was the creation of the Golden Rule Sunday project. For Vickrey, the golden rule—an ethic of responsibility derived from a statement attributed to Jesus of Nazareth (Luke 6:31, "And as ye would that men should do to you, do ye also to them likewise")—was to serve as the basis for a broad, intersectarian American renewal of support for the children of the Near East. On Golden Rule Sunday, planned for a Sunday between American Thanksgiving and Christmas, families were encouraged to eat a simple meal—approximating, they were told, what an orphan in the organization's care might consume—and give the difference between the cost of that dinner and what they would have spent on a traditional Sunday dinner to NER.

The effort gained a degree of support from elite American political and philanthropic circles, including the US president at the time, Calvin

Coolidge. By 1926 the Golden Rule Sunday had become a minor international success, with state legislatures proclaiming the holiday and celebrities pledging to participate. It was to the mid-1920s what USA for Africa ("We Are the World") was to the mid-1980s or the much-maligned Invisible Children campaign has been in the 2010s. Building on the project's success, in 1926 Vickrey published a 149-page handbook explaining how to mount the event. The book described the precepts of the Golden Rule project; provided examples of successful Golden Rule teas and luncheons, including photographs of participants from around the United States and Western Europe; included possible scripts for use on the radio; and suggested topics for newspaper editorials and sermons. Vickrey was borrowing from the playbook he and his colleagues had used to great effect during and after the war to bring the story of humanitarian need into American homes, churches, and civil society. For him, however, the Golden Rule project was much more than just a fundraising mechanism; it was also a nonideological utopian project that would help end war and, in the words of the handbook:

> A PROTECTION AGAINST INDUSTRIAL DISTURBANCES SOCIAL REVOLUTION AND ANARCHY . . . One of the best forms of insurance against the devastation and chaos that follows revolution is a reasonable observance of the Golden Rule under our present laws and orderly government. The golden rule is one of the best formulas whereby we may attain and maintain mutually helpful constructive relationships between capital and labor and other problems in our social, industrial, national, and international relationships.[1]

The embrace of the golden rule was a demonstration of American character and critical to the moral underpinnings of national prosperity: "No American can appreciate the incredible wealth of our nation and the priceless heritage of American citizenship until he has mingled with the poverty of other lands. Luxurious living and self-indulgence may be as injurious to the prosperous as undernourishment and starvation are to the less fortunate."[2] The handbook includes a brief section on the work of NER, primarily through its orphanages, but also on its development of small industries for older orphans and those who had aged out of custodial care. The most prominent of these projects was a carpet-weaving workshop in Ghazir, Lebanon, where orphan girls produced an ornate woolen carpet that was presented to Coolidge that year, with much fanfare, as the "Golden Rule Rug" (figure 7.1).

Ultimately, Vickrey imagined a Golden Rule global philanthropic mega-humanitarian organization built on the foundation of NER.

FIGURE 7.1. Charles Vickrey (on far left) presenting
President Calvin Coolidge with the orphan-made "Golden
Rule Rug" at the White House, December 1924. Source:
LC-F8- 38480, Library of Congress Prints and Photographs
Division, Washington, DC.

Clearly, in his hands, the problem of humanity that had stood at the
center of NER's initial Eastern Mediterranean–focused work had
become incidental to what seems, in retrospect, to be a grandiose, ill-
conceived, and unfocused (or, viewed less generously, cruelly delusional)
fantasy. Writing in his diary, Acheson noted in "an honest judgment . . .
the Golden Rule plans were ineffective, expensive and designed ultimately to absorb Near East Relief."[3] Vickrey, he wrote, used "hazing
and coercion . . . to compel cooperation with his plans."[4] In the end, the
project not only seemed out of touch with the professionalism exhibited
in the field (and demanded by institutional donors like RF and the Commonwealth Fund) and by the postwar educational program of American colleges and high schools in the region, but also reinforced the idea
of an infantilized and dependent population of Eastern Mediterranean
peoples. Vickrey was forced out of NER in late 1926, but he remained
at the head of a separately incorporated Golden Rule organization.

Acheson had gone to the Eastern Mediterranean partly to repair the
damage done to the organization's reputation by Vickrey. He had also
gone with an eye to shutting down parts of its operations by figuring out
how to link existing NER orphan and refugee programs with League of
Nations Nansen Commission projects—in particular its microlending—

and interfacing his organization with the French colonial administration of Lebanon and Syria, which was broadly suspicious of American philanthropy.

At the May 1927 Robert College conference, Acheson met with NER field administrators; representatives from affiliated organizations, including the Istanbul-based YMCA and YWCA; the American Missionary Board; and various American educational institutions, most notably Bayard Dodge, at the time the new president of the American University of Beirut. None of the members of the conference—in either a voting or an observing capacity—was Armenian or another object of humanitarianism. It soon became clear that a wide gulf existed between those who wanted NER to persist and those, particularly Bayard Dodge, who believed both that the institution's original purpose no longer existed and that its continuing presences in the region was detrimental to the efforts of the American University and other higher educational institutions.

Writing of his sense of the conference, and presenting a pithy analysis of prevailing American missionary and educational interests arrayed against NER, Acheson observed:

> My own feeling is that the mission board program of saving the heathen is out of date and that the mission boards would gladly abandon that conception if their constituency at home were prepared for the advance, but they are bound by their history and traditions. De luxe education for rich men's sons is also on the wane, but the colleges are bound to a continuation of this policy by their traditions, endowments, and of the personnel on the field.[5]

However, during the conference, an idea for a different humanitarian reason for NER's continued presence emerged around non-elite education. Acheson continued: "The education of the masses is just entering upon an era of popularity. . . . There is much to be said in favor of a people's foundation that will utilize all existing machinery of the foreign field, permitting each to use its own funds for the program that it has already."[6] Non-elite education—as seen, for example, in the biography of Asdghig Avakian, who had been recruited as a nursing student from an NER refugee orphanage—had been an elemental feature of NER's work, though not as important as feeding programs or its broader effort to restore Armenians in both a communal and social sense.

Following a survey mission that culminated in the humanitarian report *The Near East and American Philanthropy: A Survey, Conducted under the Guidance of the General Committee of the Near East Survey* (1929), the remaining trustees of NER incorporated the Near

East Foundation (1930).[7] The most critical element of the report was its declaration that the humanitarian *emergency* that had necessitated the form and content of the NER's work in the region was no longer present. While embracing dominant interwar social science ideas about race, it details specific regional problems according to the new political geography of the Eastern Mediterranean. The region is divided by states and ethnicities (races), with continued attention to refugees, but primarily as those refugees were a threat to social stability. The authors of the report encouraged NER to transition to mass education and technical assistance and to work in a more collaborative way with emerging public health and education bureaucracies. "The solution to the problem is mass education," the authors concluded, which is "carried to the people in their fields and in the workshops. It must be an education vital to their lives as tillers or craftsmen. . . . It should adapt to local needs all the methods of mass education which western nations have found useful. . . . Its aims should be the raising of the submerged millions to a more productive and more healthful plane of life, without which its ultimate aim, character-building cannot be achieved."[8] The foundation's transition was also accompanied by a new statement of purpose and leadership—a demand of the Istanbul conference. Bereft now of most of the missionaries who had started NER, the organization formed a new board that included the leading American educational sociologist of the interwar period, Dr. Thomas Jesse Jones. Jones, often credited as the innovator of social science education—as opposed to history—in American public education, was the educational director of the Phelps-Stokes Fund. The fund was supported by major American corporations and sought to build capacity in African American education, while opposing integration or other social transformations that might endanger existing racial hierarchies. Prior to working with NER, many of Jones's educational theories—which were built around the idea of the political and intellectual superiority of the "white race"—had also been exported to parts of Africa, in particular South Africa.[9] His influence permeated the work of the new Near East Foundation as it developed programs for mass education, in the way it saw education as a way to raise the quality of life, but not necessarily to engender political empowerment or social change. Much of the form and content of the NEF's program echoes the recommendations contained in Jones's books, *Negro Education: A Study of the Private and Higher Schools for Colored People in the United States* (1917) and *Education in Africa* (1922), both of which endorse a form of mass education that would not challenge the political and social control of whites in the southern United States, or of European colonial rulers in sub-Saharan Africa. In contrasting the proposed work of NEF with that of the American universities in the region, the report observes:

> Such students [of rural origin] as come to the universities and schools from interior villages seldom return to their homes to bring back the benefits which they as individuals have secured. There is little or nothing to call them back. By their very training, they are qualified for a fuller life and disqualified for the narrow existence of the small communities. Nor are all classes in the urban centers reached, for the students in schools and colleges are drawn very largely from what is usually called the upper middle class, or what the socialist calls the bourgeoisie. The need is for boys and girls with the kind of practical education that will equip them for leadership in the small villages in which the vast bulk of the population of the Near East lives, not the kind of education that will cause them to turn their backs upon the people from whom they came.[10]

As in Africa or the American South, education would not serve as an engine for class mobility or the growth of cities, but rather for a benign social stagnation and immobility, albeit in a way that held real promise to benefit the quality of life of the rural poor and urban underclasses.

Despite the sweeping changes in leadership, Cleveland E. Dodge (again, Bayard Dodge's father) remained the president of the foundation. Its new purpose, in the words of its prospectus, *Near East Foundation: A Twentieth Century Concept of Practical Philanthropy,* was transmitting "America's health, agriculture, child and community welfare, and leadership training techniques to the underprivileged masses of the Near East, without political or religious propaganda, but wholly in the spirit of human kindness and with the full cooperation of the peoples themselves."[11] In this new formulation, the "spiritual values of Near East Relief" would be maintained, while introducing and supporting "only projects which ultimately can be carried on by native leadership and resources, and which will stimulate similar indigenous activities." Women and children would still be central, but the projects and programs were conditioned on "the approval and cooperation of local leaders through local agencies and organizations."[12]

The problem of humanity to be addressed by NEF was no longer suffering caused by war and genocide—except to the extent that war refugees were still a focus of the organization's activities—but rather what was elaborated in the humanitarian imagination as systemic "Near Eastern" social and health problems. According to the report, NEF would "work with the peoples of the Near East to discover and remove the causes of their poverty, disease and retarded development . . . and [to] alleviate conditions arising from ignorance, famine, pestilence and war."[13] The reworking of the organization's self-imposed mandate was a response to criticisms by Bayard Dodge and others, who had been deeply troubled not only by the anti-Muslim and anti-Turkish sentiment that permeated NER's fundraising publicity but also by how deeply the organization had promoted the relief of Armenian Genocide survivors as a political act—one that might not have met the new standard of government consent and cooperation with local leaders. Indeed, one of the key outcomes of the 1927 conference at Robert College was a rejection of both that kind of publicity and the form of relief work it privileged:

> The saving of lives at times of emergency has often made it necessary to work on an emotional and opportunist basis. Unquestionably, thousands of human lives have been saved from death and demoralization because of the success of urgent publicity. . . . Opportunities to raise money at home must not mould the form of the work on the field, but a program must be thought out to meet the real needs, and money should be raised to carry out the program in a consistent way. People on the field would rather have less money and a statesman like program than large sums for objects that are not carefully thought out. . . . The Conference wishes to emphasize the absolute necessity of avoiding all forms of publicity which will do injustice to any one of the sects or governments with whom they are trying to cooperate.[14]

Moderating the language that was used by NEF to explain and describe the causes of suffering and to build support in the West for its efforts was found ultimately to be incompatible with any kind of political and social accommodation with the dominant Turkish and Arab elite. In many ways, the decision to avoid characterizing the problem of humanity in a way that might prove offensive to a state or majority recalls the initial formulation of neutrality adopted and defined by Clara Barton at the time of the Hamidian massacres. To be "statesmen like," the new organization would be silent and turn away from the forms of witness and activism that had been crucial elements of its original *humanitarian reason*.

The NEF's 1930 statement of purpose is, in many ways, a manifesto for the divorce of what, in contemporary parlance, would be called "rights-based development" from "traditional" humanitarian development practice. What was new about the NEF was its implementation of "minimally invasive" projects that would address human security issues but not engage in any action that might provide opportunities to expand political and social rights—especially not for women or ethnic and religious minorities. The NEF's plank on women and children is almost apologetic in its hesitating call to "create in Near East communities a consciousness of the needs of their neglected childhood and womanhood" and not of the political enfranchisement or social empowerment of actual *women* and *children* themselves.[15]

For Bayard Dodge, the change in NEF's posture toward reform, especially radical reform, positioned institutions like the American University in Beirut (AUB) as a conduit for modernity, but not necessarily for an aggressive American humanitarian exceptionalism—a concept consistent with ideas he had already expressed in the months after the war's end. Rather, NEF's work would challenge neither the European colonial status quo nor the dominance of the post-Ottoman Arab nationalist elite that was opposing it. Bayard Dodge had a sense, even in the 1930s, that the rising tide of Arab nationalism might translate into opposition to the entire American educational presence in the region, were that presence too at odds with the new reality.[16]

An example of the new intention of this policy is seen in the prospectus's discussion of the Antelias training school. Established in 1930, it had once been the site of a massive NER orphanage that had housed Asdghig Avakian, but now it would be used as "a demonstration of western ideals of education for leadership applied to an Eastern background and condition."[17] Alongside a picture of a successful student, Barsum Barsumian, dressed in a suit and tie, the prospectus states that the school at Antelias

> is the only indigenous institution in Syria preparing Armenian boys to teach and preach among their scattered people. Through this school, The Foundation is cooperating with local Armenian religious leaders to preserve the traditions of their race and at the same time, is interpreting to them modern experience in religious education, social welfare and education methods. Modern science and ancient culture are combining to prepare the new generation for a dual task: the re-weaving of the torn social fabric of their race, and the adjustment of Christian peoples to a Syrian and Arabic environment.[18]

The efforts by the NEF to preserve the cultural integrity of the "race," primarily through religious education, while facilitating its integration ("adjustment") to the political and religious hierarchies of the Arab Levant, parallels the efforts by the League of Nations discussed in the previous chapter. This is especially the case in the way the NEF's "Rural Life" program sought to use rural development to assuage problems of dispossession and to defuse ethnic and religious tensions. The program, similar to post–Smith-Lever Act (1914) agricultural extension work in the United States, distributed seeds, exposed farmers to expert knowledge, and introduced modest mechanization. It was employed in Macedonia, where it was thought that it could help ease the transition of Armenian refugees and Greeks transferred from Anatolia, and in Palestine, through a training program at the Kadoorie Agricultural School at Tulkarem (now the Palestine Technical University) intended to counter the "neglect of the Arab peasantry," presumably (and euphemistically) as a result of Zionist development schemes that often led to the expropriation of land held by Palestinian agricultural workers in usufruct. In Syria, the project attempted to solve a "problem [that] is complicated by racial difficulties between the [Armenian] refugees and the native Syrians and Arabs. The bitter struggle for life's necessities breeds interracial antagonisms."[19] At the core of the project in Greater Syria was a demonstration farm established near Zahle in Lebanon's Biqa' Valley, which has evolved in the intervening eighty years into the AUB's Agricultural Research and Education Center. Beyond the use of rural education to ease conflict, NEF's emphasis on improving life in the countryside helped to reinforce the rural–urban political and social divide that defined relationships of power within Eastern Mediterranean society. NEF and its leadership saw improved living conditions outside of cities as crucial to its attempts to stem urbanization—which it considered a threat to the moral underpinnings of society. For the urban elite, keeping peasants in place helped them maintain their hold on power and prevented the formation of an urban mass that might demand political and social change.

Without a doubt, the NEF's reformulation made it a more recognizable nongovernmental development organization than it had been as NER. Still, the way the foundation abandoned elements of its reform agenda indicates how easily humanitarianism can be brought into coherence with the political needs of those in power. As NEF took shape throughout the 1930s, the *problem for humanity*—its humanitarian reason—became in larger part addressing the social problems of existing colonial regimes and later independent governments, but not by seeking to solve the root problems of social and economic inequality, political disenfranchisement, or discrimination.

Looking back at the organization's history from the vantage point of the final year of World War II, James L. Barton, the official historian of both NER and NEF, wrote a valediction for the organization at the expiration of its congressional charter (1944): "Near East Relief Consummated: Near East Foundation carries on."[20] After briefly retelling a quasi-hagiographic history of NER and its transition to NEF ("So passes into history the most extensive private philanthropic venture of all time"), Barton updates us on the experience of NEF into the late 1930s and the period of war, which had taken a terrible toll on the organization's work in Nazi-occupied Greece, in particular. Yet, as postwar planning began, Barton described how NEF's experience with relief and technical assistance had already been incorporated into the work of the US government–based relief programs, such as the National War Fund and the relief arm of the nascent United Nations—the United Nations Relief and Rehabilitation Administration, the first UN humanitarian organization that would be known simply by its initials: UNRRA.[21]

NEF's technical assistance served as a model for the early Cold War–era Point Four Program promoted by US president Harry S. Truman. The purpose of Point Four was to use American-directed and -financed development projects to win "hearts and minds" in the Third World and to prevent, thereby, the spread of Communism and Soviet influence.[22] It was NEF's success working on agricultural programs in Iran under its ruler, Mohamed Reza Shah, that Truman himself identified as a model for his thinking about a US government expansion into the field of humanitarian and technical assistance abroad.[23] Arthur Zimmerman Gardiner, special assistant in the US Department of State's Bureau of Near Eastern, South Asian and African Affairs, writing in the *Middle East Journal* in 1950, placed the Point Four Program firmly into the genealogy of NEF and RF:

> In the past the Arab countries have welcomed and benefitted by technical assistance programs proffered them by such private bodies as the Rockefeller Foundation, the Near East Foundation, and the American colleges in their lands. In the Point Four program, such efforts as these are raised to the level of a national policy and a national program. In the long pages of Arab history it would be difficult to find such an offer, from abroad, of talent and resources which can be devoted to purposes selected by the free will of these nations, devoted to their own national purposes, and administered in such manner as these nations, in full agreement with their friends abroad, may determine.[24]

As Point Four technical assistance adopted the form of NEF's operations, the foundation continued to offer US humanitarian development assistance to monarchical governments—Iraq and Iran—and authoritarian regimes—Turkey and Greece. In the late 1960s John S. Badeau (1903–1995), a former president of both the American University in Cairo and the Near East Foundation, and later the US ambassador to Egypt during the John F. Kennedy administration, defined, and defended, this abstraction from the reform agenda to an apolitical—really, antipolitical—technocratic neutrality as the NEF's residual authority and humanitarian reason in the region: "There is still another factor in the nonpolitical role of the voluntary agency. It can develop a program solely concerned with the needs and opportunities of technical development. The Foundation [NEF] is unhampered by any wider question of the relationship between aid projects and political considerations. . . . It is free to design and support programs simply because they are technically sound and desperately needed, and not because they serve any other purpose."[25]

In retrospect, there is a purposeful naiveté to the assertion made by Badeau, who was a contemporary and colleague of Stanley Kerr and Bayard Dodge. Badeau's explanation is a précis of what the economist William Easterly calls the *technocratic illusion*—the mistaken assessment that "poverty results from a shortage of expertise, whereas poverty is really about a shortage of rights. The emphasis on the problem of expertise makes the problem of rights worse."[26] NEF's own emphasis on working exclusively through states, no matter the degree to which those states abused the rights of their citizens, only at their invitations and only through their bureaucracies, expanded the authority, legitimacy, and power of those states to continue to violate the rights of their citizens in the name of development and in association with the organization.[27] This is especially the case in what the NEF saw as its crowning achievement in the post–World War II period—namely, its outsized role in the evolution of the Iranian educational system in general and its agricultural colleges in particular. "The Foundation has consistently maintained a position of disinterest in politics," explained William Fuller, the NEF country director for Iran in the mid-1950s. "Because of its purely private, humanistic character, it has never been involved in furthering vested interests."[28] NEF's "disinterested politics" did not occur in a political vacuum, but were part and parcel of efforts to extend the control of Iran's Mohammad Reza Pahlavi, who had recently been returned to power following a coup assisted by the US Central Intelligence Agency against the democratically elected government of Prime Minister Mohammad Mosaddegh (1953). It strains credulity to believe that NEF technical advisors were unaware of the antidemocratic and authoritarian nature of the regime they were helping or the fact that Americans had been at the center of returning the Shah to power.

Among the most troubling assessments of interwar modern humanitarianism is that what was a fundamentally decent and humane, but deeply paternalistic, act of organized compassion delivered by Americans who had come of age in the Great Depression and who brought into the field advanced understandings of soil science, irrigation, agriculture, and teacher training could become an instrument of Cold War politics and a tool to help preserve antidemocratic governments and brutal dictatorships.

BAGHDAD: AUGUST 26, 1936

There is something unsettlingly familiar in the accounts from Iraq in the late summer of 1933. Newspapers reported that, fresh from putting down an insurgent force of what the newly independent Iraqi state considered recalcitrant Assyrian Christian separatists in the rough and mountainous borderlands adjacent to both Syria and Turkey, the Iraqi army had been greeted as heroes as they paraded on al-Rashid Street in downtown Baghdad. Women poured confetti and streamers from second-floor balconies and crowds of young men chanted nationalist slogans while waving sticks, swords, and daggers from the shade of the arcade that lined both sides of the street; meanwhile, a marching band accompanied the troops with strains of the US Civil War–era tune "Marching through Georgia." One is left wondering if the song was chosen because of lyrics like "Treason fled before us, for resistance was in vain" or just because it is a catchy tune. As those soldiers marched down al-Rashid Street, accounts of massacres, especially in the Assyrian village of Simele, began to surface. These accounts, while denied by the Iraqi state, told a very different story: one in which the army had used the opportunity of a minor uprising to mount a pogrom against civilians with both religious and nationalist overtones.

Many members of the Assyrian population of Simele were originally refugees from Anatolia and the Caucasus Mountain region who had experienced genocide alongside the Armenians in 1915 and fled to Iraq in the wake of World War I. In Iraq they joined an ancient community of Arabic- and Aramaic-speaking Assyrians—a mix of Nestorian and Chaldean Christians. By the 1930s, the refugees were viewed by the post-Ottoman Arab Sunni Muslim political elite as outsiders, and moreover as collaborators with the British, as they often served in British military units. Britain had left Iraq and the Assyrians in 1932. Their colonial protectors gone, the non-Muslim, non-Arab, "foreign" Assyrians were an easy target for ambitious nationalist demagogues or those hoping to assert Iraqi sovereignty in the face of limitations imposed by the League and Britain at the time of independence.

The League and the Kingdom of Iraq had stipulated that the Assyrian refugees would be afforded an opportunity for final settlement along the same lines as the Armenians in neighboring Syria. As understood by the Iraqi state, that meant that the semi-autonomy the Assyrians had enjoyed during the years of the British mandate would no longer apply, and that Assyrian men who had served in units of the colonial military would be disarmed and their weapons surrendered. To enforce that policy, the Iraqi army was sent to the Syrian-Iraqi borderlands, where many Assyrian refugees had settled. Subsequent investigation would show that Kurdish and Arab bedouin irregulars, with the tacit and active support of the Iraqi Army, conducted systematic attacks on several Assyrian villages, engaging in rape; targeted killing of religious and secular leaders, including teachers; and the desecration of schools and churches. Credible estimates place the number of civilian victims of these massacres at three thousand, with another ten thousand made homeless. While the actual intent of the atrocities is unclear—and may have been to exterminate, to discipline, or to pillage—what is clear is that life for many Assyrians in Iraq became intolerable and the process of emigration from Iraq to Syria, Europe, and the Americas accelerated. What is also clear is that the "victory" over the Assyrians made its chief architect, General Bakr Sidqi, very popular, and he used that popularity when, three years later, he mounted the first successful military coup d'état in an Arab country.[29] More critically, the massacres and the official responses in Baghdad and Geneva evidence the formulation of an "official" conclusion that societies like Iraq should and would eventually be homogenized through emigration—forced or otherwise. The plans that the League formulated for the Assyrians fit into the larger emerging principle that the un-mixing of diverse populations was a humanitarian act in and of itself.

Responding to a request by longtime Iraqi prime minister Nuri al-Said to the League that Assyrians who no longer wished to stay Iraq be helped to leave, the League established a special committee on October 16, 1933 (figures 7.2 and 7.3). Its task was nothing less than to investigate the possibility of transferring the Assyrians (estimated at twenty thousand families) out of Iraq to a third country. Already, many

FIGURE 7.2. A League of Nations expert (in pith helmet) speaks with Assyrian men through a translator during a visit to their village prior to transfer, ca. 1937. Source: Enclosure in c.387.m.258.1937.VII, ALON-UNOG. Courtesy of the United Nations.

FIGURE 7.3. The belongings—including several traditional wooden rocking cribs—of Assyrian refugees being loaded by Iraqi soldiers during the transfer of Assyrians to Syria, ca. 1937. Source: Enclosure in c.387.m.258.1937.VII, ALON-UNOG. Courtesy of the United Nations.

198 | Chapter 7

Assyrians—two thousand families—had resettled in Syrian Mesopotamia on the Khabur River, a small tributary of the Euphrates, but the new plans envisioned the wholesale movement of all the Assyrians beyond Iraq's borders to the Western Hemisphere.

Early in 1934, the League dispatched a delegation to Brazil, which had signaled its willingness to accept the Assyrians as settlers in the Parana region. In the plan, it was envisioned that, with international assistance, five hundred Assyrian families per month would settle as farmers on the Brazilian frontier, becoming self-sufficient within a year. In May 1934 the League authorized its representatives to begin final negotiations. While those negotiations seemed to be proceeding apace, anti-Assyrian editorials and screeds began to appear in Brazil's significant Arabic-language press and, owing to the potential cost, the Brazil plan was abandoned. For a short period, the League explored the possibility of settling the Assyrians in the southern portion of British Guiana (now Guyana). Eventually, this plan would be abandoned as well, again due to costs and to the fear that Assyrians would not be able to adapt to the climate.[30]

Thereafter, the League refocused its attention on the refugees who had been evacuated to Syria, providing agricultural resources and helping to establish schools and primary health facilities. Despite these services, in the end Syrian citizenship was opposed by the Arab nationalist elite in Damascus, as Syria was not independent; the settlement was accomplished because real power in Syria was held by the French high commissioner. Seen as a success, this limited transfer would be reproduced by the League again in 1939, when it resettled Armenians from the province of Alexandretta—turned over by the League to Turkey from Syria—to Lebanon.[31] That episode of "soft" ethnic cleansing came at the end of the last of the League's operations in the Eastern Mediterranean and certainly its nadir. Turkey's Mustafa Kemal Atatürk had claimed the Syrian province of Alexandretta, which was inhabited primarily by Alawite Arabs and Armenians, for his state. The French mandate authorities agreed to a League-administered plebiscite that returned a verdict in favor of continued union with Syria. Rejecting the League's results, the Turkish government, threatening force, oversaw a new election with a pro-Turkish outcome. The relative ease with which Turkey was able to invalidate the efforts of the League confirmed how marginal the organization had become on the eve of World War II. The resettlement of the Assyrians, likewise, occurred in that space of the broad collapse of the League's moral authority.

Tellingly, the whole process of transfer was initiated without consulting the Assyrians in any meaningful way (or, for that matter, the indigenous inhabitants of the Parana and Rupununi districts of Brazil and Guyana, respectively). There is no evidence of any attempt to moderate the Iraqi state's position on the Assyrians. Instead, the need to save this population through transfer was presented as a self-evident fact, suggesting that, within humanitarian circles, the impossibility of reconciliation between Assyrians and Iraqis—and perhaps by extension between Muslim majorities and Christian minorities—was not possible; rather, their conflict—evidence to the contrary notwithstanding—was inherent, timeless, and essential. Critically, the program of transferring Iraq's Assyrians was scuttled not because it was found to be unsound, but rather primarily because of a lack of available resources during the Great Depression. There was no theoretical objection raised to it—it appeared to be a reasonable and rational solution to the problem of "minorities." By 1939, discussions similar to those that had occurred between the League and Brazil would be reproduced by various interlocutors on behalf of Eastern European and German Jews.

Population transfer, a euphemism that includes in its definition another euphemism, "ethnic cleansing," is generally considered illegal under international humanitarian law. Nonetheless, "population transfer" was a key component of the practice of humanitarianism in the interwar world. It was one of the implications of Wilsonianism, and not just on the theory and practice of humanitarianism, but also on the emerging diplomatic notion of "collective security": less diversity within the nation-state created a better basis for national development and fewer opportunities for civil strife between subnational groups that might drag the world back into war. Indeed, accounting for its role is a critical element of any attempt to understand humanitarianism's evolution. Part of that effort is trying to unravel the very vocabulary of "population transfer" and divorce it from the diplomatic and Orwellian language in which it is often couched. As the scholarship on humanitarianism and refugees in the interwar Eastern Mediterranean evolves, the need to account for the several episodes during which the *unmixing* of populations occurred or was attempted and generally supported or facilitated by the League of Nations is acute. Critically, the various acts of unmixing were seen as being based on humanitarian reason and necessary for the promotion of peace and stability. It is important to recall that the "removed" were not the perpetrators or the powerful, but rather the victims and the abject.

Humanitarian transfer always benefitted those in power and always rewarded perpetrators for committing atrocity. The pattern as it emerged began with the targeting of a minority for a host of reasons (perceived rebellion or disloyalty, unwillingness to surrender autonomy), often followed by massacres and atrocity. The group in power emerged victorious, gaining prestige and sometimes the property of the victims. The international humanitarian community then removed the victim group with little or no cost and no penalty to the perpetrator. This pattern of humanitarianism—soft ethnic cleansing—remains a possible feature of the humanitarian subject's range of action. Consider the role Dutch peacekeepers played in facilitating the transfer of Bosnian women in the days before the 1995 Srebrenica genocide of the Yugoslav war.

There is an important implication of the larger history of the Assyrian massacres to the history of human rights and international human rights law. The case of the Assyrians had been followed closely by Raphael Lemkin (1901–1959), the Polish jurist who coined the term *genocide* and advocated fiercely for its banning under international law. In the wake of the Simele massacre, during the League of Nations' Conference for the Unification of Penal Law (Madrid, 1933), Lemkin proposed adding to the growing corpus of international law the crimes of "vandalism and barbarity." These new laws would recognize and punish a category of crimes committed against people *as groups* during peacetime, or at least in the absence of a recognized international conflict. "Vandalism" would mean an attack against what would now be termed "cultural heritage"; "barbarity" roughly equates to the contemporary notion of ethnic cleansing and anticipates one of the key components of genocide, primarily mass killing.[32]

Lemkin's proposal reflected his concerns about Europe's Jews in the face of growing attacks on their communities and institutions. Yet it was also based—as Lemkin's unfinished memoir and research notes show—on a more immediate example of the crime he sought to codify and punish that had occurred in the weeks preceding the conference: the pogrom of the Iraqi Assyrian community. Equally, his ideas were derived from his understanding of the causes and origins of the genocide of the Ottoman Armenians seventeen years earlier, and the compound practical *humanitarian failures* to achieve justice on their behalf. As a student in Lwów, Lemkin had followed closely the 1921 trial in Berlin of an Armenian survivor of 1915, Soghomon Tehlirian, for the murder of an Ottoman official generally considered an architect of the

Armenian Genocide, Talaat Pasha; and at the time of his death, Lemkin had assembled a large inventory of primary and secondary materials on the destruction of the Armenian community and the massacre of the Assyrians in anticipation of writing a global history of genocide.[33]

NAHR IBRAHIM, LEBANON: SEPTEMBER 9, 1923

Stanley Kerr had left Marash for Beirut in July 1922. He and his wife, Elsa Reckman (1896–1985), whom he had met and married during his second tour, had been assigned to run NER's boys orphanage at Nahr Ibrahim. In the fall of 1923, most of the boys became sick with malaria—a disease against which they had little natural immunity. Elsa, who was pregnant with their first child, also became sick, and Kerr feared that they would lose both her and the baby. "I nursed her all the time, night and day, and was pretty much worn out myself and then had to return to Nahr Ibrahim to see what the state of affairs was there," he wrote to his family.[34] The epidemic had brought the work of the orphanage to a halt. The teachers worked as nurses, and Kerr was forced to dismiss the artisans who were providing vocational education to the boys. The Abraham River, which gives its name to the orphanage's location, slows to a trickle as it reaches the sea, leaving stagnant pools of fetid water in which the mosquitoes bred. "If the same thing occurs next year we will have to abandon the orphanage," Kerr explained. In the midst of this terrible personal strain, he drew on the reservoir of professionalism that sustained him in Marash and described in the same letter how he would use the expert knowledge of an American sanitary engineer, Walter Ernest Hardenberg (1886–1942), to start an antimosquito campaign, and in particular to import a kind of fish to eat the larvae. Elsa Kerr survived the epidemic, as did most of the orphans. Nevertheless, NER closed the facility and transferred the boys to the massive orphanage at Antelias.

In another letter, a few weeks later, Kerr described the otherwise uneventful birth of their child. He also told of a dream Elsa had in the maternity hospital: "When Elsa was going under the chloroform she dreamed that her baby was in the orphanage in Aleppo, and that she was in [New York]. She had the idea it was going to be put out [of the orphanage], so started for Aleppo by flying, travelling with the speed of a cablegram! On reaching Aleppo she found the baby had been put out of the orphanage!"[35] The anxiety evident in the dream may have been a result of the fact that, just before she had gone into labor, Elsa and her husband had been forced to discharge orphans from the facility due to lack of funds. But the dream was also evidence of the depth of identification these young Americans—both still in their twenties—had with the children and mothers they had cared for, taught, fed, and protected, and whose stories of trauma they had listen to, recorded, and shared.

In the same letter Kerr told his family he had been offered a permanent position at AUB by its president, Bayard Dodge. Both Kerrs remained in Lebanon for much of the remainder of their lives, Stanley as a chair of biochemistry at AUB—a position endowed by the Rockefeller Foundation—and Elsa as a mathematics teacher at the Beirut College for Women, now the Lebanese American University. In the mid-1950s she was appointed dean of women at AUB. It was not uncommon up to the 1990s to encounter American-trained physicians and scientists—even older Israelis who had gone to school at AUB before 1948—who remembered studying with Stanley Kerr.

The Kerrs could not imagine leaving unfixed the problem of humanity they had first encountered together in Marash. This was a problem that evolved with time; it became the central organizing principle for their careers as well as definitive of their *humanity,* and the searing events of 1920, which had been such a failure for the American humanitarian enterprise, still nonetheless formed the basis of their personal and professional commitment to the peoples of the Eastern Mediterranean. Both Kerrs lived long enough to watch as the American humanitarian presence in the region changed from the Progressive idealism of NER's efforts to repair the lives and communities of genocide survivors, complete with the misplaced utopian project of the "New Near East," to the emphasis on technical assistance and advanced secondary education. Surely, those projects improved people's lives, and derived from a more pragmatic understanding of the possible reach of humanitarian action, but most often they put Americans on the wrong side of history as that technical assistance buttressed some of the region's worst human rights offenders. I imagined that the Kerrs watched in great disappointment as American prestige in the region—a prestige that derived in no small part from the kind of work they did as humanitarians, educators, mentors, colleagues, and friends—collapsed in the face of ill-conceived Cold War policies that viewed the Eastern Mediterranean through the lens of a bipolar world and without the nuance and compassion their generation of humanitarians had brought; official American indifference to Palestinian suffering; and cruel ideologies like Baathism and then radical Islamism. The rise of those ideologies and abandonment of principles visited renewed suffering on both subjects and objects of humanitarianism, sometimes exacting the ultimate cost in the process. Modern humanitarianism had locked the Kerrs into a relationship with place and peoples in such a way that they too were exposed to forms of deep suffering. And while it is assumed that the humanitarian subject can go home, as it were, it is remarkable how many choose to stay as they did. Stanley Kerr died in 1975, shortly after completing his memoir of his time in Anatolia, *The Lions of Marash*. Elsa Kerr lived long enough to see her youngest son, the political scientist Malcolm Kerr (1931–1984), who had been born in Beirut, leave the safety of a faculty position at the University of California, Los Angeles, to serve as AUB's president during the turmoil and inhumanity of the last years of the Lebanese Civil War. He would be killed in an act of political violence just a few months after his return to Lebanon in an assassination that targeted him as symbol of the American presence in the Eastern Mediterranean his own parents had helped define and shape over the course of their lifetimes.[36]

Notes

ABBREVIATIONS

ALON-UNOG   Archive of the League of Nations, Geneva, Switzerland

A-AUB   Archive of the American University of Beirut, Beirut, Lebanon

A-NER   Archives of Near East Relief, American University of Beirut, Beirut, Lebanon

CADN-MAE   Centre des archives diplomatiques, Ministère des affairs etrangères, Nantes, France

PRO FO   371 General Correspondences Aleppo Consulate, Public Record Office, Foreign Office, Kew, United Kingdom

RAC   Rockefeller Archive Center, Sleepy Hollow, NY

RAC-NER   Archives of Near East Relief and Near East Foundation, Rockefeller Archive Center, Sleepy Hollow, NY

RAC-RF   Archives of the Rockefeller Foundation, Rockefeller Archive Center, Sleepy Hollow, NY

USNA II   Decimal File 867, Internal Affairs of Turkey, Record Group 59, Records of the Department of State, United States National Archive, Department of State, College Park, MD

1. THE BEGINNINGS OF THE HUMANITARIAN ERA IN THE EASTERN MEDITERRANEAN

1. Stanley Kerr to parents, February 9, 1920, Kerr Family Letters Collection, Stanley Kerr and Elsa Reckman Kerr Letters.

2. In many critical ways, this book is the product of the emergence of a new history of the late Ottoman Empire, including work on the destruction of the Ottoman Armenians. A remarkable transformation in the subfield of late Ottoman history has occurred over the last decade. Much of that change has happened because historians and intellectuals of Turkish origin have brought new archival and primary sources, methods, and ways of thinking to bear on the history of the destruction of the Ottoman Armenian communities of Anatolia during World War I. Salient works in this new history include Fatma Müge Göçek, *The Transformation of Turkey: Redefining State and Society from the Ottoman Empire to the Modern Era* (London: Tauris Academic Studies, 2011) and *Deciphering Denial: Ottoman Past, Turkish Present, and Collective Violence against Armenians, 1789–2009* (Oxford: Oxford University Press, 2014); Taner Akçam, *The Young Turk's Crime against Humanity: The Armenian Genocide and Ethnic Cleansing in the Ottoman Empire* (Princeton: Princeton University Press, 2012); Fuat Dündar, *Crime of Numbers: The Role of Statistics in the Armenian Question (1878–1918)* (New Brunswick: Transaction Publishers, 2010); Ugur Ümit Üngör, *The Making of Modern Turkey: Nation and State in Eastern Anatolia, 1913–1950* (Oxford: Oxford University Press, 2011); and Ugur Ümit Üngör and Mehmet Polatel, *Confiscation and Destruction: The Young Turk Seizure of Armenian Property* (London: Bloomsbury Academic, 2011). This transformation has also been possible because of the achievement of broad historical consensus on the genocide of the Ottoman Armenians—foreclosing the need to argue that it happened and instead using the fact of genocide as a starting point for historical analysis. The best evidence for this consensus is the publication in the *American Historical Review,* generally considered the journal of record for the international community of historians, of several articles and essays on the history of aspects of the Armenian Genocide. These include Eric D. Weitz, "From the Vienna to the Paris System: International Politics and the Entangled Histories of Human Rights, Forced Deportations, and Civilizing Missions," *American Historical Review* 113, no. 5 (2008): 1313–1343; Ronald Grigor Suny, "Truth in Telling: Reconciling Realities in the Genocide of the Ottoman Armenians," *American Historical Review* 114, no. 4 (2009): 930–946; and my article, "The League of Nations' Rescue of Armenian Genocide Survivors and the Making of Modern Humanitarianism, 1920–1927," *American Historical Review* 115, no. 5 (2010): 1315–1339.

3. For example, Michael Barnett, in his *Empire of Humanity: A History of Humanitarianism* (Ithaca: Cornell University Press, 2011) devotes little if any attention to the relief and development operations that took place in the Eastern Mediterranean in the interwar period; beyond that, he also avoids the work of the UN, national government development agencies, and independent aid organizations that worked among the Palestinians displaced in the wake of the creation of the state of Israel.

4. See Jan Herman Burgers, "The Road to San Francisco: The Revival of the Human Rights Idea in the Twentieth Century," *Human Rights Quarterly* 14, no. 4 (1992): 447–477; and Weitz, "From the Vienna to the Paris System."

5. Craig Calhoun, "The Imperative to Reduce Suffering: Charity, Progress and Emergencies in the Field of Humanitarian Action," in *Humanitarianism in*

Question: Politics, Power, Ethics, ed. Michael Barnett and Thomas G. Weiss (Ithaca: Cornell University Press, 2008), 78–79.

6. "Although hardly a new idea in the *fin-de-siecle,* the civilizing mission acquired greater currency in the age of democratic empire; ruling elites in France sought to reconcile themselves and the recently enfranchised masses to intensified overseas conquest by claiming that the newly restored republic, unlike the more conservative European monarchies, would liberate Africans from moral and material want." Alice L. Conklin, "Colonialism and Human Rights, A Contradiction in Terms? The Case of France and West Africa, 1895–1914," *American Historical Review* 103, no. 2 (1998): 420.

7. Gary Bass, *Freedom's Battle: The Origins of Humanitarian Intervention* (New York: Knopf, 2008).

8. Samuel Moyn, "Spectacular Wrongs: Gary Bass's *Freedom's Battle,*" *The Nation,* October 13, 2008, www.thenation.com/doc/20081013/moyn (accessed December 5, 2014).

9. This transition was noted and endorsed at the time. For example, Frank Carlton made the observation that "the opening years of the twentieth century are witnessing the development of a new and powerful humanitarian movement. The economic developments of the preceding quarter of a century furnished the germ. This movement is concerned with social settlements, charity work, educational reform, municipal betterment, civil service reform and socialism." Frank T. Carlton, "Humanitarianism, Past and Present," *International Journal of Ethics* 17, no. 1 (1906): 54.

10. On the evolution of philanthropy, see Merle Curti, "The History of American Philanthropy as a Field of Research," *American Historical Review* 62, no. 2 (1957): 352–363.

The shift to the "scientific" management of humanitarian crises or disasters accompanied the emergence of the social sciences in the second half of the nineteenth century. See Thomas Haskell, *The Emergence of Professional Social Science: The American Social Science Association and the Nineteenth-Century Crisis of Authority* (Baltimore: Johns Hopkins University Press, 2000).

11. Merle Curti, "The Changing Pattern of Certain Humanitarian Organizations," in "Pressure Groups and Propaganda," ed. Harwood L. Childs, special issue, *Annals of the American Academy of Political and Social Science* 179 (May 1935): 59–67.

12. Barnett, *Empire of Humanity,* 39–41.

13. Davide Rodogno, *Against Massacre: Humanitarian Interventions in the Ottoman Empire, 1815–1914* (Princeton: Princeton University Press, 2012), 23.

14. Rodogno writes: "The European powers' nonintervention in favor of the Ottoman Armenians is important, for it reveals that despite the extent and incontrovertible evidence of massacre, atrocity and extermination, the nature of the international system prevented intervention from taking place. The horror that these massacres aroused in 'civilized' Europe was not enough to trigger a humanitarian intervention. . . . Saving strangers, even Christian coreligionists, was an international practice subordinated to the maintenance of peace and the security of Europe" (ibid., 209–210).

15. See Amy Singer, *Constructing Ottoman Beneficence: An Imperial Soup Kitchen in Jerusalem* (Albany: State University of New York Press, 2002) and *Charity in Islamic Societies* (Cambridge: Cambridge University Press, 2008); Mine Ener, *Managing Egypt's Poor and the Politics of Beneficence, 1800–1952* (Princeton: Princeton University Press, 2003); and Nadir Özbek, "The Politics of Welfare: Philanthropy, Volunteerism and Legitimacy in the Ottoman Empire, 1876–1914" (PhD diss., Binghamton University, 2001).

16. See Juan R.I. Cole's discussion of Rifah al-Tahtawi (1801–1873) in "Al-Tahtawi on Poverty and Welfare," in *Poverty and Charity in Middle Eastern Contexts*, ed. Michael Bonner, Mine Ener, and Amy Singer (Albany: State University of New York Press, 2003), 236.

17. Nadir Özbek, "Defining the Public Sphere during the Late Ottoman Empire: War, Mass Mobilization and the Young Turk Regime (1908–18)," *Middle Eastern Studies* 43, no. 5 (2007): 795–809.

18. See Isa Blumi, *Ottoman Refugees, 1878–1939: Migration in a Post-Imperial World* (London: Bloomsbury Academic, 2013); and James H. Meyer, "Immigration, Return, and the Politics of Citizenship: Russian Muslims in the Ottoman Empire, 1860–1914," *International Journal of Middle East Studies* 39, no. 1 (2007): 15–32.

19. Nesim Şeker, "Demographic Engineering in the Late Ottoman Empire and the Armenians," *Middle Eastern Studies* 43, no. 3 (2007): 461–474.

20. See the comparative cases of 1830s America and 1915 Anatolia as discussed by Hans-Lukas Kieser in "Removal of American Indians, Destruction of Ottoman Armenians: American Missionaries and Demographic Engineering," *European Journal of Turkish Studies: Social Sciences on Contemporary Turkey* 7 (2009), http://ejts.revues.org/2873 (accessed January 2, 2015).

21. Bedross Der Matossian, "The Taboo within the Taboo: The Fate of 'Armenian Capital' at the End of the Ottoman Empire," *European Journal of Turkish Studies: Social Sciences on Contemporary Turkey* (2011), http://ejts.revues.org/4411 (accessed January 2, 2015).

22. Ugur Ümit Üngör and Mehmet Polatel document at great length how organized dispossession and the theft of Armenian property accompanied mass killing in *Confiscation and Destruction*.

23. "Coded telegram from the Interior Ministry's General Directorate of Tribal and Immigrant Affairs to the Province of Aleppo, and to the Provincial Districts of Urfa and Marash, February 26, 1916, BOA/DH.ŞFR, no. 61/117, cited in Akçam, *The Young Turks' Crime*, 357.

24. The trope of Western indifference to Muslim suffering figures prominently in the project of Armenian Genocide denial, in part to portray perpetrator communities as victims—an inversion of victims and perpetrators, which is a feature of all genocide denial literatures regardless of origin. For example, in response to an early public discussion of my 2010 *American Historical Review* article, "The League of Nations' Rescue of Armenian Genocide Survivors and the Making of Modern Humanitarianism, 1920–1927," Günay Evinch [Övünç], past president of the Assembly of Turkish American Associations (ATAA) and a Washington, DC–based attorney whose international law clients include the Turkish embassy, attacked my work in the alumni magazine of the University of

California, Davis. In his review, he noted that the article about my work "would have been better titled, 'Humanitarianism for Christians Only'" *UC Davis Magazine* 29, no. 1 (Fall 2011). My reply to Evinch placed the counterfactual, but nonetheless telling, nature of his letter in the context of the Turkish governments' broader policy of denying the Armenian Genocide. As a consequence, Evinch and the ATAA wrote a series of letters to colleagues and administrators on my campus that was interpreted as a threat to bring a lawsuit if I did not retract my statement. That view was supported by the Committee on Academic Freedom of the Middle East Studies Association, which wrote to the ATAA on my behalf: "We are concerned that your letters' specific references to legal action initiated in another case involving the question of what happened to the Armenians of the Ottoman empire during the First World War may have a chilling effect on academic inquiry and discourse about this important historical episode." I did not issue a retraction, and a lawsuit never materialized. See Scott Jashcik, "Refusing to Back Down," *Inside Higher Education*, December 6, 2011, www.insidehighered.com/news/2011/12/06/new-dispute-between-historian-and-turkish-american-group (accessed November 14, 2013).

25. Akçam, *The Young Turks' Crime*, 444.

26. Edward R. Stoerer, "Report of Constantinople Office 1 June 1916–May 1917," RAC-RF, International Projects, 1:100, box 76, folder 719, p. 4.

27. See chapters 2 and 4 in this book.

28. See Giorgio Agamben, *Homo Sacer: Sovereign Power and Bare Life,* trans. Daniel Heller-Roazen (Stanford: Stanford University Press, 1998). "From the perspective of the social group that has cast him out, the homo sacer no longer has any of the customary forms or qualifications of specific lives (bios) in a community. Stripped of them, all that remains is a human creature, a bare life (zoe)." Leland de la Durantaye, *Giorgio Agamben: A Critical Introduction* (Stanford: Stanford University Press, 2009), 207.

29. Stoerer, "Report of Constantinople Office," 4.

30. M. Salbi, *Aleakner ew khleakner: Hay vranak'aghak'in taregirk'ě* [Waves and wrecks: Almanac of the Armenian tent city] (Alexandria: Tpagrut'iwn A. Gasapean, 1919). A fictionalized account of that resistance forms the basis of Franz Werfel's novel *The Forty Days of Musa Dagh* (London: G. Dunlop, 1934).

31. "This will lead us to regard the camp not as a historical fact and an anomaly belonging to the past (even if still verifiable) but in some way as the hidden matrix and *nomos* of the political space in which we are still living." Agamben, *Homo Sacer*, 166. See also Zygmunt Bauman, *Modernity and the Holocaust* (Ithaca: Cornell University Press, 1989).

32. Ussama Makdisi, *Artillery of Heaven: American Missionaries and the Failed Conversion of the Middle East* (Ithaca: Cornell University Press, 2008) and "Reclaiming the Land of the Bible: Missionaries, Secularism, and Evangelical Modernity," *American Historical Review* 102, no. 3 (1997): 680–713; Ellen Fleischmann, "The Impact of American Protestant Missions in Lebanon on the Construction of Female Identity, c. 1860–1950," *Islam and Christian-Muslim Relations* 13, no. 4 (2002): 411–426; "'Our Moslem Sisters': Women of Greater Syria in the Eyes of American Protestant Missionary Women," *Islam*

and *Christian-Muslim Relations* 9, no. 3 (1998): 307–323; Inger Marie Okken-haug, *The Quality of Heroic Living, of High Endeavour and Adventure: Angli-can Mission, Women, and Education in Palestine, 1888–1948* (Leiden: Brill, 2002); Nefissa Naguib and Inger Marie Okkenhaug, eds., *Interpreting Welfare and Relief in the Middle East* (Leiden: Brill, 2008); Heather Jane Sharkey, *American Evangelicals in Egypt: Missionary Encounters in an Age of Empire* (Princeton: Princeton University Press, 2008); and Nazan Maksudyan, *Orphans and Destitute Children in the Late Ottoman Empire* (Syracuse: Syracuse University Press, 2014).

33. On the history of the Syrian Protestant College and its successor, see Stephen Beasley Linnard Penrose, *That They May Have Life: The Story of the American University of Beirut, 1866–1941* (Beirut: American University of Beirut, 1970); and Betty S. Anderson, *The American University of Beirut* (Austin: University of Texas Press, 2011).

34. Didier Fassin, *Humanitarian Reason: A Moral History of the Present,* trans. Rachel Gomme (Berkeley: University of California Press, 2012).

35. According to Hannah Arendt's conception of the role of compassion in revolution, "history tells us that it is by no means a matter of course for the spectacle of misery to move men to pity; even during the long centuries when the Christian religion of mercy determined moral standards of Western civiliza-tion, compassion operated outside the political realm and frequently outside the established hierarchy of the Church." What is crucially distinctive about moder-nity is the capability of being moved to action rather than pity by the suffering of others. Arendt, *On Revolution* (New York: Penguin, 1977), 60–61.

36. In the words of Michael N. Barnett,

> There is a great need for a proper genealogy of humanitarianism. Humanitarian gov-ernance was produced by institutions, discourses, and contingency. Meanings and complexes of humanitarianism were produced not only by strategic and sincere actors—by political communities, moral communities, and expert communities—but also by the creation of boundaries between "humanitarianism" and other kinds of aspirational activities. For instance, although human rights and humanitarianism share common origins, they now constitute two different fields of action. In fact, many in the relief community insist that they have little to do with human rights because they want to keep people alive by giving them the bare necessities, whereas rights activists are so interested in the spread of a culture of rights that they are even willing to use food as a tool to force needy societies to accept new norms. What are the origins of their initial distinction and how (and by whom) were such distinctions produced, amended, and refined?

Barnett, "Humanitarian Governance," *Annual Review of Political Science* 16 (2013): 383.

37. In the words of Eleanor Davey, with John Borton and Matthew Foley: "At such a juncture, a renewed regard for the history of the humanitarian sys-tem offers the prospect of a more balanced reflection upon its future. At the core of HPG's project on 'A Global History of Modern Humanitarian Action' is the belief that a better understanding of the past will help ensure a humanitarian system that is more self-aware, clearer about its identity and better prepared for engagement with the world in which it operates." See Davey, Borton, and Foley,

"A History of the Humanitarian System of Western Origins and Foundations," working paper, Humanitarian Policy Group of the Overseas Development Institute (London: 2013), 1.

38. In a provocative revision with great promise, historian of genocide Dirk Moses argues that rightsspeak in the years after World War II was used to justify the forced deportation of German minorities, the exchange of populations in the Indian subcontinent, and the partition of Palestine. See Moses, "Partitions, Population 'Transfers,' and the Question of Human Rights and Genocide in the 1930s and 1940s," *Genocide and the Terror of History* (Cambridge: Cambridge University Press, 2016).

39. See, for example, United States Agency for International Development, "USAID Strategy on Democracy, Human Rights and Governance" (2013, 5), which states:

> Elevates human rights as a key USAID development objective. USAID has a long history of supporting human rights under a variety of reporting labels, including rule of law, civil society, vulnerable populations, property rights and access to justice. This strategy makes human rights an explicit component of the Agency's approach to democratic development. It builds on USAID's existing portfolio of human rights programming, while elevating human rights, including economic, social and cultural rights, as a critical element of a development strategy that leverages the inclusion and dignity of all. USAID places particular emphasis on inclusive development, expanding rights and opportunities for women, persons with disabilities, displaced persons, LGBT persons, indigenous peoples and other historically marginalized populations, including ethnic and religious minorities. Additionally, this strategy enshrines the prevention of human rights abuses as an important part of human rights programming.

40. Bruno Cabanes, *The Great War and the Origins of Humanitarianism, 1918–1924* (Cambridge: Cambridge University Press, 2014), 9.

41. See, in particular, my discussion of the Nansen passport in chapter 6 of this book and my "Between Communal Survival and National Aspiration: Armenian Genocide Refugees, the League of Nations, and the Practices of Interwar Humanitarianism," *Humanity: An International Journal of Human Rights, Humanitarianism, and Development* 5, no. 2 (2014): 159–181.

42. Michelle Tusan, " 'Crimes against Humanity': Human Rights, the British Empire, and the Origins of the Response to the Armenian Genocide," *American Historical Review* 119, no. 1 (2014): 77.

43. Jeanne Morefield, *Empires without Imperialism: Anglo-American Decline and the Politics of Deflection* (Oxford: Oxford University Press, 2014).

44. Ernest Gellner, *Nations and Nationalism* (Ithaca: Cornell University Press, 1983); and Benedict Anderson, *Imagined Communities: Reflections on the Origin and Spread of Nationalism* (London: Verso, 1983).

45. See Shaloma Gauthier and Davide Rodogno, "The Near East Relief's Caucasus Branch Operation (1919–1920)," Rockefeller Archive Research Report, 2011, www.rockarch.org/publications/resrep/gauthier-rodogno.pdf (accessed December 2, 2013).

46. James L. Barton's *The Story of Near East Relief: An Interpretation* (New York: MacMillan, 1930) is exemplary of this genre—and also an exhaustive narrative account of the origins, work, and eventual disestablishment of Near

East Relief. Based on Barton's own experience with the organization, and on access to archives that are now much more incomplete, the book has been broadly influential in shaping the received history of the organization. It still stands as a remarkable institutional history of NER and how it saw its origins, activities, and role—at times, it is a very honest and self-critical book.

47. This process of emblemizing anticipates a phenomenon observed by Liisa Malkki in the way the international community treated Hutu refugees in 1970s Tanzania. For Malkki, bureaucratic humanitarian intervention transformed the political and social categorization of the refugees in a profound manner that had far-ranging implications for their assistance. In Malkki's case: "Refugees stop being specific persons and become pure victims in general: universal man, universal woman, universal child. . . . The problem is that the necessary delivery of relief . . . is accompanied by a host of other, unannounced social processes and practices that are dehistoricizing. This dehistoricizing universalism creates a context in which it is difficult for people in the refugee category to be approached as historical actors rather than simply as mute victims." Malkki, "Speechless Emissaries: Refugees, Humanitarianism, and Dehistoricization," *Cultural Anthropology* 11, no. 3 (1996): 377–404.

48. See my "The Human Rights Historian and the Trafficked Child: Writing the History of Violence and Individual Trauma," *Perspectives on History,* October 2013.

49. An example of the emergence of this new social history is the work of Elizabeth Thompson and Mustafa Aksakal with the National Endowment for the Humanities–supported seminar "World War One in the Middle East and North Africa," which took place in 2013 and 2014: "The Great War's impact on the Middle East [was] as critical as the Civil War was to American history. The fall of the Ottoman Empire, the expulsion of non-Muslims from Anatolia, Europeans' violent denial of Arabs' demands for independence, and the war's vast social traumas have defined Middle Eastern politics, forced radical social change, and caused violent conflict for the past century." https://blogs .commons.georgetown.edu/world-war-i-in-the-middle-east/ (accessed November 24, 2013).

2. THE HUMANITARIAN IMAGINATION AND THE YEAR OF THE LOCUST

1. Salim Tamari, *Year of the Locust: A Soldier's Diary and the Erasure of Palestine's Ottoman Press* (Berkeley: University of California Press, 2011), 93–94.

2. Bayard Dodge to C. H. Dodge, "Relief Work in Syria during the Period of the War: A Brief and Unofficial Account," New York, 1918, A-AUB, folder AA:2.3.3.18.3, Howard Bliss Collection 1902–1920, p. 3.

3. See the recent work of Zach Foster, "Can the Locust Speak? Explaining the Famine in Greater Syria" (unpublished paper, 2012). Foster engages the question of the plague with a growing body of environmental historical literature.

4. Amartya Sen, "Food, Economy, and Entitlement," in Jean Drèze and Amartya Sen, *The Political Economy of Hunger,* vol. 1, *Entitlement and Well-*

Being (Oxford: Oxford University Press, 1991), 34–51. This cascade of causes— mostly human in origin—is reinforced by Linda Schatkowski Schilcher in her classic discussion of the plague and famine, "The Famine of 1915–1918 in Greater Syria," in *Problems of the Modern Middle East in Historical Perspective*, ed. John P. Spagnolo (Oxford: Oxford University Press, 1992), 229–258.

5. Foster, "Can the Locust Speak?," 5.

6. Dominique Marshall, "International Child Saving," in *The Routledge History of Childhood in the Western World*, ed. Paula S. Fass (London: Routledge, 2013), 469–490.

7. David Rieff, *A Bed for the Night: Humanitarianism in Crisis* (New York: Simon and Schuster, 2002), 78.

8. This idea builds from the thinking of Thomas W. Laqueur:

> The fact that sympathy for characters in literature does not necessarily translate to sympathy for real live people; that sentimental feelings for distant strangers can bind us to suffering at home for all sorts of self-serving reasons . . . that human rights as a history narrative tends to short change the history of political and legal change—these facts do not diminish the core insight of the theses. . . . [I]n the late eighteenth century the ethical subject was democratized. More and more people came to believe it was their obligation to ameliorate and prevent wrongdoing to others; more and more people were seen as eligible to be members of "the circle of we."

Thomas W. Laqueur, "Mourning, Pity and the Work of the Narrative in the Making of Humanity," in *Humanitarianism and Suffering: The Mobilization of Empathy*, ed. Richard Ashby Wilson and Richard D. Brown (Cambridge: Cambridge University Press, 2009), 37–38.

9. Charles F. Brissel (Baghdad) to Henry Morgenthau (Constantinople), December 3, 1914, USNA II, 867.48/36.

10. Jonathan Sciarcon, "Unfulfilled Promises: Ottomanism, the 1908 Revolution and Baghdadi Jews," *International Journal of Contemporary Iraqi Studies* 3, no. 2 (2009): 155–168.

11. J.W. Davis (Washington, DC) to Secretary of State (Washington, DC), December 26, 1914, USNA II, 867.48/24.

12. For a broader survey of American Jewish Committee (AJC) organizing efforts in both Palestine and Eastern Europe, see Jaclyn Granick, "Waging Relief: The Politics and Logistics of American Jewish War Relief in Europe and the Near East (1914–1918)," *First World War Studies* 5, no. 1 (2014): 55–68.

13. See Abigail Jacobsen, "American 'Welfare Politics': American Involvement in Jerusalem During World War I," *Israel Studies*, 18, no. 1 (2013): 56–76.

14. Louis Levin (Baltimore) to Robert Lansing (Washington, DC), July 23, 1915, USNA II, 867.48/158.

15. Ibid.

16. U.O. Schmelz, "Population Characteristics of Jerusalem and Hebron Regions According to the Ottoman Census of 1905," in *Ottoman Palestine, 1800–1914: Studies in Economic and Social History*, ed. Gad G. Gilbar (Leiden: Brill, 1990), 25.

17. See Hilton Obenzinger, *American Palestine: Melville, Twain and the Holy Land Mania* (Princeton: Princeton University Press, 1999).

18. Stephen Wise, *Challenging Years: The Autobiography of Stephen Wise* (New York: G. P. Putnam's Sons, 1949), 49.

19. Ibid., 48.

20. Ibid., 185.

21. Ibid., 185.

22. Ibid., 186.

23. Ibid., 187. See also Frank W. Brecher, "Woodrow Wilson and the Origins of the Arab-Israeli Conflict," *American Jewish Archives* 39 (1987): 23–47.

24. Wise, *Challenging Years*, 47.

25. *Jewish Relief Work in Palestine: A Summary of Reports Received up to Date, October 1918* (London: Palestine Relief Board, 1918), 4.

26. Ibid., 9–11.

27. Jennifer Johnson Onyedum, "'Humanize the Conflict': Algerian Health Care, Organizations and Propaganda Campaigns, 1954–62," *International Journal of Middle East Studies* 44, no. 4 (2012): 713–731.

28. Wise, *Challenging Years*, 55.

29. Melanie Tanielian's work is the most important discussion of the famine and the local and global response to its effects. She effectively shows how the famine was created and what insititions—civic or otherwise—were mobilized to meet the need that resulted; moreover, she locates the history of famine in Beirut in the larger literature on economic development and humanitarianism uniquely in the field. See Tanielian, "The War of Famine: Everyday Life in Wartime Beirut and Mount Lebanon (1914–1918)" (PhD diss., University of California, Berkeley, 2012). Also see Tanielian's recent "Politics of Wartime Relief in Ottoman Beirut (1914–1918)," *First World War Studies* 5, no. 1 (2014): 69–82; and Nicholas Z. Ajay's "Mount Lebanon and the Wilayah of Beirut, 1914–1918: The War Years" (PhD diss., Georgetown University, 1972).

30. W. Stanley Hollis (Beirut) to William Bryan (Washington, DC), April 21, 1915, USNA II, 867.48/126.

31. Ibid.

32. Elizabeth Thompson describes the social effects of the famine:

These war and famine memories evoke a wrenching, nightmarish experience of the world gone awry, of families not simply abandoned and split apart, but actually turned against each other. Men who had prided themselves on protecting their families could no longer do so. Mothers and wives, soldiers' inspiration or life and love of country, were selling themselves to strangers and devouring their children. Women habituated to social norms of seclusion howled in the streets, naked, or were attacked in their homes by strange men. All social and familial norms seemed suspended.

Thompson, *Colonial Citizens: Republican Rights, Paternal Privilege, and Gender in French Syria and Lebanon* (New York: Columbia University Press, 2000), 25.

33. For a detailed discussion of the college's humanitarian relief work, see A. Tylor Brand, "Lives Darkened by Calamity: Enduring the Famine of World War I in Lebanon and Western Syria" (PhD diss., American University of Beirut, 2014).

34. Bayard Dodge to C. H. Dodge, "Relief Work in Syria," 4.

35. Paul Knabeshue (Cairo) to Secretary of State (Washington, DC), July 7, 1916, USNA II, 867.48/324.

36. Gibran Khalil Gibran (New York) to Robert Lansing (Washington, DC), June 17, 1916, USNA II, 867.48/306.

37. Margaret McGilvary, *The Dawn of a New Era Syria* (New York: Fleming H. Revell, 1920), 95. A. Tylor Brand suggests that the American publicity used to raise funds for the "Christmas Ship" contributed to Cemal Pasha's ultimate refusal to allow its disembarkation or the distribution of foodstuffs directly by Americans: "As supportive as Jamal [Cemal] had been of the relief work that the SPC had conducted in the country, . . . *Caesar*'s mix of foreign aid and wide publicity made the humanitarian relief a political liability. While . . . *Caesar* was at sea, he issued the demand that the cargo unload at Jaffa, where he would personally oversee the distribution to those in need." Brand, "'That They May Have Life': The Practice and Practicality of the Syrian Protestant College's Humanitarian Relief Projects in Beirut and Lebanon during the Famine of World War I," in *AUB 150th Anniversary Festschrift* (forthcoming).

38. Tanielian, "War of Famine," 309–321.

39. McGilvary, *The Dawn of a New Era Syria*, 268.

40. Ibid., 288.

41. Ibid., 268.

42. McGilvary wrote,

During the Ottoman regime there was no political cohesion among the Syrians. Racial and sectarian disagreements were paramount over national considerations, and the true patriot despaired, doubting whether anything could weld together these antagonistic factions. The curse of Syria has always been the religious fanaticism of her various sects. The increasing nationalistic tendency of to-day is, therefore, by far the most hopeful sign that Syria possesses latent elements of strength, and a spark of that divine fire which, if properly fostered, will flame into national enthusiasm and patriotism.

McGilvary, *The Dawn of a New Era Syria*, 293.

43. Bayard Dodge to C. H. Dodge, "Relief Work in Syria," 15.

44. Ibid.

45. Branden Little, "Humanitarian Relief in Europe and the Analogue of War, 1914–1918," in *Finding Common Ground: New Directions in First World War Studies*, ed. Jennifer Keene and Michael Neiberg (Leiden and Boston: Brill, 2010), 145.

3. THE FORM AND CONTENT OF SUFFERING

1. See Fredrick Starr, *The Truth about the Congo* (Chicago: Forbes and Company, 1907).

2. Quoted in Séamas Ó Síocáin and Michael O'Sullivan, eds., *The Eyes of Another Race: Roger Casement's Congo Report and 1903 Diary* (Dublin: University College Dublin Press, 2003), 71.

3. See Eleni Coundouriotis's reading of the legacy of Casement's report on the writing of contemporary human rights history, "Congo Cases: The Stories

of Human Rights History," in *Humanity: An International Journal of Human Rights, Humanitarianism, and Development* 3, no. 2 (2012): 133–153.

4. Raymond Kévorkian, *The Armenian Genocide: A Complete History* (London: I.B. Tauris, 2011), 11.

5. Michele Tusan, *Smyrna's Ashes: Humanitarianism, Genocide and the Birth of the Middle East* (Berkeley: University of California Press, 2012), 9–11.

6. See Ann Marie Wilson, "In the Name of God, Civilization, and Humanity: The United States and the Armenian Massacres of the 1890s," *Le mouvement social* 2 (2009): 27–44.

7. Taner Akçam, *A Shameful Act: The Armenian Genocide and the Question of Turkish Responsibility* (New York: Macmillan, 2006), 44.

8. See, for example, Janet Klein, *The Margins of Empire: Kurdish Militias in the Ottoman Tribal Zone* (Palo Alto: Stanford University Press, 2011).

9. Donald Bloxham, *The Final Solution: A Genocide* (Oxford: Oxford University Press, 2009), 61.

10. Clara Barton, *Report: America's Relief Expedition to Asia Minor under the Red Cross* (Meriden, CT: Journal Publishing Company, 1896), 9.

11. Ibid.

12. Marion Moser Jones, *The American Red Cross from Clara Barton to the New Deal* (Baltimore: Johns Hopkins University Press, 2012), 74.

13. Barton, *Report*, 43.

14. Ibid.

15. See Margaret Lavinia Anderson, "'Down in Turkey, Far Away'": Human Rights, the Armenian Massacres, and Orientalism in Wilhelmine Germany," *The Journal of Modern History* 79, no 1 (2007): 80–111.

16. See Hans-Lukas Kieser, "Johannes Lepsius: Theologian, Humanitarian Activist and Historian of Völkermord: An Approach to a German Biography (1858–1926)," in *Logos im Dialogos: Auf der Suche nach der Orthodoxie*, ed. A. Briskina-Müller, A. Drost-Abgarjan, and A. Meissner (Münster: LIT Verlag, 2011), 209–229.

17. Johannes Lepsius, *Armenia and Europe: An Indictment* (London: Hodder and Stoughton, 1897), 142.

18. Ibid., 240–242.

19. Ibid., 145. Lepsius's account is similar in that his fear that a "final answer" to the Eastern Question would be an exterminationist policy is shared by George Hepworth, a leading Protestant intellectual who went to the Ottoman state on behalf of the New York *Herald*, one of the city's main papers. Hepworth traveled through the provinces most affected by the massacres and spoke (through an interpreter) to a wide range of Ottoman society. What is most striking in Hepworth's account is the degree to which he identifies social and legal causes among the roots of Armenian suffering, and indeed his observations may have reflected some of his own thinking about racial prejudice and inequality in the United States. In a chapter entitled "An Armenian's View," he relates a conversation he had with an anonymous Armenian intellectual—identified as a composite out of fear that his informants might be targeted for speaking with him—and uses it to make sense of how late Ottoman society had incorporated a whole range of discriminatory practices into the way it treated Armenians, but

Armenians, for their part, were loyal citizens. The anonymous Armenian details legal discrimination in property disputes, the use of torture, and censorship, but also how unrepresentative Armenian separatists were. George Hughes Hepworth, *Through Armenia on Horseback* (New York: E. P. Dutton, 1898.)

20. Lepsius, *Armenia and Europe*, 150.

21. Ibid., 252.

22. Kévorkian, *Armenian Genocide*, 88.

23. Marc Nichanian, *Writers of Disaster: Armenian Literature in the Twentieth Century*, vol. 1, *The National Revolutions* (Princeton: Gomidas Institute Press, 2002), 190.

24. Zapēl Esayean [Zabel Yesayan], *Awheraknerun mēj* [Among the ruins] (Istanbul: K. Polis, 1911), 7–9.

25. Arshakuhi T'ēodik [Archakouhi Téodik], *Amis mě i Kilikia: Kts'ktur nōt'er* [A month in Cilicia: Some notes] (Istanbul: 1910), 94.

26. Kévorkian, *Armenian Genocide*, 95.

27. Esayean, *Awheraknerun mēj*, 206.

28. "When assessing women's benevolent work in Cilicia, it is evident that ... preservation of national identity among Armenian Children and orphans [was the primary goal]. ... After 1909 the Armenian children of Cilicia were seen as the responsibility of the Armenian nation, and women's organizations ... sought to extend maternal care through the establishment to national schools designed to take the place of lost parents." Victoria Rowe, "Cilicia: The View from the Constantinople Women's Organizations," in *Armenian Cilicia,* ed. Richard G. Hovannisian and Simon Payaslia (Costa Mesa: Mazda Publishers, 2008), 389.

29. "Any publication at the present time of this report as coming from the Foundation would probably react on our informants whether mentioned or not, as the sources from which we obtained information would be known in Constantinople." E. Wadsworth and J. Smith, Jr., "Report of the War Relief Commission to the Rockefeller Foundation on Conditions in Turkey," 1917, RAC-RF, International Projects, 1:100, box 76, folder 719, p. 21.

30. Ibid., 22.

31. Ibid., 23.

32. Ibid., 25.

33. Ibid., 27.

34. Ibid., 29 (emphasis added).

35. See David Miller's discussion of Toynbee's body of historical writing on Armenians and its larger reception in British political circles, "The Treatment of Armenians in the Ottoman Empire: A History of the 'Blue Book,'" *The RUSI Journal* 150, no. 4 (2005): 36–43. Miller, building from Toynbee's memoirs, argues that the British Foreign Office commissioned the report in order to paint the Ottoman State as as great a violator of human rights as its ally the Russian Empire following its massacre of Jews in the Jewish Pale. There is some suggestion that this was done to elicit Jewish support for the American entrance into World War I. Miller concludes that Toynbee and Lord Bryce, who supported and promoted the historian's efforts, were both unaware of this purpose. See also Michele Tusan, "'Crimes against Humanity': Human Rights, the British

Empire, and the Origins of the Response to the Armenian Genocide," *American Historical Review* 119, no. 1 (2014): 47–77.

36. Arnold J. Toynbee, *Acquaintances* (London: Oxford University Press, 1967), 242.

37. Arnold J. Toynbee, *Armenian Atrocities: The Murder of a Nation* (London: Hodder and Stoughton, 1915), 24.

38. Ibid., 28.

39. Ibid., 30.

40. Ibid., 31.

41. Ibid., 40, 50.

42. By the fall of 1916, the Rockefeller Foundation had contributed $290,000 to Armenian and Syrian relief. More than $300,000 in additional funds had been contributed by other donors. It is important to note that, as the various American relief committees began to produce public reporting on the situation in Anatolia, the Rockefeller Foundation commissioned a confidential report by a British group that visited the Caucasus and Eastern Anatolia. This report reassured Jerome D. Greene and others at Rockefeller that the reports of mass violence were accurate and that the Protestant missionary network was capable of distributing cash assistance. The report also emphasized that the American relief agents were committed to promoting "self-help." See Jerome D. Greene, "Armenian and Syrian Relief," October 1916, RAC-RF, International Projects, 1:100, box 76, folder 718, p. 18.

43. American Committee for Armenian and Syrian Relief, "The Cry of a Million: Exiled Destitute Dying" (ca. 1916), RAC-NER.

44. Ibid., 1–2.

45. Ibid., 4.

46. Ibid., 3–4.

47. Fridtjof Nansen, *Scheme for the Settlement of Armenian Refugees: General Survey and Principal Documents* (Geneva: Kundig, 1927), 5.

48. James Dawes, *That the World May Know: Bearing Witness to Atrocity* (Cambridge: Harvard University Press, 2009), 9–10.

4. "AMERICA'S WARDS"

1. Mabel Elliott, *Beginning Again at Ararat* (New York: Fleming H. Revell, 1924), 122–123.

2. Stanley Kerr to family, June 20, 1920, Kerr Family Letters Collection, Stanley Kerr and Elsa Reckman Kerr Letters.

3. Near East Relief, "Coaching and Utilizing Speakers" (ca. 1921), RAC-NER.

4. While without a doubt at this time in their lives both Kerr and Elliott identified as mainline Protestant Christians, and occasional references to religion appear in their writing, mentions of Christianity, evangelism, conversion, pietism, and religious redemption, which course through the missionary writing of the time, are absent. Typical of missionary thought at the time was the statement by Reverend James Lyman, American Board of Foreign Missions representative at Marash, who, writing at around the same time as Kerr and Elliott,

explained the attacks on NER infrastructure and efforts in Cilicia in much different terms:

> God has heard the cry of his people and is answering. What the next move will be we cannot say, but we pray God will help us to meet whatever comes, in faith. We need your prayers very much these days. Tell all your friends to pray, not only that the hand of evil men will be stayed, but that to the Armenian and Turkish peoples there will be a spirit of repentance given. Our enemies are many and the worst of them are not our neighbors, but the evil spirit that leads us to wish to revenge, to be jealous, to seek our own wills instead of His will. So pray for us that we may be set free from the power of the evil spirit.

James K. Lyman (Marash) to James L. Barton (Boston), February 8, 1921, Stanley Kerr Archives, no. 139, Zoryan Institute, Arlington, MA.

5. Elliott, *Ararat*, 13.

6. On the American Relief Administration, see Bertrand Patenaude, *The Big Show in Bololand: The American Relief Expedition to Soviet Russia in the Famine of 1921* (Palo Alto: Stanford University Press, 2002).

7. For a detailed narrative description of the repatriation process, see Vahram Shemmassian, "The Repatriation of Armenian Refugees from the Arab Middle East, 1918–1920," in *Armenian Cilicia*, ed. Richard G. Hovannisian and Simon Payaslian (Costa Mesa: Mazda Publishers, 2008), 419–456. Shemmasian's historical discussion is drawn from British and archival sources and the records of the Armenian National Delegation. Citing a report by the American consul in Aleppo, Jesse Jackson, Shemmassian states that a total of 74,431 refugees had been repatriated by the fall of 1919 and only a few thousand remained in Aleppo. Well over half that number were sent into southern Cilicia.

8. On French policy in Cilicia, see Vahé Tachjian, *La France en Cilicie et en Haute-Mésopotamie: Aux Confins de la Turquie, de la Syrie et de l'Iraq* (Paris: Karthala, 2004).

9. On the institutional history of AWHS, see Esther Pohl Lovejoy, *Certain Samaritans* (New York: MacMillan, 1933).

10. Near East Relief, "Near East Bibliography" (ca. 1922), RAC-NER.

11. Stanley E. Kerr, *The Lions of Marash: Personal Experiences with American Near East Relief, 1919–1922* (Albany: State University of New York Press, 1975), 47.

12. Ibid.

13. Stanley Kerr to James Kerr, November 23, 1919, Kerr Family Letters Collection, Stanley Kerr and Elsa Reckman Kerr Letters.

14. Stanley Kerr to James Kerr and family, December 16, 1911, Stanley Kerr Archives, no. 131, Zoryan Institute, Arlington, MA.

15. Kerr, *Lions*, 49. In his introduction to *The Lions of Marash*, Bayard Dodge reflects on his recognition during the war and its aftermath that the accounts of suffering were so great that Western publics might not believe them. "Conditions were so horrible that people in America thought that the accounts about them were exaggerated." Bayard Dodge in Kerr, *Lions*, x.

16. Even after a lapse of nearly a century, I found working with similar documents deeply and emotionally unsettling and painful. See my essay "The

Human Rights Historian and the Trafficked Child: Writing the History of Mass Violence and Individual Trauma," *Perspectives on History*, October 2013.

17. Stanley Kerr to family, November 23, 1919, Kerr Family Letters Collection, Stanley Kerr and Elsa Reckman Kerr Letters.

18. On the emerging scholarship on land and property transfer, see Ugur Ümit Üngör, *The Making of Modern Turkey: Nation and State in Eastern Anatolia, 1913–1950* (Oxford: Oxford University Press, 2011); and Ugur Ümit Üngör and Mehmet Polatel, *Confiscation and Destruction: The Young Turk Seizure of Armenian Property* (London: Continuum, 2011).

19. See Lerna Ekmekcioglu's critical essay "A Climate for Abduction, a Climate for Redemption: The Politics of Inclusion during and after the Armenian Genocide," *Comparative Studies in Society and History* 55, no. 3 (2013): 522–553.

20. Elliott, *Ararat*, 21–22.

21. Ibid., 22.

22. Ibid., 16.

23. Ibid., 17.

24. Ibid.

25. Ibid.

26. Ibid., 19.

27. Mabel Elliott to Mary Crawford (Marash), September 2, 1919, Records of American Women's Hospitals, 1917–1982, American Women's Hospitals series, Near East correspondence, no. ACC-144–010, Drexel University College of Medicine.

28. Kerr, *Lions*, 75.

29. Elliott, *Ararat*, 66.

30. Stanley Kerr to family, February 9, 1920, Kerr Family Letters Collection, Stanley Kerr and Elsa Reckman Kerr Letters.

31. See Richard G. Hovannisian, "The Postwar Contest for Cilicia and the 'Marash Affair'," in *Armenian Cilicia*, ed. Richard G. Hovannisian and Simon Payaslian (Costa Mesa: Mazda Publishers, 2008), 495–518.

32. On the post-Marash political climate for Armenians, see Levon Marashlian, "Finishing the Genocide: Cleansing Turkey of Armenian Survivors, 1920–1923," in *Remembrance and Denial: The Case of the Armenian Genocide*, ed. Richard G Hovannisian (Detroit: Wayne State University Press, 1999), 113–146.

33. Elliott, *Ararat*, 120–121.

34. Ibid., 137.

35. E.R. Applegate (Aleppo) to Chairman (New York), "The Armenian Refugee Schools in Aleppo," October 25, 1923, RAC-NER, p. 1.

36. Ibid.

37. See my discussion of French policy toward Armenian refugees in interwar Syria in *Being Modern in the Middle East: Revolution, Nationalism, Colonialism, and the Arab Middle Class* (Princeton: Princeton University Press, 2006), 279–288.

38. E.R. Applegate, "The Near East Relief Armenian Orphanage Industrial Department," October 25, 1923, RAC-NER.

39. Near East Relief, "Overseas Disbursement in All Areas" (ca. 1924), RAC-NER.

40. In a caustic report on the organization prepared for the Commonwealth Fund that was circulated at the Rockefeller Foundation, NER's orphan relief was criticized:

> ... Near East Relief has chosen to select from great numbers of destitute as many promising orphans as it could accommodate in institutions or could help otherwise and has devoted itself in great part to caring for these orphans on the basis which should result in their becoming not only trained artisans, farmers etc. but also good Protestants. Apparently larger numbers of children could have been kept alive had the Near East chosen to concentrate on child feeding operations but the discussion of such a question as this is academic at present.

Barry C. Smith to the Commonwealth Fund, June 9, 1922, RAC, Laura Spellman Collection, LSRMo series 3.8, NER subseries, box 8, folder 100.

41. Near East Relief, "America We Thank You" (ca. 1924), A-NER.

42. Ibid.

43. I discuss the process of becoming "uncomfortable" by becoming modern in a developing society more extensively in "The Uncomfortable Inhabitants of French Colonial Modernity: Mandate Syria's Communities of Collaboration (1920–1946)," in *Transnational Spaces and Identities in the Francophone World*, ed. Hafid Gafaïti, Patricia Lorcin, and David Troyansky (Lincoln: University of Nebraska Press, 2007), 24–52.

44. On the emergence of a new Armenian intellectual community in diaspora, see Nicola Migliorino, *(Re)Constructing Armenia in Lebanon and Syria: Ethno-Cultural Diversity and the State in the Aftermath of a Refugee Crisis* (New York: Berghahn Books, 2007), 123.

45. Ashdghig Avakian, *Stranger among Friends: An Armenian Nurse from Lebanon Tells Her Story* (Beirut: Catholic Press, 1960), 81.

46. Ibid., 116.

47. Garnig Banian [Karnig Panian], "Addendum to Memories of Childhood and Orphanhood" (ca. 1980), trans. Vahe Habeshian, in Karnig Panian, *Goodbye Antoura: A Memoir of the Armenian Genocide* (Palo Alto: Stanford University Press, 2015).

48. Ibid.

49. Ibid.

50. Nefissa Naguib was able to interview several elderly Armenians who had lived at the orphanages, including the "Birds Nest." Their oral histories reinforce the sense that interaction between orphans and NER officials was rare and that Armenian educators and administrators played a major role in their care and training. See her "A Nation of Widows and Orphans: Armenian Memories of Relief in Jerusalem" in *Interpreting Welfare and Relief in the Middle East*, ed. Nefissa Naguib and Inger Marie Okkenhaug (Leiden: Brill, 2008), 47.

51. Antranik Zaroukian, *Men Without Childhoods*, trans. Elise Bayizian and Marzbed Margossian (New York: Ashdod Press, 1985), 5. Originally published as Andranik Tsaṛukean, *Mankut'iwn ch'unets'ogh mardik* (Peyrut: K. Tōnikean ew Ordik', 1980).

52. Ibid., 43.

53. See *Ēndardzak grpani ergaran: Azgayin, heghap'okhakan, sirayin, zhoghovrdakan ew geghjkakan erger* (Boston: H. G. Berberian, 1919), 140. I thank the ethnomusicologists Melissa Billal and Mari Akbaş for helping me locate this early version of the song.

5. THE LEAGUE OF NATIONS RESCUE OF TRAFFICKED WOMEN AND CHILDREN AND THE PARADOX OF MODERN HUMANITARIANISM

1. Yervant Odian, *Accursed Years: My Exile and Return from Der Zor, 1914–1919*, trans. Ara Stepan Melkonian (London: Gomidas Press, 2009), 99–100.

2. Taner Akçam, *The Young Turks' Crime against Humanity: The Armenian Genocide and Ethnic Cleansing in the Ottoman Empire* (Princeton: Princeton University Press, 2012), 314.

3. Odian, *Accursed Years,* 120.

4. Zabel Yessayan, "La libération des femmes et enfants nonmusulmans en Turquie," 1919, Nubarian Library, National Delegation Archives, pp. 1–15, correspondence.

5. Dame Rachel Crowdy, head of the "Opium and Social Questions" section of the League Secretariat, observed, "You may disarm the world, you may reduce your troops or abolish your battleships, but unless you introduce better economic conditions, better social conditions and better health conditions into the world, you will not be able to maintain peace." Rachel E. Crowdy, "The Humanitarian Activities of the League of Nations," *Journal of the Royal Institute of International Affairs* 6, no. 3 (1927): 153.

6. "Registers of Inmates of the Armenian Orphanage in Aleppo," 1922–1930, 4 vols., Records of the Nansen International Refugee Office, 1920–1947, ALON-UNOG .

7. Ibid, no. 961, March 25, 1926.

8. Ibid.

9. A rich literature based on oral history and first-person memoirs has emerged around the topic of rescued captives. Notable works include Donald E. Miller and Lorna Touryan Miller, *Survivors: An Oral History of the Armenian Genocide* (Berkeley: University of California Press, 1999); Mae Derdarian, *Vergeen: A Survivor of the Armenian Genocide* (Los Angeles: Atmus Press, 1997); and Aram Haygaz's autobiographical *Ch'ors tari K'iwrtistani lernerun mej* [Four years in the hills of Kurdistan] (Antilias: 1972).

10. It is important to emphasize that the League's adoption and internationalization of the work of rescue followed earlier efforts by Near East Relief, as described in previous chapters, as well as Armenian communal efforts. In addition, many informal rescues took place, and relatives would locate and negotiate the release of children or relatives. The adoption of this humanitarian practice by the League placed rescue in a different political context and appended to it a broader meaning. On Armenian rescue efforts, see Levon Yotnakhparian's memoir, *Crows of the Desert: The Memoirs of Levon Yotnakhparian* (Tujunga: Parian Photographic Design, 2012).

11. "Deportation des femmes et des enfants en Turquie, en Asie Mineure et dans les territoiries avoisinants," Report of the Fifth Commission, Geneva, September 21, 1921, ALON-UNOG, 12/15998/4631.

12. *Treaty of Peace with Turkey, Signed at Sèvres,* August 10, 1920 (London: H.M. Stationary Office, 1920), article 142.

13. H.M. Swanwick to Robert Cecil, May 20, 1920, ALON-UNOG 638 12/4631/647, and "1924 Letter from Emily Robinson, Secretary of the Armenian Red Cross and Refugee Fund (Great Britain)," ALON-UNOG 638 12/4631/647.

14. Alan Duben, "Household Formation in Late Ottoman Istanbul," *International Journal of Middle East Studies,* 22, no. 4 (1990): 422–424.

15. Ferhunde Özbay et al., "Adoption and Fostering," *Encyclopedia of Women and Islamic Cultures,* ed. Suad Joseph (Leiden: Brill, 2009).

16. While some recent scholarship has emerged on surfacing children post-rape, the larger question of transfer—which is an element of the crime of genocide—remains largely unstudied. See Charlie R. Carpenter, "Surfacing Children: Limitation of Genocidal Rape Discourse," *Human Rights Quarterly* 22 (2000): 428–477.

17. The phrase is used in Fethiye Çetin's memoir, *My Grandmother,* trans. Maureen Freeley (London: Verso, 2008), 102. Originally published as *Anneannem: Anlatı* (Istanbul: Metis Yayinları, 2004).

18. Slavery in the Ottoman Empire, especially trans-Saharan trade in Africans via the Nile, had ended under pressure from Britain in the mid-nineteenth century. However, the practice of de facto enslavement persisted at an extralegal level well into the Republican period, despite being outlawed by the Young Turks in 1908. Because social taboos persist about acknowledging this form of slavery and servile concubinage, and because banning it pushed it underground, precious little scholarly attention has been paid to it beyond random cases where this practice intersected with the criminal justice system and memoirs of former slaves. See Y. Hakan Erdem, *Slavery in the Ottoman Empire and Its Demise, 1800–1909* (London: Palgrave, 1995); and Ehud Toledano, *Slavery and Abolition in the Ottoman Middle East* (Seattle: University of Washington Press, 1998).

19. Karen Jeppe, Baalbek to Geneva, August 24, 1922, enclosure in Records of the Nansen International Refugee Office, 1920–1947, ALON-UNOG, p. 10.

20. Barbara Metzger, "The League of Nations and Human Rights: From Practice to Theory" (PhD diss., University of Cambridge, 2001).

21. For a comprehensive description of the rescue movement in Aleppo, see Vahram L. Shemmassian, "The League of Nations and the Reclamation of Armenian Genocide Survivors," in *Looking Backward, Moving Forward,* ed. Richard G. Hovannisian (Rutgers: Transaction Press, 2003), 81–111.

22. On accounts of early rescue efforts by Armenian organizations, see ibid., in particular, 107n2.

23. Johannes Lepsius (1858–1926) was witness to some of the worst atrocities during the war and published two firsthand accounts in addition to his earlier humanitarian reporting: *Bericht über die Lage des armenischen Volkes* (Potsdam: Tempelverlag, 1916) and *Der Todesgang des armenischen Volkes* (Potsdam: Missionshandlung und Verlag, 1919).

24. See Matthias Bjørnlun, "Karen Jeppe, Aage Meyer Benedictsen, and the Ottoman Armenians: National Survival in Imperial and Colonial Settings," *Haigazian Armenological Review* 28 (2008): 9–43.

25. Ibid., 9.

26. Calhoun observes that this phenomenon is also a reflection of the changing nature of religion and religious vocation in the late nineteenth century. See Craig Calhoun, "The Imperative to Reduce Suffering: Charity, Progress and Emergencies in the Field of Humanitarian Action," in *Humanitarianism in Question: Politics, Power, Ethics,* ed. Michael Barnett and Thomas G. Weiss (Ithaca: Cornell University Press, 2008), 79.

27. Karen Jeppe, "Account of the situation of the Armenians in Syria and of my own work amongst them from the 1st of May til the 1st of September 1922," enclosure in Records of the Nansen International Refugee Office, 1920–1947, ALON-UNOG, p. 18.

28. Ibid., 15.

29. Ibid., 14–15.

30. Kamil al-Ghazzi, *Kitab nahr al-dhahab fi tarikh Halab* [River of Gold in the History of Aleppo], 2nd ed., 3 vols. (Aleppo: Arab Pen Press, 1991–1993).

31. Ibid., 3:557.

32. Ibid.

33. Ibid., 3:558.

34. Ibid.

35. "Deportation des femmes et des enfants," 356.

36. Ibid., 358–359.

37. "Obituary of Emma Cushman," *The American Journal of Nursing* 31, no. 4 (1931): 417–419.

38. See Zaruhi Pahri [Zarouhi Bahri], *Keank'is vepe* [My biography] (Beirut: 1995). Bahri recounts in her memoir one case from the Neutral House: A very pretty young woman was brought from a Turkish home, and Bahri arranged to have her marry rather than be institutionalized. The future husband asked Bahri and his bride to keep her background secret, even from his parents, presumably to conceal the shame of her rape and lost virginity. The lack of a larger body of Armenian-language sources is due in no small part to the tendency of accounts of trafficking and sequestration to evoke a series of responses, ranging from shame to outright denial, in the Armenian diaspora. At the time, as Bahri's story indicates, there were clear practical reasons for concealment in social situations that placed a premium on modesty. Her story also signaled how the rescued women and female children were caught between two patriarchal systems.

39. "Letter from Armenian Patriarch of Istanbul to Major Arnold," August 7, 1919, ALON-UNOG 12/15100/4631.

40. "Letter from Miss Cushman," August 25, 1921, ALON-UNOG, C. 281m.218.

41. Ibid.

42. "Index of Children Brought to the Neutral House," July 1920, ALON-UNOG, 12/15100/4631.

43. Ibid.

44. Halide Edip, *Memoirs of Halidé Edib* (New York: The Century Co., 1926).

45. On prewar Ottoman orphanages and workhouses, see Nazan Maksudyan, "Orphans, Cities, and the State: Vocational Orphanages (Islahhanes) and Reform in the Late Ottoman Urban Space," *International Journal of Middle East Studies* 43, no. 3 (2011): 493–511.

46. Garnik Banian [Karnik Panian], *Husher antourayi vosbanotse* (Beirut: Hamazkain, 1992).

47. Bayard Dodge to C.H. Dodge, "Relief Work in Syria during the Period of the War: A Brief and Unofficial Account," New York, 1918, A-AUB, folder AA:2.3.3.18.3, Howard Bliss Collection 1902–1920, p. 13.

48. Halidé Edip, *The Turkish Ordeal: Being the Further Memoirs of Edib* (New York: The Century Co., 1928), 17.

49. Ibid., 16.

50. Ibid., 18.

51. For a lengthy and fascinating discussion of the intercommunal dimensions of the Neutral House's operations, see Lerna Ekmekçioğlu, "A Climate for Abduction, a Climate for Redemption: The Politics of Inclusion during and after the Armenian Genocide," *Comparative Studies in Society and History* 55, no. 3 (2013): 522–553.

52. W.A. Kennedy, "Interim Report," August 25, 1921, p. 6, ALON-UNOG 12/15100/4631.

53. Hüsnü Ada, "The First Ottoman Civil Society Organization in the Service of the Ottoman State: The Case of the Ottoman Red Crescent" (MA thesis, Sabancı University, Istanbul, 2004), 100–101.

54. "Deportation des femmes et des enfants," 359–360.

55. See, for example, Vacaresco's collection *The Bard of the Dimbovitza: Romanian Folk Songs Collected from the Peasants* (New York: Osgood, McIlvaine and Co., 1897).

56. Florence Brewer Boeckel, "Women in International Affairs," in *Annals of the American Academy of Political and Social Science*, vol. 143, *Women in the Modern World* (May 1929), 232–233.

57. "Deportation des femmes et des enfants," 360.

58. Ibid.

59. "Deportation des femmes et des enfants," 361.

60. Ibid.

61. Turkish National Congress, *The Turco-Armenian Question: The Turkish Point of View* (Istanbul: National Congress of Turkey, 1919). A distinctive element of the reporting of this period is the acknowledgment that the massacres and deportations of Armenians took place and were justified, nonetheless, for *raisons d'etat*. For example, in a pivotal passage, the author of *The Turco-Armenian Question* explained that "no doubt the forcible transplantation of an entire people at short notice is a cruel measure. But consider the circumstances. . . . Turkey found herself confronting an internal enemy. . . . As a matter of fact, was the transportation of the Armenians an iniquitous measure? The exigencies of war know no law" (82).

62. Ministry of the Interior, Department of Refugees, *Cemiyet-i Akvam ve Türkiyede Ermeni ve Rumlar* [The League of Nations and Greeks and Armenians in Turkey] (Istanbul: Ahmed Hassan: 1921), 5. References are to the simultaneously published English-language version.

63. Ibid., 7. On the trials, see Vahakn Dadrian, "The Documentation of the World War I Armenian Massacres in the Proceedings of the Turkish Military Tribunal," *International Journal of Middle East Studies* 23, no. 4 (1991): 549–576.

64. Ibid., 29–30.

65. Djevad [Cevat] to Secretary General (Geneva), March 31, 1922, p. 4, ALON-UNOG, RG 638 C.181.m.99.1922.IV (emphasis added).

66. See attached note in ibid.

67. Ministry of the Interior, *Cemiyet-i Akvam ve Türkiyede Ermeni ve Rumlar,* 21.

68. A measure of the reach of this attitude throughout the Muslim world was the degree to which South Asian Muslims lobbied the British Empire on behalf of the Turks in the lead-up to the Treaty of Lausanne. Indeed, in a parallel to the way in which Western Protestants had taken up the cause of the Armenians, the South Asian Islamist intellectual and later founder of the Jamaat-e-Islami, Abu al-A'la' al-Mawdudi, authored pamphlets defending Turkey with titles like *The Christians in Turkey* (1922) and the *Tyrannies of the Greeks in Smyrna* (1922). Cited in Seyyed Vali Reza Nasr, *Mawdudi and the Making of Islamic Revivalism* (Oxford: Oxford University Press, 1996), 19.

69. "Relationship between the Resolution Adopted by the Assembly of the League of Nations at its meeting held on Wednesday 15 December, 1920 (Morning), and Article 142 of the Turkish Treaty," memorandum to the secretary-general, Geneva, December 18, 1920, Records of the Nansen International Refugee Office, 1920–1947, ALON-UNOG, internal document no. 9771.

70. "Report of the Commission for the Protection of Women and Children in the Near East," ALON-UNOG, Publications of the League of Nations IV. Social. 1927.IV.6, p. 1.

71. This idea of "chaos" resonates with the similar Indian and Pakistani efforts to reverse the abduction and sequestration of Hindu and Muslim women at the time of India's partition: "The proper regulation of women's sexuality had to be restored, and the sexual chaos that mass abduction represented had to be reversed. Thus, the individual and collective sins of men who behaved without restraint or responsibility in a surge of communal 'madness' had to be redeemed by nations who understood their duty in, once again, bringing about secular discipline and, through it, the desired reinforcement of community and national identities." Ritu Menon and Kamla Bhasin, *Borders and Boundaries: Women in India's Partition* (New Brunswick: Rutgers University Press, 1998), 108.

72. A recent example of the entrance of these discussions into contemporary Turkish historical discourse was the Hrant Dink Foundation's November 2013 conference on "Islamized Armenians."

6. BETWEEN REFUGEE AND CITIZEN

This chapter is drawn from a paper delivered at the conference "Towards a New History of the League of Nations," held August 23–25, 2011, at the Graduate Institute, Geneva, Switzerland. I thank Mark Toufayan for his help in understanding some elements of French legal thought. Portions of this paper were delivered at the 2010 annual meeting of the Middle East Studies Association, during which I benefited from the comments of Benjamin Thomas White; at the workshop "Humanitarianism to Human Rights," Stanford University, June 1, 2012; and at the September 27, 2012, meeting of the Tufts University seminar series "Exploring the History of Humanitarianism and Development."

1. Donald Bloxham explores the gradual shift in support of the Great Powers away from Armenia toward the successor state of the Ottoman Empire, Kemalist Turkey, and its territorial ambitions and desire for regional influence. See Donald Bloxham, *The Great Game of Genocide: Imperialism, Nationalism, and the Destruction of the Ottoman Armenians* (Oxford: Oxford University Press, 2005).

2. See Lloyd E. Ambrosius, "Wilsonian Diplomacy and Armenia: The Limits of Power and Ideology," in *America and the Armenian Genocide,* ed. Jay Winter (Cambridge: Cambridge University Press, 2003), 1131–1145.

3. See Daniel Gerard Cohen, *In War's Wake: Europe's Displaced Persons in the Postwar Order* (Oxford: Oxford University Press, 2011).

4. Jules Pam et al., *Scheme for the Settlement of Armenian Refugees: General Survey and Principal Documents,* publication of the League of Nations, C. 699. M. 264. 1926. IV.

5. The archive of the Armenian National Delegation is held, in part, at the Nubarian Library in Paris. The delegation was dominated by the Armenian General Benevolent Union, which, through the course of the interwar period, cooperated with the League of Nations as a quasi-state in terms of representing diasporan Armenian interests, but also as the primary collaborator in resettlement and educational projects. See Raymond Kévorkian and Vahé Tachjian, eds., *The Armenian General Benevolent Union: One Hundred Years of History,* trans. G.M. Goshgarian, 2 vols. (Cairo: AGBU Central Board, 2006).

6. André Mandelstam, *La Société des nations et les puissances devant le problème arménien* (Paris: Pédone, 1926), 322 (emphasis in original).

7. Raymond Kévorkian, *The Armenian Genocide: A Complete History* (London: I.B. Tauris, 2011), 155.

8. Fuat Dündar, *Crime of Numbers: The Role of Statistics in the Armenian Question (1878–1918)* (Piscataway: Transaction Publishers, 2010), 103–104.

9. Levon Marashlian, "Finishing the Genocide: Cleansing Turkey of Armenian Survivors, 1920–1923," in *Remembrance and Denial: The Case of the Armenian Genocide,* ed. Richard Hovannisian (Detroit: Wayne State University Press, 1998), 113–146.

10. Mandelstam, *Société des nations,* viii.

11. Ibid.

12. See, for example, "Protection of Minorities in Turkey," ALON-UNOG, C.508.1929. In this complaint, the Armenian patriarch of Cilicia, Paul Terzian, describes at length attacks on Armenians in southeastern Anatolia, including the extrajudicial execution of an Armenian Catholic priest. The penultimate sentence of Terzian's note is suggestive of how these attacks were understood as an assault on the Armenian national community: "Nous sommes dans l'espoir que la Société des Nations, par sa haute Intervention, pourra obtenir justice des attentats et des spoliation dont sont victimes les Chrétiens, et améliorer la condition des épaves survivantes de notre Nation en Anatolie" (We hope that the League of Nations, by its great intervention, can obtain justice for the attacks

against and thefts from Christian victims, and improve the conditions of poor survivors of our nation in Anatolia).

13. For a largely narrative account of the League's activities based on a close reading of the archive, see Dzovinar Kévonian, *Réfugiés et diplomatie humanitaire: Les acteurs européens et la scéne proche-orientale pendant l'entre-deux-guerres* (Paris: Publications de la Sorbonne, 2004).

14. "Deportation des femmes et des enfants en Turquie, en Asie Mineure et dans les territoiries avoisinants," Report of the Fifth Commission, Geneva, September 21, 1921, ALON-UNOG, 12/15998/4631.

15. See Nansen's Nobel lecture, "The Suffering People of Europe," delivered on December 19, 1922, at http://nobelprize.org/nobel_prizes/peace/laureates /1922/nansen-lecture.html (accessed September 20, 2012).

16. Michael Barnett, *Empire of Humanity: A History of Humanitarianism* (Ithaca: Cornell University Press, 2011), 88–89.

17. League of Nations, *Arrangement of 30 June 1928 Relating to the Legal Status of Russian and Armenian Refugees,* June 30, 1928, League of Nations Treaty Series, vol. 89, no. 2005, www.refworld.org/docid/3dd8cde56.html (accessed January 2, 2015).

18. League of Nations, *Arrangement of 12 May 1926 Relating to the Issue of Identity Certificates to Russian and Armenian Refugees,* League of Nations Treaty Series, vol. 89, no. 2004, www.refworld.org/docid/3dd8b5802.html (accessed January 2, 2015).

19. League of Nations, *Convention Relating to the International Status of Refugees,* October 28, 1933, League of Nations Treaty Series, vol. 159, no. 3663, www.unhcr.org/refworld/docid/3dd8cf374.html (accessed June 22, 2012).

20. Ibid.

21. James C. Hathaway, "The Evolution of Refugee Status in International Law, 1920–1950," *International and Comparative Law Quarterly* 33, no. 2 (1984): 353.

22. "It does not provide for equal treatment with citizens in regard to labor permits, social security, taxation, and other matters, but an Arrangement of June 30, 1928, recommends favorable treatment for the refugees in regard to these matters." Louise W. Holborn, "The League of Nations and the Refugee Problem," *Annals of the American Academy of Political and Social Science* 203 (1939): 126.

23. Ibid.

24. Barnett, *Empire of Humanity*, 89.

25. "Russian and Armenian Refugees: Report to the Eighth Ordinary Session of the Assembly by the High Commissioner for Refugees (Fridtjof Nansen)," ALON-UNOG A.48.1927.VIII, pp. 4–5.

26. Pachalian also led early efforts to use legal recourse to recover lost Armenian property seized by the Republic of Turkey, collaborating in this effort with Mandelstam. See *Confiscation des Biens des Refugiés Arméniens par the Gouvernement Turc: Consultation of M.M. Gilbert Gidel, Albert De Lapradelle, Louis Le Fur, André N. Mandelstam* (Paris: Imprimerie, Massis, 1929).

27. See Keith David Watenpaugh, *Being Modern in the Middle East: Revolution, Nationalism, Colonialism, and the Arab Middle Class* (Princeton: Princeton University Press, 2006), 211–308.

28. Ibid.

29. Keith David Watenpaugh, "Towards a New Category of Colonial Theory: Colonial Cooperation and the Survivors' Bargain—The Case of the Post-Genocide Armenian Community of Syria under French Mandate," in *The British and French Mandates in Comparative Perspective*, ed. Nadine Méouchy and Peter Sluglett (Leiden: Brill, 2004), 597–622.

30. "Rapport de M. B. Nicolsky sur l'oeuvre d'établissement de réfugiés arméniens en Syrie," June 30, 1936, CADN-MAE, Nantes, Fonds Unions Internationales, 2ème versement, no. 1902.

31. "Comité de secours aux refugiés arméniens, Procès-verbal," June 24, 1931, CADN-MAE, Nantes, Fonds Beyrouth, carton 575 (emphasis added).

32. "Rapport de M. B. Nicolsky." See also Raymond Kévorkian et al., eds., *Les Arméniens, 1917–1939: La quête d'un refuge* (Beirut: Presses de l'Université Saint-Joseph, 2006).

33. "A total of 36,016 refugees were settled in 5,576 houses and 1,090 refugees installed in five large agricultural colonies by the end of December 1937." Holborn, "League of Nations and the Refugee Problem," 128.

34. Monck-Mason (Aleppo) to Lord Cushendon, October 30, 1928, PRO FO [Foreign Office] FO 371/ 13074, E 5338/1 41/8.

35. See Avi Shlaim, "Husni Za'im and the Plan to Resettle Palestinian Refugees in Syria," *Journal of Palestine Studies* 15, no. 4 (1986): 68–80; and Abbas Shiblak, "Residency Status and Civil Rights of Palestinian Refugees in Arab Countries," *Journal of Palestine Studies* 25, no. 3 (1996): 36–45.

36. *Report of the Advisory Committee of the High Commissioner for Refugees for Russian, Armenian, Assyrian, Assyro-Chaldean, and Turkish Refugees,* ALON-UNOG A.23.1929, VI, p. 27.

37. "At the same time, the possibilities of increasing the movement of refugees to South America should not be disregarded. In spite of the passport, visa and transport difficulties, some 1000 refugees have been transferred to South American countries, and there are indications that those refugees are now applying for assistance to bring out their friends in increasing numbers" (ibid., 17).

38. See Dzovinar Kévonian, "Question des réfugiés, droits de l'homme: Éléments d'une convergence pendant l'entre-deux-guerres," *Matériaux pour l'histoire de notre temps* 72 (2003): 40–49. See also Eric D. Weitz, "From the Vienna to the Paris System: International Politics and the Entangled Histories of Human Rights, Forced Deportations, and Civilizing Missions," *American Historical Review* 113, no. 5 (2008): 1313–1343.

39. Daniel Whelan, *Indivisible Human Rights: A History* (Philadelphia: University of Pennsylvania Press, 2010), 50–51; Jan Herman Burgers, "The Road to San Francisco: The Revival of the Human Rights Idea in the Twentieth Century," *Human Rights Quarterly* 14, no. 4 (1992): 451–454.

7. MODERN HUMANITARIANISM'S TROUBLED LEGACIES

1. Charles Vernon Vickrey, *International Golden Rule Sunday: A Handbook* (New York: George H. Doran Company, 1926), 18–19.

2. Ibid., 23.

3. "Diary of Barclay Acheson," January 1–April 29, 1927, inclusive, RAC-NER, box 134.

4. Ibid.

5. Ibid., May 20, 1927.

6. Ibid., May 20, 1927.

7. Frank Alexander Ross et al., *The Near East and American Philanthropy: A Survey, Conducted under the Guidance of the General Committee of the Near East Survey* (New York: Columbia University Press, 1929).

Robert L. Daniel provides a lucid narrative account of the transition of Near East Relief into the Near East Foundation. See his *American Philanthropy in the Near East, 1820–1960* (Athens: Ohio University Press, 1970), 199–224.

8. Ross et al., *The Near East and American Philanthropy*, 8.

9. Consider Donald Johnson's assessment:

Jones' construction of the field of social studies fit easily into the dominant worldview of colonialism. He shared with a majority of English and American leaders and scholars the notion that, because of the slow progress of evolution, the "higher" nations were obliged to bring "civilization" to the lesser breeds while continuing to provide orderly government for the peoples of Asia and Africa. In his extensive writings on Africa based on several visits, Jones constantly argued that the 'native' peoples of Africa will be " . . . able to realize the advantages and disadvantages of the European colonization of Africa, and to contrast both with the advantages and disadvantages of independent countries like Abyssinia and Liberia." If introduced into Africa, his new field of social studies would insure that the natives, " . . . will learn that the progress and civilization of all nations have required the assistance of other nations, that hermit peoples have usually been stagnated people, that the principle of self-determination is an important half-truth, the complementary half-truth is altruism or brotherhood, which passes on experiences and achievements to others."

Donald Johnson, "W.E.B. Du Bois, Thomas Jesse Jones and the Struggle for Social Education, 1900–1930," *The Journal of Negro History* 85, no. 3 (2000), 11.

See also William H. Watkins, "Thomas Jesse Jones, Social Studies, and Race," *International Journal of Social Education* 10, no. 124–134 (1995–1996): 34.

10. Ross et al., *The Near East and American Philanthropy*, 8.

11. Near East Foundation, *Near East Foundation: A Twentieth Century Concept of Practical Philanthropy* (New York: Near East Foundation, 1931), 3.

12. Ibid., 4.

13. Ibid.

14. Ross et al., *The Near East and American Philanthropy*, 288.

15. Ibid.

16. Among the various social needs outlined by Ross et al. in *The Near East and American Philanthropy* was an observation about the possible positive role American institutions and philanthropy could play in shaping nationalism: "One constantly hears of the 'new nationalism' so widespread in the area, and probably in the long run patriotism will yield food results to humanity. . . . American philanthropy should not work to the destruction of nationalism, but it should direct its efforts to an appreciation of the value of social relationships, personal and national—to the development, in fact, of the genuine social consciousness" (6).

17. Near East Foundation, *Near East Foundation,* 25.

18. Ibid.

19. Ibid., 8.

20. James L. Barton, "Near East Relief Consummated: Near East Foundation Carries On," a supplement to *Story or Near East Relief* (1944), enclosed in RAC-NER, box 136.

21. United Nations Relief and Rehabilitation Administration and George Woodbridge, *UNRRA: The History of the United Nations Relief and Rehabilitation Administration* (New York: Columbia University Press, 1950).

22. See Halford L. Hoskins, ed., "Point Four with Reference to the Middle East," *Annals of the American Academy of Political and Social Science* (March 1950): 85–95.

23. Joseph Grabill, *Protestant Diplomacy and the Near East: Missionary Influence on American Policy, 1810–1927* (Minneapolis: University of Minnesota Press, 1971), 301.

24. Arthur Z. Gardiner, "Point Four and the Arab World: An American View," *Middle East Journal* 4, no. 3 (1950): 306.

25. John S. Badeau, "The Big Idea," in *Bread from Stones: Fifty Years of Technical Assistance,* ed. John Stothoff Badeau and Gerogiana G. Stevens (Englewood Cliffs: Prentice-Hall, 1966), 5.

26. William A. Easterly, *The Tyranny of Experts: How the Fight against Global Poverty Suppressed Individual Rights* (New York: Perseus, 2014), 7.

27. As Easterly writes, "By this technocratic illusion, the technical experts unintentionally confer new powers and legitimacy on the state as the entity that will implement the technical solutions. The economists who advocate the technocratic approach have a terrible naiveté about power—that as restraints on power are loosened or even removed, that same power will be benevolent on its own accord" (ibid., 6).

28. William Fuller, "From Village School to Agricultural College in Iran," in *Bread from Stones: Fifty Years of Technical Assistance,* ed. John Stothoff Badeau and Gerogiana G. Stevens (Englewood Cliffs: Prentice-Hall, 1966), 47.

29. On the broader meaning of the massacre of the Assyrians and the politics of Iraqi anticolonialism, see Sami Zubaida, "Contested Nations: Iraq and the Assyrians," *Nations and Nationalism* 6, no. 3 (2000): 363–382.

30. "League of Nations: Settlement of the Assyrians of Iraq," September 26, 1934, ALON-UNOG c.427,1934.VII; "Report of the Committee of the Council, with detailing annexes concerning the settlement of the Assyrians of Iraq in the region of the Ghab (French mandated territories of the Levant)," September 12, 1935, ALON-UNOG c.352.Mm.179.1935.VII; "Report of the Committee of the Council, with annexes, discussing the complications which have arisen from the abandonment of the plan for the settlement of the Assyrians of Iraq in the Ghab plain and considering the settlement of the Assyrians in Khabur, together with a text of an erratum, Sept. 28, which is contained within the report," September 25, 1937, ALON-UNOG c.387.m.258.1937.VII/.

31. See Keith David Watenpaugh, "'Creating Phantoms': Zaki al-Arsuzi, the Alexandretta Crisis, and the Formation of Modern Arab Nationalism in Syria," *International Journal of Middle East Studies* 28 (1996): 363–389; and Sarah D.

Shields, *Fezzes in the River: Identity Politics and European Diplomacy in the Middle East on the Eve of World War II* (Oxford: Oxford University Press, 2011).

32. On the Madrid Conference, see Raphael Lemkin, "Acts Constituting a General (Transnational) Danger Considered as Offences against the Law of Nations," in *5th Annual Conference for the Unification of Penal Law in Madrid, 1933*; also see his autobiography, *Totally Unofficial: The Autobiography of Raphael Lemkin* (New Haven: Yale University Press, 2013).

33. See Steven Leonard Jacobs, *Lemkin on Genocide* (Lanham: Lexington Books, 2012), in particular the second chapter of the third part, "Modern Times," entitled "Assyrians in Iraq . . . Christians" (223–260).

34. Stanley Kerr to family, September 9, 1923, Kerr Family Letters Collection, Stanley Kerr and Elsa Reckman Kerr Letters.

35. Stanley Kerr to family, October 11, 1923, Kerr Family Letters Collection, Stanley Kerr and Elsa Reckman Kerr Letters.

36. The letters of Malcolm Kerr, contained in the memoirs of his widow, Ann Z. Kerr, *Come with Me from Lebanon* (Syracuse: Syracuse University Press, 1994), confirm his sense of professional responsibility to lead the university. He was in Beirut at the time of the Israeli occupation of Lebanon and was witness to the city's occupation as well as the massacre of three thousand Palestinian refugees in the Sabra and Shatila neighborhoods in September 1982. The letters bear an uncanny resemblance to those of his father from Marash in the 1920s in the mix of accounts of the mundane to a frank consciousness of the risk to his own life. See also Susan Van de Ven's account of postassassination attempts to identify the assailant and achieve justice, *One Family's Response to Terrorism: A Daughter's Memoir* (Syracuse: Syracuse University Press, 2008).

Select Bibliography

ARCHIVES
Republic of France

Centre des archives diplomatiques, Ministère des affairs etrangères, Nantes (CADN-MAE).
Fonds Unions Internationales, 2ème versement

United Kingdom

371 General Correspondences Aleppo Consulate, Public Record Office, Foreign Office, Kew (PRO FO)

United Nations Organization

Archive of the League of Nations, Geneva, Switzerland (ALON-UNOG)
   League of Nations Secretariat, 1919–1946
   Records of the Nansen International Refugee Office, 1920–1947
   Refugees Mixed Archival Group (Nansen Fonds), 1919–1947

United States of America

Decimal File 867, Internal Affairs of Turkey, Record Group 59, Records of the Department of State, United States National Archive, Department of State, College Park, MD (USNA II)

University and Foundation Archives

Archive of the American University of Beirut, Beirut, Lebanon (A-AUB)

Archives of Near East Relief (A-NER)
Howard Bliss Collection, 1902–1920
La Bibliothèque Nubarian, Paris, France
  National Delegation Archives
Rockefeller Archive Center, Sleepy Hollow, NY (RAC)
  Archives of Near East Relief and Near East Foundation (RAC-NER)
  Archives of the Rockefeller Brothers Foundation
  Archives of Rockefeller Family Members, including Laura Spelman Rockefeller
  Archives of the Rockefeller Foundation (RAC-RF)
    International Projects

Private Memoirs and Collections

Kerr Family Letters Collection
  Stanley Kerr and Elsa Reckman Kerr Letters
Memoirs and Private Papers of Karnig Panian
Zohrab Information Center Digital Collection, New York, NY
Zoryan Institute, Arlington, MA
  Stanley Kerr Archives

ARTICLES, DOCTORAL DISSERTATIONS, AND BOOKS

Agamben, Giorgio. *Homo Sacer: Sovereign Power and Bare Life.* Translated by Daniel Heller-Roazen. Stanford: Stanford University Press, 1998.
Ajay, Nicholas Z. "Mount Lebanon and the Wilayah of Beirut, 1914–1918: The War Years." PhD diss., Georgetown University, 1972.
Akçam, Taner. *The Young Turks' Crime against Humanity: The Armenian Genocide and Ethnic Cleansing in the Ottoman Empire.* Princeton: Princeton University Press, 2012.
Anderson, Betty S. *The American University of Beirut.* Austin: University of Texas Press, 2011.
Anderson, Margaret Lavinia. "'Down in Turkey, Far Away': Human Rights, the Armenian Massacres, and Orientalism in Wilhelmine Germany." *The Journal of Modern History* 79, no. 1 (2007): 80–111.
Arendt, Hannah. *On Revolution.* New York: Penguin, 1977.
Avakian, Ashdghig. *Stranger among Friends: An Armenian Nurse from Lebanon Tells Her Story.* Beirut: Catholic Press, 1960.
Badeau, John Stothoff, and Gerogiana G. Stevens, ed. *Bread from Stones: Fifty Years of Technical Assistance.* Englewood Cliffs: Prentice-Hall, 1966.
Banian, Garnik [Karnik Panian]. *Husher antourayi vosbanotse.* Beirut: Hamazkain, 1992.
Barnett, Michael N. *Empire of Humanity: A History of Humanitarianism.* Ithaca: Cornell University Press, 2011.
———. "Humanitarian Governance." *Annual Review of Political Science* 16 (2013): 379–398.
Barton, Clara. *Report: America's Relief Expedition to Asia Minor under the Red Cross.* Meriden, Conn.: Journal Publishing Company, 1896.

Barton, James L. *Story of Near East Relief, 1915–1930: An Interpretation.* New York: Macmillan, 1930.

Bauman, Zygmunt. *Modernity and the Holocaust.* Ithaca: Cornell University Press, 1989.

Bloxham, Donald. *The Final Solution: A Genocide.* Oxford: Oxford University Press, 2009.

Burgers, Jan Herman. "The Road to San Francisco: The Revival of the Human Rights Idea in the Twentieth Century." *Human Rights Quarterly* 14, no. 4 (1992): 451–454.

Cabanes, Bruno. *The Great War and the Origins of Humanitarianism, 1918–1924.* Cambridge: Cambridge University Press, 2014.

Çetin, Fethiye. *Anneannem: Anlatı.* Istanbul: Metis Yayinları, 2004. Translated by Maureen Freely as *My Grandmother* (London: Verso, 2008).

Cohen, Daniel Gerard. *In War's Wake: Europe's Displaced Persons in the Postwar Order.* Oxford: Oxford University Press, 2011.

Coundouriotis, Eleni. "Congo Cases: The Stories of Human Rights History." *Humanity: An International Journal of Human Rights, Humanitarianism, and Development* 3, no. 2 (2012): 133–153.

Curti, Merle. "The History of American Philanthropy as a Field of Research." *American Historical Review,* 62 no. 2 (1957): 352–363.

Daniel, Robert L. *American Philanthropy in the Near East, 1820–1960.* Athens: Ohio University Press, 1970.

Dawes, James. *That the World May Know: Bearing Witness to Atrocity.* Cambridge: Harvard University Press, 2009.

de la Durantaye, Leland. *Giorgio Agamben: A Critical Introduction.* Stanford: Stanford University Press, 2009.

Easterly, William A. *The Tyranny of Experts: How the Fight against Global Poverty Suppressed Individual Rights.* New York: Perseus, 2014.

Edip, Halidé. *Memoirs of Halidé Edib.* New York: Century Co., 1926.

Ekmekcioglu, Lerna. "A Climate for Abduction, A Climate for Redemption: The Politics of Inclusion during and after the Armenian Genocide." *Comparative Studies in Society and History* 55, no. 3 (2013): 522–553.

Elliot, Mabel E. *Beginning Again at Ararat.* New York: Fleming H. Revell, 1924.

Esayean, Zapēl [Zabel Yesayan]. *Aweraknerun mēj* [Among the ruins]. Istanbul: K. Polis, 1911.

Fassin, Didier. *Humanitarian Reason: A Moral History of the Present.* Translated by Rachel Gomme. Berkeley: University of California Press, 2012.

Feldman, Ilana. "Refusing Invisibility: Documentation and Memorialization in Palestinian Refugee Claims." *Journal of Refugee Studies* 21, no. 4 (2008): 498–516.

Ghazzi, Kamil, al-. *Kitab nahr al-dhahab fi tarikh Halab* [River of gold in the history of Aleppo]. 2nd ed., 3 vols. Aleppo: Arab Pen Press, 1991–1993. Originally published by Maronite Press in 1923–1926.

Hathaway, James C. "The Evolution of Refugee Status in International Law, 1920–1950." *International and Comparative Law Quarterly* 33, no. 2 (1984): 348–380.

Hepworth, George Hughes. *Through Armenia on Horseback*. New York: EP Dutton, 1898.

Holborn, Louise W. "The League of Nations and the Refugee Problem." *Annals of the American Academy of Political and Social Science* 203 (1939): 124–135.

Hoskins, Halford L. "Point Four with Reference to the Middle East." In "Aiding Underdeveloped Areas Abroad," special issue, *Annals of the American Academy of Political and Social Science* 268 (March 1950): 85–95.

Irwin, Julia F. *Making the World Safe: The American Red Cross and a Nation's Humanitarian Awakening*. Oxford: Oxford University Press, 2013.

Jacobsen, Abigail. "American 'Welfare Politics': American Involvement in Jerusalem during World War I." *Israel Studies* 18, no. 1 (2013): 56–76.

Jewish Relief Work in Palestine: A Summary of Reports Received up to Date, October 1918. London: Palestine Relief Board, 1918.

Jones, Marion Moser. *The American Red Cross from Clara Barton to the New Deal*. Baltimore: Johns Hopkins University Press, 2012.

Kerr, Ann Z. *Come with Me from Lebanon*. Syracuse: Syracuse University Press, 1994.

Kerr, Stanley E. *The Lions of Marash: Personal Experiences with American Near East Relief 1919–1922*. Albany: State University of New York Press, 1975.

Kévonian, Dzovinar. "Question des réfugiés, droits de l'homme: Éléments d'une convergence pendant l'entre-deux-guerres." *Matériaux pour l'histoire de notre temps* 72 (2003): 40–49.

———. *Réfugiés et diplomatie humanitaire: Les acteurs européens et la scène proche-orientale pendant l'entre-deux-guerres*. Paris: Publications de la Sorbonne, 2004.

Kévorkian, Raymond. *The Armenian Genocide: A Complete History*. London: I. B. Tauris, 2011.

Kévorkian, Raymond, and Vahé Tachjian, eds., *The Armenian General Benevolent Union: One Hundred Years of History*. Translated by G. M. Goshgarian, 2 vols. Cairo: AGBU Central Board, 2006.

Lepsius, Johannes. *Armenia and Europe: An Indictment*. London: Hodder and Stoughton, 1897.

Little, Branden. "Humanitarian Relief in Europe and the Analogue of War, 1914–1918." In *Finding Common Ground: New Directions in First World War Studies*, edited by Jennifer Keene and Michael Neiberg, 139–160. Leiden: Brill, 2010.

Makdisi, Ussama. *Artillery of Heaven: American Missionaries and the Failed Conversion of the Middle East*. Ithaca: Cornell University Press, 2008.

Maksudyan, Nazan. *Orphans and Destitute Children in the Late Ottoman Empire*. Syracuse: Syracuse University Press, 2014.

Malkki, Liisa. "Speechless Emissaries: Refugees, Humanitarianism, and Dehistoricization." *Cultural Anthropology* 11, no. 3 (1996): 377–404.

Mandelstam, André. *La Société des nations et les puissances devant le problème arménien*. Paris: Pédone, 1926.

McGilvary, Margaret. *The Dawn of a New Era Syria*. New York: Fleming H. Revell, 1920.

Migliorino, Nicola. *(Re)Constructing Armenia in Lebanon and Syria: Ethno-Cultural Diversity and the State in the Aftermath of a Refugee Crisis.* New York: Berghahn, 2007.

Miller, David. "The Treatment of Armenians in the Ottoman Empire: A History of the 'Blue Book.'" *The RUSI Journal* 150, no. 4 (2005): 36–43.

Morefield, Jeanne. *Empires without Imperialism: Anglo-American Decline and the Politics of Deflection.* Oxford: Oxford University Press, 2014.

Morgenthau, Henry. *Ambassador Morgenthau's Story.* New York: Doubleday, Page, 1919.

Nansen, Fridtjof. *Scheme for the Settlement of Armenian Refugees: General Survey and Principal Documents.* Geneva: Kundig, 1927.

Nichanian, Marc. *Writers of Disaster: Armenian Literature in the Twentieth Century.* Vol. 1, *The National Revolutions.* Princeton: Gomidas Institute Press, 2002.

Obenzinger, Hilton. *American Palestine: Melville, Twain and the Holy Land Mania.* Princeton: Princeton University Press, 1999.

Odian, Yervant. *Accursed Years: My Exile and Return from Der Zor, 1914–1919.* Translated by Ara Stepan Melkonian. London: Gomidas Press, 2009. Originally published in 1919.

Ottoman Ministry of the Interior, Department of Refugees. *Cemiyet-i Akvam ve Türkiyede Ermeni ve Rumlar* [The League of Nations and Greeks and Armenians in Turkey], no. 6 (Istanbul: Ahmed Hassan, 1921).

Pahri, Zaruhi [Zarouhi Bahri]. *Keank'is vepe* [My biography]. Beirut: 1995.

Penrose, Beasley Linnard. *That They May Have Life: The Story of the American University of Beirut, 1866–1941.* Beirut: American University of Beirut, 1970.

Rodogno, Davide. *Against Massacre: Humanitarian Interventions in the Ottoman Empire, 1815–1914.* Princeton: Princeton University Press, 2012.

Ross, Frank Alexander, Charles Luther Fry, Elbridge Sibley, and Otis William Caldwell. *The Near East and American Philanthropy: A Survey, Conducted under the Guidance of the General Committee of the Near East Survey.* New York: Columbia University Press, 1929.

Salbi, M. *Aleakner ew khleakner: Hay vranak'aghak'in taregirk'ě* [Waves and wrecks: Almanac of the Armenian tent city]. Alexandria: Tpagrut'iwn A. Gasapean, 1919.

Shields, Sarah D. *Fezzes in the River: Identity Politics and European Diplomacy in the Middle East on the Eve of World War II.* Oxford: Oxford University Press, 2011.

Ó Síocháin, Séamas, and Michael O'Sullivan, eds. *The Eyes of Another Race: Roger Casement's Congo Report and 1903 Diary.* Dublin: University College Dublin Press, 2003.

Tamari, Salim. *Year of the Locust: A Soldier's Diary and the Erasure of Palestine's Ottoman Past.* Berkeley: University of California Press, 2011.

Tanielian, Melanie. "Politics of Wartime Relief in Ottoman Beirut (1914–1918)." *First World War Studies* 5, no. 1 (2014): 69–82.

———. "The War of Famine: Everyday Life in Wartime Beirut and Mount Lebanon (1914–1918)." PhD diss., University of California, Berkeley, 2012.

Thompson, Elizabeth. *Colonial Citizens: Republican Rights, Paternal Privilege, and Gender in French Syria and Lebanon.* New York: Columbia University Press, 2000.

Toynbee, Arnold Joseph. *The Treatment of Armenians in the Ottoman Empire: Documents Presented to Viscont Grey of Fallodon, Secretary of State for Foreign Affairs. Viscount Bryce. Laid Before the Houses of Parliament as An Official Paper.* London: Hodder and Stoughton, 1916.

Toynbee, Arnold Joseph, and James Bryce Bryce. *Armenian Atrocities: The Murder of a Nation.* London: Hodder and Stoughton, 1915.

Tsaṛukean, Andranik [Antranik Zaroukian]. *Mankut'iwn ch'unets'ogh mardik.* Peyrut: K. Tōnikean ew Ordik', 1980. Translated by Elise Bayizian and Marzbed Margossian as *Men without Childhoods* (New York: Ashdod, 1985).

Turkish National Congress. *The Turco-Armenian Question: The Turkish Point of View.* Istanbul: Turkish National Congress, 1919.

Tusan, Michele. "'Crimes against Humanity': Human Rights, the British Empire, and the Origins of the Response to the Armenian Genocide." *American Historical Review* 119, no. 1 (2014): 47–77.

———. *Smyrna's Ashes: Humanitarianism, Genocide and the Birth of the Middle East.* Berkeley: University of California Press, 2012.

Üngör, Uğur Ümit. *The Making of Modern Turkey: Nation and State in Eastern Anatolia, 1913–1950.* Oxford: Oxford University Press, 2012.

Üngör, Uğur, and Mehmet Polatel. *Confiscation and Destruction: The Young Turk Seizure of Armenian Property.* London: Bloomsbury Academic, 2011.

Vickrey, Charles Vernon. *International Golden Rule Sunday: A Handbook.* New York: George H. Doran, 1926.

Watenpaugh, Keith David. "'Are There Any Children for Sale?': Genocide and the Transfer of Armenian Children (1915–1922)." *Journal of Human Rights* 12, no. 3 (2013): 283–295.

———. *Being Modern in the Middle East: Revolution, Nationalism, Colonialism, and the Arab Middle Class.* Princeton: Princeton University Press, 2006.

———. "Between Communal Survival and National Aspiration: Armenian Genocide Refugees, the League of Nations, and the Practices of Interwar Humanitarianism." *Humanity: An International Journal of Human Rights, Humanitarianism, and Development* 5, no. 2 (2014): 159–181.

———. "'Creating Phantoms': Zaki al-Arsuzi, the Alexandretta Crisis, and the Formation of Modern Arab Nationalism in Syria." *International Journal of Middle East Studies* 28 (1996): 363–389.

———. "The League of Nations' Rescue of Armenian Genocide Survivors and the Making of Modern Humanitarianism, 1920–1927." *The American Historical Review* 115, no. 5 (2010): 1315–1339.

———. "Towards a New Category of Colonial Theory: Colonial Cooperation and the Survivors' Bargain—The Case of the Post-Genocide Armenian Community of Syria under French Mandate." In *The British and French Man-*

dates in Comparative Perspective, edited by Nadine Méouchy and Peter Sluglett, 597–622. Leiden: Brill, 2004.

Whelan, Daniel. *Indivisible Human Rights: A History*. Philadelphia: University of Pennsylvania Press, 2010.

Wise, Stephen. *Challenging Years: The Autobiography of Stephen Wise*. New York: G. P. Putnam's Sons, 1949.

Index

Page references in italics indicate illustrations, and t indicates a table.

CPSIA information can be obtaine
at www.ICGtesting.com
Printed in the USA
LVOW03s0640230917

549715LV00002B/3